Antarctica, My Destiny

A Personal History by the Last of the Great Polar Explorers

by CAPTAIN FINN RONNE

"Finn Ronne's appreciation of the raw beauty and hazards of those South Polar regions and his adventures in mapping much of it makes his story one of the most exciting tales of exploration of our day."—*LOWELL THOMAS*

BEFORE scientists were able to start geophysical research in Antarctica, the job of exploring the continent's unknown surface was led by a handful of courageous pioneers — Shackleton, Amundsen, Scott, Wilkins, Ellsworth and Captain Finn Ronne.

During nine trips to Antarctica Finn Ronne logged more miles on skis and sledding with dog teams and discovered more territory than any man before or since. The Ronne Ice Shelf, one of Antarctica's largest geographical features, is a tribute to his exploits. During his own Ronne Antarctic Research Expedition in 1946-48, which was the last privately sponsored "man-against-the-ice" effort in Antarctica, over 250,000 square miles of land were discovered and over 14,000 aerial photographs were taken of 450,000 square miles of the continent's surface.

(Continued on back flap)

Antarctica, My Destiny

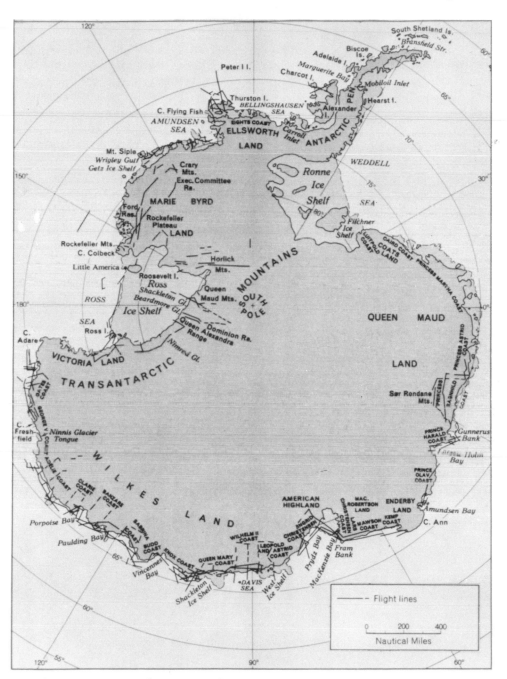

Antarctica as it was known in 1958.

Captain Finn Ronne, US Navy (Ret.) as military commander of the Ellsworth Station during the International Geophysical Year program, 1956–58.

ANTARCTICA
MY DESTINY

A Personal History by the
Last of the Great Polar Explorers

by

FINN RONNE

Captain, USN

Illustrated with photographs and maps

HASTINGS HOUSE • PUBLISHERS

New York, N.Y. 10016

Other Books by Captain Finn Ronne
ANTARCTIC CONQUEST
ANTARCTIC COMMAND
RONNE EXPEDITION TO ANTARCTICA

Library of Congress Cataloging in Publication Data
Ronne, Finn.
    Antarctica, my destiny.
    Includes index.
    1. Ronne, Finn.   2. Antarctic regions.
3. Explorers — United States — Biography.   I. Title.
G875.R66A32   919.8′9′040924   79-18037
ISBN 0-8038-0485-7

Published simultaneously in Canada by
Saunders of Toronto, Ltd., Don Mills, Ontario
Printed in the United States of America

To My Father Martin,
who broke trail for me into
the frigid unknown,
and to My Mother, Maren,
whose devotion to her family
was unexcelled

RONNE ANTARCTIC

FRENCH BASE

INDIAN OCEAN

WILKES LAND

VICT

SOUTH
Amundsen

AMERICAN
HIGHLAND

ANTARC C

AUSTRALIAN BASE

FIELD BASE

MAIN FLIGHT TRACK

FIELD BASE

Q
U
E
E
N

ENDERBY
LAND

M
A
U
D

LAND

COATS

N E W
S C H W A B E N L A N D

NORWEGIAN BASE

Stonington

Punta Arenas

Valparaiso

Panama

New York

ROUTE OF VESSELS

Area previously explored
or photographed

A
T
L

A N T I C

William Briesemeister, 1949

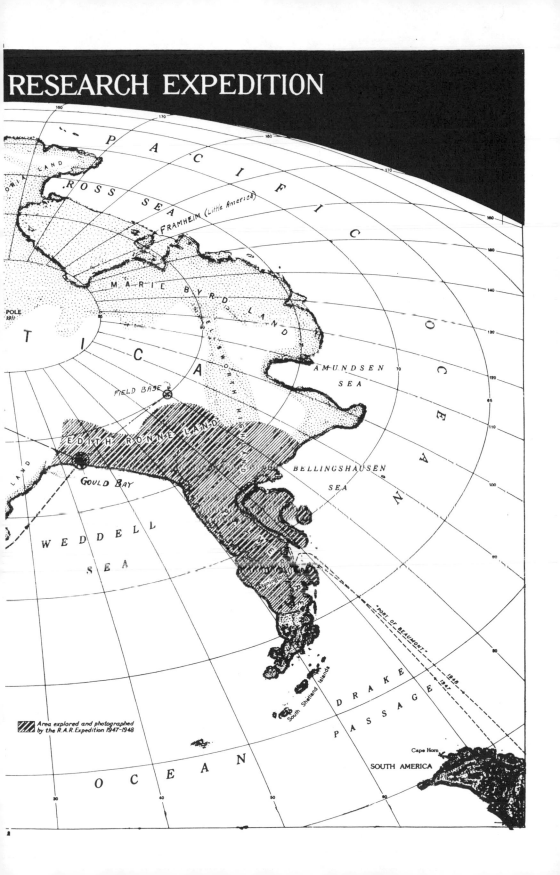

RESEARCH EXPEDITION

Area explored and photographed
by the R.A.R. Expedition 1947-1948

SOUTH ORKNEY
ISLANDS

Sanae (RSA)

0°

Bellingauzen (USSR)
Capitán Arturo Prat (Ch.)
─DECEPTION ISLAND

Novolazarevskaya
(USSR)

Showa (Jap.)
Molodezhnaya (USSR)

SØR
RONDANE
MOUNTAINS

Q U E E N

M A U D

L A N D

WEDDELL SEA

Halley Bay (UK)

INDIAN OCEAN

Palmer (USA)

General Belgrano
(Arg.)

LASSITER
COAST

Mawson (Aust.)

SHACKLETON RANGE

Plateau (USA; closed)

RONNE
ICE
SHELF

ELLSWORTH STATION
(U.S.A.) Ronne's Wintering Base

90° W

BELLINGSHAUSEN SEA

ELLSWORTH
LAND

Siple (USA)

Amundsen-Scott
South Pole (USA)

QUEEN MAUD
MOUNTAINS

Mirnyy (USSR)

90° E

Vostok (USSR)

Byrd (USA)

MARIE BYRD LAND

QUEEN ALEXANDRA
RANGE

Casey (Aust.)

ROSS ICE SHELF

AMUNDSEN SEA

Scott Base (N.Z.)
McMurdo (USA)

DRY VALLEYS

WILKES LAND

ROSS ISLAND

ROSS SEA

Hallett (USA)

VICTORIA LAND

Dumont d'Urville (Fr.)

500   0   500   1000

Leningradskaya (USSR)

KILOMETERS

180°

The International Bases on the Antarctic continent and the adjacent islands
during the International Geophysical Year Program, 1956–1958.

Introduction

by LOWELL THOMAS

One of the greatest joys — yes, the greatest — of a life spent roaming the world is the people you meet. My long time friendship with Norwegian born Finn Ronne is one that strikingly illustrates this. I've known our indefatigable, incorrigible, widely enthusiastic explorer for half a century.

His accomplishments in the Antarctic are legendary. Today scientifically advanced equipment has taken some of the danger — and maybe some of the high adventure — out of Arctic and Antarctic research, but for pioneering Finn Ronne the challenge was to attack head on the mysteries of this most forbidding continent.

His courage and intuition, his knowledge of nature's idiosyncracies and most important his boundless desire to do what had never been done before, to search the unknown, makes him truly an explorer's explorer.

During his nine trips to the Ultimate South he believes he logged more miles sledding with dog teams and on skis and discovered more territory than any man before or since. (In fact he has discovered so much territory that while on his highly successful expedition of 1946–1948 he paid me the somewhat breathtaking compliment of naming a mountain range for me, at the top of what is now known as The Antarctic Peninsula, formerly on your maps either as Graham Land or Palmer Land.)

Finn Ronne's appreciation of the raw beauty and hazards of those South Polar regions and his adventures in mapping much of it makes his story one of the most exciting tales of exploration of our day.

Finn says each time you go to The Antarctic it puts a "hole in your head." So he now has nine of them and I suspect there soon will be a tenth!

FOREWORD

THE LOVE OF THE SEA and the spirit of seeking new fields to conquer have long been a part of my family history. Up to the middle of the 14th century, my ancestors lived on the island of Bornholm, just off the Danish coast, the capital of which still bears the name Ronne. Around 1600, one branch of the family moved to the Trondheim area in central Norway. From this Norwegian group of Ronnes came my amazing great-grandfather. At the age of 90 years, he retired from the sea as master of his own sailing vessel, a 2,000-ton barque, which he had been sailing for 20 years. His lifetime of sailing the seven seas made a lasting impression on his grandson, my father Martin Ronne. When only a boy of nine, my father began to spend his summers under his grandfather's tutelage sailing the Baltic and Mediterranean in small barquentines. By the time he was 13, Martin Ronne had left for a four-year voyage on a full-rigged sailing ship. He told me that he rounded Cape Horn when he was 15, and hit ports such as Valparaiso and Antofagasta as well as San Francisco, where he was in 1876. At 17, he returned to Norway, went through a ships' school, and received his certificate as a navigator. He served on various ships engaged in world trade, advancing to top mate. That was about as high as it was possible to go in those days unless you were related to the owners.

It was in 1884 that the ship he was on stopped at a small town of Horten, Norway, to load "props" for Newcastle, England. The props were timbers used to shore up the overhead in the coal mines. On a Sunday, when the ship's crew was not working,

Martin Ronne was introduced to one of the three daughters of the chief accountant at the Navy Yard at Horten. The two must have liked each other, because they kept a correspondence going after my father left. Two years later his ship called at Holmestrand, about nine miles north of Horten. While in port, my father and a shipmate — who also had a girl in Horten — used to walk every evening the dusty road to Horten; then walk back late at night.

My mother thought those fellows were crazy, stating that she did not particularly like Martin anyway. Nevertheless, on September 24, 1887, they were married in Horten Cathedral. My mother's age was 24; my father's 26.

As is the case with men of the sea, much of Martin Ronne's life was spent away from home. However, every time he returned home from the "far away places across the sea" — there was another little Ronne crawling around, spaced about three years apart. Of the five boys and two girls, I was the middle son and the one most fascinated by his adventurous life.

My mother, Maren Gurine Ronne, a God-fearing woman, attended services every Sunday in the Norwegian Lutheran church. She preached and practiced the highest standards in dignity, always looked at things in a positive way, and was equal to my father in strength and resourcefulness. These qualities served her well when my father was at sea. For example, she would paper and paint the rooms in our house, climb up on the roof to fix tiles, mix cement to patch the chimney or a garden wall, and do light carpenter work around the property. In addition, she hand-sewed clothing for all her seven children. She also found time to raise vegetables, preserve fruits and berries from the garden, and she grew the prettiest flowers in Horten. A member of the Tuberculosis Society, she raised funds for the sick and needy and attended their regular monthly meetings, and special events.

Her family's welfare was always uppermost in her mind as she prepared hearty meals for five sons and two daughters. This remarkable woman, who lived to be 73 years old, sustained me with unyielding faith in God. My rigorous standards of conduct — not always appreciated by those who served with me — as well as my capacity for enduring harsh conditions, stem from qualities inherited from my mother no less than from my father.

Roald Amundsen

This was the exciting era when history was being made on the world's two polar continents, the Arctic and the Antarctic. I devoured the books of Nansen, Nordenskjold, Franklin expedition, Amundsen, Scott and Shackleton, and the newspaper accounts of Peary's first sledging with dog teams to the North Pole on April 6, 1909. In Norway, Roald Amundsen was a national hero. He had just completed a three-year expedition on Gjoa, proving that a ship could sail through the Northwest Passage. Prior to Peary's announcement, he was making final plans for his expedition to conquer the North Pole. I was electrified when my father broke the news to us that Amundsen had selected him as a member of the expedition. This was my earliest direct contact with polar expeditions.

What ten-year-old boy wouldn't be overwhelmed with joy when he learned that preparations for this historic expedition would involve his own home? I listened to discussions on the merits of the lightly constructed Nansen sledge, and my eyes lingered on the various skis and ski boots being tried. Already I was taking part in ski-jumping contests and cross-country racing. How I wished I were old enough to go along with my father and Amundsen. By the time the expedition sailed, I was as familiar with the supplies, equipment, sledge-dogs, and the loading plan of Amundsen's ship *Fram* as any of those aboard her.

When Peary's North Pole feat became known, Amundsen changed his plans and headed for the Antarctic continent instead. History has recorded his sledge trip to the South Pole as one of the best-planned achievements in all polar exploration.

From 1914 to 1918, I watched once again as Amundsen outfitted a new polar ship — *Maud,* destined for fame with her six-year voyage through the Northeast Passage. My father, who was to remain with Amundsen on expeditions for 20 years, helped with preparations and planning.

During those years, I remained at home in Norway and obtained an education in mechanical and marine engineering at Horten Technical College; I took post-graduate courses in naval architecture and boiler construction. My outside interests were always in athletics, and they continued during my years prior to embarking for the United States.

Soccer-football, track, cross-country ski racing, ski jumping and gymnastics were enjoyed in their seasons. The spirit of competition invariably drove me forward. Even though I did not always win, I had the satisfaction of having done my utmost.

In 1923 I emigrated to the United States and filled out citizenship papers the first day after arrival. My first employment in America was as a designer of ship machinery and equipment with the Bethlehem Ship Yard in the Elizabeth, New Jersey, plant.

Martin Ronne, *right*, with Byrd's second in command Dr. Laurence McKinley Gould at Little America during the Byrd expedition of 1928–1930.

After a year there, I went to Pittsburgh to work for the Westinghouse Electric Corporation as a mechanical engineer, a position I held for 15 years.

Meanwhile, in Norway during the years 1925 and 1926, my father was busily working on various types of equipment needed for the successful flights of the Dornier-Whal seaplanes in 1925 and the dirigible *Norge* in 1926. In 1925 Amundsen and the American explorer Lincoln Ellsworth reached a point within 150 miles of the North Pole. The next year the Italian General Umberto Nobile joined the two men. On this *Norge* flight they completed their mission from Kings Bay, Spitsbergen, across the North-polar basin and landed at Teller, Alaska. This was the great explorer's last expedition. In 1928, Amundsen flew from Tromso, Norway, toward Spitsbergen in an attempt to rescue Nobile, who had crash-landed on the ice north of this isolated island-group. Amundsen was never heard from.

In the year of Amundsen's death, Commander Richard Byrd was planning his first venture to the Antarctic. He had met my father first at Kings Bay in 1926, when he and pilot Floyd Bennett made their controversial North Pole flight. Byrd, who knew of Martin Ronne's work with Amundsen, asked my father to accompany him on his first Antarctic expedition.

Among more than 100 men on this expedition, including Byrd himself, my father proved to be the only one who had been in the Antarctic before. He was unique in that sense, and Byrd told me many times that he leaned on him heavily for advice when the going was rough. He was a man of the old school.

While my father was at Little America with the expedition from 1928 to 1930, I received a radio message from Byrd stating that he would be delighted to have me come with him on his next expedition. By this time, I had been living in the United States some ten years and had become a citizen. Byrd's message pleased me, and although another expedition at that time looked very remote due to the world-wide depression, I viewed the possibility with considerable anticipation.

During a visit to Norway in 1931, I learned that Byrd had invited Martin to go to Antarctica again the next year despite his age of 70 years. My father was young in spirit, sharp of mind and looked forward to the trip, but in the spring of 1932 a cerebral hemorrhage caused his death.

Byrd selected me as a member of his second expedition to the Antarctic in the capacity of ski expert, dog-driver and trail-radio operator. My first assignment was to learn the art of driving sledge dogs. It is infinitely harder than it looks. A dog-team is not born, it is made; and the same applies to the driver. Successful training requires an enormous amount of patience. When I became irritated with my team, I would often switch from cursing them in English to Norwegian. As a result, my dogs soon gained the reputation of being the only group to understand two languages fluently.

On my nine expeditions to the Antarctic I skied behind a dog-team more than six thousand miles. Bridging the pioneering and modern eras of polar exploration, I have seen the dogs replaced by airplanes, helicopters and tracked vehicles. The full cycle of polar achievement has passed before my eyes. But I was

The barquentine *Bear of Oakland* moored along the ice edge in the Bay of Whales.

Finn Ronne

not content to be a passive observer; from the beginning I was determined to be a participant, willing to risk everything to be an explorer of the world's unknown.

My early experience as deck-hand and able-bodied seaman hardened me to danger at sea. I was aboard the *Bear of Oakland* in September 1933 when a hurricane off Cape Hatteras battered the 75-year-old wooden barquentine for about 40 hours, opening her seams and flooding holds and engine room. A powerless derelict, her well-deck awash, the *Bear* could have easily capsized. Miraculously she survived, sparing a young emigrant in quest of his destiny.

Undaunted by danger and disappointments, I progressed through the grades — ultimately becoming an expedition leader and a military captain in the United States Navy. I had chosen this life because of my father's influence. I wanted to follow in his footsteps and explore the unknown. It was therefore natural for me to understand his love for the sea and for Antarctica. There was something mysterious and beautiful about that endless expanse of ice and snow.

Within my life span the geographical conquest of both the North and South polar regions has been accomplished. A scientific onslaught sponsored by the great resources of national governments has since left little of major geographical significance uncaptured by eye or camera. My 1946–48 polar venture was the last private one ever to go to the Antarctic because expeditions are too costly. Only governments can now afford the tremendous expenses involved. I feel fortunate that time and circumstances enabled me to enter into the exploration field — the last of an exclusive fraternity . . .

◆ ◆ ◆

The 150 foot high Ross Ice Shelf, or the Great Barrier, named after Sir James Ross who discovered it in 1841.

CHAPTER *1*

SHIMMERING IN BRILLIANT SUN, fields of sea ice stretched beyond my range of sight. Spread before me was an ocean paved with ice ten feet thick. Zigzags of indigo water, called leads, widened or narrowed as the heaving crust pulled apart or buckled upon itself. Jutting from the horizon were flotillas of noble bergs. Two dimensional in white and inky shadow, they looked like grotesque cutouts pasted against the sky. I stood in awe on the fo'c'sle and watched these dreadnoughts in their cold shining armor pass by as we pressed into the unknown.

By the end of January 1934, we broke through to the ice-free Ross Sea. Ahead loomed the Ross Ice Shelf, 150 feet high and stretching some 400 miles in an east-west direction across our path. Surely the most spectacular of nature's wonders, the barrier cliff was a mighty presence, its sheer face rising from the waterline as though sheared off by a giant's saw. It was a massive flat-topped wall of ice, a ribbon of glistening cliff reflecting its prodigious length in the darkness of the dull, cobalt sea. Most of the men on board beheld the great spectacle for the first time. We could only stare; there were no words to describe the awesome sight facing us.

With the ice wall now to our starboard, less than quarter of a mile away, the steel-plated expedition ship, *Jacob Ruppert*, sliced through the water towards an identation in the barrier — the Bay of Whales. Carsten Borchgrevink first landed here in 1898. Robert Scott followed in 1902, found it unsafe to build a base, and steamed west to McMurdo Sound. Ernest Shackleton stopped here in 1908 to set up a wintering base but abandoned the idea because he feared the ice might drift out to sea. Roald Amundsen in 1911 came next, built his winter-base Framheim, and made his historic dash to the South Pole. Richard Byrd came to the Bay of Whales in 1929 to establish an American foothold in Antarctica, choosing a spot within four miles of Amundsen's original base. First to fly to the South Polar Plateau, Byrd, a retired naval commander basking in a hero's aura, now returned to Little America.

The main engine stopped and I was struck by the immense hush of the moment. To break that silence seemed almost blasphemous. Others also sensed the mood and spoke softly, even whispered, as if in a holy place. A group was selected to go ashore and lined up along the railing on the main deck. I was included. Warm in fur-lined parkas, we moved slowly down the gangway. A motorboat idled impatiently as we stepped aboard. Byrd, I noticed, was last in line — strictly Navy protocol. His face betrayed no emotion, no expression of delight. How could that be? I was barely able to control the excitement welling inside me.

The crowded boat moved toward shore — actually the edge of an ice floe that connected to heavier ice southward. "Finn," the helmsman yelled, "jump ashore with the bowline and pull us in." I pushed my way through a dozen eager men and flung over my skis and ski poles. Then I grabbed the line and leaped to the firm snow — my first landing on the Antarctic continent.

Shattering the stillness, men in the boat suddenly began screaming at me. I was bewildered. What was the matter? Had I committed some major sin? I heard someone say, "The Admiral was supposed to be the first one ashore." Another voice, more subdued, retorted, "To hell with the Admiral." I, in my enthusiasm, had forgotten the protocol. Apparently I should have stepped back onboard after pulling the boat in.

Two men quickly followed me ashore, protocol or not. But I heard no complaints. They set up tripods and began cranking their cameras, filming Byrd in his teddy-bear suit as he stepped on the ice. Suddenly it dawned on me that I was witnessing history in the making. Newsreels in theaters from Maine to California would soon reveal that magic moment Byrd came back to Antarctica.

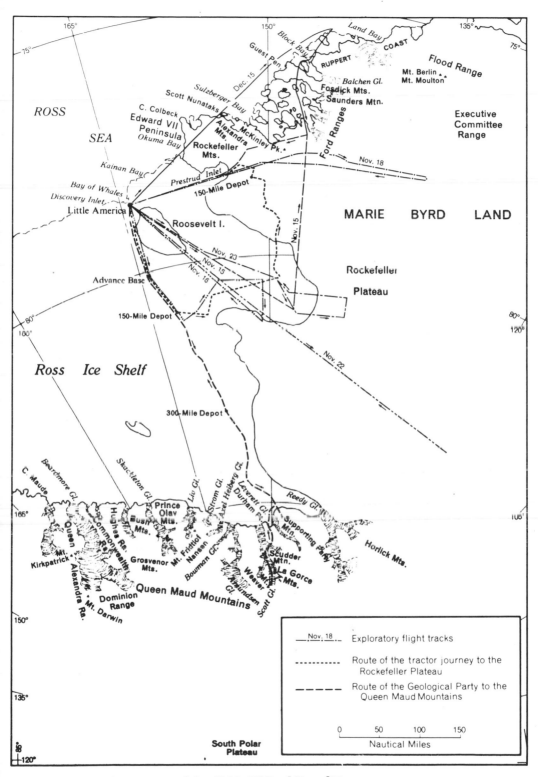

Air and land operations of the 1933–35 Byrd Expedition.

I strapped on my skis and headed for a slope leading to the high barrier. From there I spotted Little America's three radio masts. The rest of the group followed in my ski tracks, and in about 20 minutes we reached the base site of Byrd's first expedition. Stove pipes poking above the snow marked the location of the buried buildings. With pick and shovels we started digging for the entrance ten feet below. Probing with a long pole, we finally hit a roof, cut a hole through it, and lowered ourselves into the old mess hall, banked with tiers of crudely built bunks. Icicles hung down everywhere. Byrd asked me if I would like to see my father's bunk. Of course I would. We crawled through a narrow snow-tunnel to the tomb-like administration building fifty yards away.

In the eerie setting, one of the strangest experiences of my life unfolded. The event was reported in our mimeographed camp newspaper *LITTLE AMERICA TIMES*, datelined Saturday, January 27, 1934:

> It was dark in the big room, but where the hard ice was packed against the windows there was a bright blue fluorescence. Carl Petersen struck a match and pieces of paper on the floor were twisted into torches.
>
> Then Admiral Byrd found a fruit jar half full of kerosene which had been his reading lamp during his first winter here. He lit that and the shadows fell back.
>
> The empty bunks against the wall were draped with some loose clothing thrown aside when the camp was abandoned on Feb. 19, 1930. On the table was a pot of coffee, frozen, and a side of roast beef . . . a fork was stuck into one side of the beef.
>
> There were 1929 calendars on the walls and on the floor Byrd found a rubber ball with which his famous fox terrier, Igloo, now dead, used to play. It still gave the same annoying squeak. . .
>
> The group, chuckling over these familiar relics, suddenly turned to Finn Ronne. The young Norwegian was standing beside the bunk where his father, Martin Ronne, used to sleep. Martin Ronne first came to the Bay of Whales with Amundsen in 1911. He returned with Admiral Byrd in 1929 when he was 69 years old. He died last year.
>
> Where the son held the light to the wall you could

Finn Ronne in his bunk at Little America, 1933.

see where he (Martin Ronne) had printed out his son's name. . . . Finn Ronne. Nobody remembered seeing it before. Apparently Martin Ronne had written it just before he left.

Finn Ronne's eye's blazed.

"The old man," he said, "must have known I'd come here."

Why my name? Of five sons, why had I been chosen by my father? Had he foreseen before his death that I would be the one to take his place?

◆ ◆ ◆

The ends of the earth exerted a powerful pulling force on Martin Ronne. He was a veteran of high latitudes in both the Arctic and Antarctic. In 1908, when Roald Amundsen, fresh from his conquest of the Northwest Passage, was interviewing men for his forthcoming North Pole expedition, he selected Martin Ronne to be a member of his crew as sailmaker on the sailing ship *Fram*.

I remember well the evening my father came home after his meeting with Amundsen. We were sitting around the kitchen table in our small house in Horten, Norway. Father outlined on a small map the track Amundsen would take in order to reach the North Pole ahead of anyone else. How proud I was that he had been chosen for such a famous expedition.

Before *Fram* sailed, my father invited all the expedition members to our home for a last get-together. Beer flowed freely, and my mother served sandwiches and cakes. Late in the evening twilight, when it was time to leave, the men lined up outside the gate. Then they raced down the street to the ship. That was the last time I saw some of them.

One can well imagine my excitement, as a boy of ten, to see in the harbor of my hometown the tall masts of Fridtjof Nansen's old ship *Fram*. The Norwegian government, whose property it had become, had loaned it to Amundsen. Now it was tied up there to be fitted out for another polar expedition.

The three-masted barquentine-rigged sailing ship was a marvel to me. I explored it from stem to stern and climbed high in its rigging. I went below too, to watch mechanics work on the diesel engine. When it started up, it boomed with a hollow sound, as if steel drums were being slammed together. The hull of the ship was round-bottomed like a soup bowl; the pressure of the thick ice floes would lift her up rather than crush her sides. My father would write us later that the gunwales were constantly awash as the ship moved into the Antarctic seas; but, happily, *Fram* "bounced like a cork."

Her modest size limited the expedition's complement to 18 men. Therefore, the more trades a man knew, the more valuable he would be to the expedition. My father, a sailor since the age of 13, soon learned a new trade: aerial observer.

The usual method of piloting a ship through the pack ice was from the crow's-nest on the foremast. The resourceful Amundsen sought a much higher vantage point. He introduced box kites to navigation. Ten or so kites attached to one another were able to carry a man aloft to a height of 300 meters. Such an observer, standing in a light canvas covered frame suspended from the kites, would guide a ship through leads in the ice much as helicopters assist icebreakers today. Martin Ronne made numerous practice ascents before the ship departed. But Amundsen, not one to gamble with men's lives when the chips were down, left the kites behind.

He intended to sail around Cape Horn, proceed to San Francisco, pass through the Bering Strait, then drift with the current that sweeps across the North Polar basin into the Atlantic Ocean between Iceland and Greenland. His plan was based on Nansen's original idea. Amundsen would have succeeded. In the summer of 1909 world headlines announced that an American explorer, Robert Peary, claimed he had reached the North Pole.

When Amundsen heard the news, he secretly junked his plan to drift across the Arctic Ocean and trained his sights instead on the South Pole, still waiting to be conquered. The English explorer Ernest Shackleton had come within 97 miles of it in 1909. In the summer of 1910 another Englishman, Robert Falcon Scott, was on his way to New Zealand. From there he would head south and establish his wintering quarters at McMurdo Sound in the Ross Sea. Two months after Scott's departure from England, Amundsen left Norway. When *Fram* reached her last port of call at Funchal on the island of Madeira, Amundsen broke his long silence and cabled Scott in New Zealand: "Am going south." Before he departed, the Norweigan offered each member of his crew the opportunity to return home. There were no takers. Like the other men, Martin Ronne was eager for the new challenge. *Fram*, the winds of destiny in her sails, was put on a course for the south polar continent.

Amundsen, in one of history's great dramas, beat Scott to the heart of that windswept wasteland of snow and ice at the southernmost point where all meridians merge. The small silk tent he left at the Pole was made by my father, who had remained on *Fram*. On leather tongs inside the tent Martin Ronne had tooled the names of his wife, two daughters and five sons. He had also scribed a prescient message to Amundsen: "Good luck on the trip and welcome to 90° South." One month later the tent was found by Scott's party of five, all of whom perished on their return journey.

Over a period of twenty years Martin Ronne sailed with Amundsen to both polar regions. "He was one of the teeth in the gear that pulled the engine forward to the goal," Amundsen wrote. "I dare safely say that if that tooth had been missing, the result would have been in doubt."

After the death of Amundsen in 1928, my father was coaxed out of retirement to go to the Antarctic again, this time with Byrd's first expedition 1928–30. When my father came to the United States to join the expedition, I was with him. My image of Byrd, based on his flights in Greenland as a member of Donald MacMillan's expedition, over the Arctic Ocean, and over the Atlantic, was of heroic proportions. I had expected to find a rugged outdoors man, the type who would eat raw meat, drink seal blood, and sleep in an igloo. I was soon disillusioned. Well mannered, nattily dressed in naval aviators' green uniform with leather leggings, smooth shaven and with manicured fingernails, Byrd was a man of slight build with Errol Flynn looks. He was smoking a cigaret in a long holder.

Martin was the only one of the wintering party of 43 men who had ever been in the Antarctic before. Four years later I would stand wonder-struck beside my father's bunk.

My frozen feet brought me painfully back to the fact that I was still in that desolated building beneath the ice. I noticed that my companions had gone, leaving me to my thoughts. What a dismal place! I shivered. Climbing up a makeshift ladder, I stumbled into the glaring sunlight with a great feeling of relief.

Byrd asked me if I wanted my father's bunk; and, of course I accepted. Sentiment aside, that proved to be a mistake, for I soon discovered that it occupied the coldest spot in the settlement. Located near the door leading into the tunnel, kept open at night for ventilation, my bunk caught the brunt of the Antarctic blizzard, sometimes blasting me with temperatures of 60 to 70 below. How typical of that tough Viking to choose such a place to sleep. But many times I wished my father had picked another bunk on Byrd's 2nd expedition to Little America.

CHAPTER *2*

"I F YOU ARE HALF AS MUCH a man as your daddy," Byrd had cabled me from Little America, "I shall be delighted to have you come with me on my next expedition." He knew from my father that I had learned to ski almost as soon as I could walk. All my life, unknowingly had been spent preparing for the time when I would be summoned to break trails in a virgin continent. That time was now at hand.

The barrier was not a safe place to moor the *Ruppert:* huge icebergs could break off and smash into her. We had to find a safer place somewhere along the bay ice. I was assigned the task of breaking new trails over the ice, across and through the pressure ridges, on up to the top of the barrier. The route had to be safe for tractors and loaded sledges, each carrying a ton of cargo or more.

With a bundle of orange flags under one arm, a ski pole in the other hand, and my lunch — a sandwich and a thermos bottle of hot tea — in a canvas bag slung over my shoulder, I beat a straight track toward an overturned iceberg. Skiing over the rippled bay ice, I encountered dangerous pressure ridges impossible to cross, and gaping holes were everywhere. Small lakes had been formed in the cracking and sinking of the ice; in many of them I saw Weddell seals playing. Pups, knowing no fear, followed me with their large brown eyes.

Many times I retraced my steps and searched in another direction. Finally I reached a high ridge from where I could see the surrounding area. From there it was about five miles to the

Ruppert. Eastward lay Little America with its radio beacons towering over the barrier. To the south, about a mile and a half distant, I could see a fairly even stretch of sloping snow and ice. It seemed to be knit together more smoothly than any area I had explored — exactly what I had been searching for.

I skied rapidly along this stretch of bay ice, marking the trail with flags attached to bamboo sticks about 30 inches in height. The orange guideposts stood out in bold relief against the stark white vista. Although there were many small cracks in the ice, the dog teams and tractors would be able to cross them without difficulty, I judged — if they were careful. Still, there was no denying that real danger is never more than a step away. I tossed a chunk of ice through a crack and heard it splash in the water 35 feet below. I quaked at the thought of slipping through a fissure.

Back on the ship, I reported my findings. Anxious to test my trail I suggested we hitch up two dog teams for a practice run. Stu Paine and Alton Wade were the drivers. I was to precede them on skis to point out the route already marked with flags.

Half a ton of cargo was loaded onto each sledge; and at the command "Yake!" off went the dogs. But not very far. They crossed paths, triggering in seconds one of the worst dog fights I had ever seen. The snarling huskies tore into each other, and soon there were bleeding dogs, yelping dogs, lame dogs, frightened dogs all over the ice floe. I skied back to the ship for help, summoning Allan Taylor with his first-aid kit. But the dogs chewed off the bandages as fast as he put them on. Harnesses — gang lines, neck and tail traces — were all tangled up. It took us an hour to get the mess straightened out.

Only the butt end of a whip, swung with a harsh hand, could force the huskies apart. Order was at last restored, and the sledges again began moving. I kept well ahead of the dogs so they could easily follow my tracks. The route soon became known as Misery Trail, because of the perils of the ever-changing ice. When we reached the top of the barrier the drivers indicated they could find their way to Little America.

Wearily I returned to the ship. On the move continuously for 49 hours, I generated enough body heat to keep my ski boots pliable. But once I stopped moving, they froze solid. I spent an hour prying them off. After a hearty meal, I dragged myself forward to the fo'c'sle and fell exhausted in my bunk. When I awoke 15 hours later, the ship had moved to its new mooring, and off-loading was in full swing.

Not even in this relatively protected place would *Ruppert* be safe for long. With the Antarctic winter closing in rapidly, the ship risked being icebound while waiting for the sledges shuttling supplies to Little America. We quickly set up a halfway station between Ruppert and Little America. Supplies could be dropped off at this temporary depot, enabling the dog teams to make more round trips in less time. Of course we had to make sure that the depot was located atop the barrier, in a place where there were no pressure ridges. It didn't take long for the men to pin a label on the supply dump — "Pressure Camp." Here we were introduced to rigorous trail life in the Antarctic.

◆ ◆ ◆

The first vehicles to traverse "Misery Trail" were tractors loaded with mail bags. These were stacked on the snow behind a small building with specific orders for immediate attention. The ship would leave within a couple of weeks, and the cancelled mail had to be on board. Unfortunately, a blizzard roared in and buried the sacks of mail under ten feet of snow. Out of sight, out of mind was never proved truer. With everybody working 12 hours a day, the mail was quickly forgotten.

Six months later, during the darkest part of the year, carpenter Edgar Cox uncovered the canvas sacks while digging a pit outside the cow barn. Yes, we had cows at Little America. They were a gift to Byrd from the Guernsey Cattle Association, to provide us with milk. One of the three cows even presented us a bonus — a bull calf born the day we sighted the first iceberg outside the Ross Sea. Predictably, he was named Iceberg. The pit, incidentally, was for his benefit; the growing bull needed an exercise yard. So, thanks to Iceberg and hard working Cox, the mail eventually went through. But none of the recipients ever knew why it took more than a year for their letters to reach them.

Meanwhile, Byrd had found a way to cash in on the U.S. mails by persuading the Post Office Department to issue a special Byrd stamp. It sold nation-wide for 53 cents, of which Byrd received 50 cents to help finance the expedition. Without those funds — several hundred thousand dollars — we could never have left the Boston harbor.

Returning to Misery Trail, heavily loaded sledges were in constant use for six weeks, ferrying cargo to the high barrier. In the fore was my powerful dog team. It was on Misery Trail that I really learned to drive dogs. Back at the kennels in New Hampshire, the animals had been trained to pull a log across green meadows. How different the white meadows of Antarctica, where I skied alongside a loaded sledge, steering it with the G pole, as the dogs raced across the broken ice.

I knew my dogs well, far better than I knew most of the men on the expedition. "Power" was a big brown husky with strong legs, a wide chest, and ears that hung down. A mixture of many breeds — but with very little Malamute or Siberian — he was smart, dependable, and eager to work. He was to be my

Over 125,000 pieces of stamp collectors' mail were sent through the Little America post office during the spring of 1935 to help raise funds for the Byrd expedition of 1933–1935.

Finn Ronne with his nine-dog husky team and a load of supplies reaching the top of the ice barrier on the 15 mile "Misery Trail" from the moored *Ruppert* to Little America.

companion over hundreds of miles of sledging. "Harold" was a Manitoba, a wolflike dog, grayish in color, weighing about 75 pounds. Unlike Power's ears, Harold's stood straight up. "Spring" was a mixture of every type of husky born within the Arctic Circle. Black and white spots covered his thin, shaggy fur; I doubted that he would be able to withstand extremely low temperatures. "Brutus" was black, with a foxlike face, and was probably the best fighter of the team. "Ski," smaller than the rest, was born in Little America during Byrd's first expedition. This was to be his second trip south. He had been brought back to New Hampshire, and later spent some time on a farm in Indiana. But he killed so many chickens and turkeys that he had to be returned to the kennels.

Ski was black, and his coat was really too thin for cold latitudes. His mischievous eyes fooled many other dogs into thinking he would be an easy mark in a fight. But, to their sorrow, they

♦ 23 ♦

learned that he feared no creature on earth. Even Brutus re-spected Ski's fighting ability. "Hip" was perhaps the second best fighter of the team. He seemed to stay awake constantly, as if on the lookout for an opponent. More peace-loving were "Standard" and "Woody." Each weighed about 80 pounds and had heavy legs and curling tails.

"Mounty" was larger and well muscled, a fine pulling dog. At first he seemed to me the best choice for the lead dog spot, and that's where I hitched him. It proved to be a mistake, even though he understood the command to go right or left. Mounty had the peculiar habit of stopping in the middle of the trail when another team approached. He just stood there, his ears high, as every dog came under his piercing gaze. Suddenly, seeing one that he didn't like — perhaps because of an earlier encounter — he would dive into the enemy with teeth bared. The other dogs needed no coax-ing, and soon there was a pileup of snarling huskies.

Hardly a day passed that I did not have to untangle trace lines and break up free-for-alls. To add to the confusion, penguins sometimes picked fights with the dogs. But I did not fault the birds; this was their world, and we were the intruders.

At Pressure Camp we suddenly became godfathers. With the temperature registering 30 deg. below zero, seven puppies were born in one of the crates that had housed the huskies during the voyage. The mother was a malamute named Taku, the father a part-Labrador named Milton. The pups were very much alike — grayish, wolflike with erect ears. We named them Kim, Mike, Mascara, Cleo, Ten-Ten, Ray and Fritz. Frisky, alert, with bright button eyes, the pups grew rapidly. After the long Antarctic night, I would take charge of their training and eventually work them into my own team.

The unloading operation was but one part of our preparation for the winter night approaching. Some of the men, myself in-cluded, lived in tents at Pressure Camp. As sledges moved up and down Misery Trail, other men and dog teams were busy at Little America, badly damaged by weight of accumulated snow and shifting ice. To shelter the animals, we dug eight trenches, each one six feet deep, three feet wide, and about 40 to 50 yards in length. We placed wooden slats across the top of the trenches and nailed down heavy canvas to prevent snow from sifting

"Dogtown" in Little America consisted of eight trenches, each one six feet deep, three feet wide and 40 to 50 yards in length.

through. The tunnels intersected, forming a maze we dubbed "Dogtown." We dragged the dog crates inside and placed them along the snow walls about ten feet apart. Iron pipes anchored the crates to the snow floor. Each dog was fastened to his crate with a three-foot neck chain. All the dogs in a team were kept together, so that the driver knew exactly where to find them.

Early blizzards slowed our progress. At times snow drifted into the tunnels faster than we could shovel it out. But we persisted, and finally the last husky was taken from the tethering lines and led inside.

For months the dogs remained in total darkness. The only light they would see would be the beam of a flashlight or the glow of a kerosene lantern at feeding time and during checkups. After a few hours in the dark tunnels, the dogs went wild with delight at the approach of a human visitor, leaping up at him, playfully nipping at his heels, yelping shrilly.

The mothers and their offspring — several litters were born at Little America — were kept separate from the other dogs, at least to start with. For example, Taku nursed her brood in a snowy cave, isolated from other dogs that might harm the helpless pups. But quite the contrary would happen. The huskies, so vicious in a fight, would make attentive surrogate parents. On two occasions when I discovered that a puppy was missing, I searched through the crates and both times found the runaway lying snug against a hospitable husky. I shined my light on the big dog and he clumsily tried to hide the pup by twisting his body to block my view.

The puppies were allowed free run of the camp. They didn't mind the cold at all, having literally cut their teeth in below zero temperatures. But the little rascals would abuse their privileges and soon become nuisances. At night we let the fires in the coal stoves die out and, in order to let fresh air into our quarters, opened the doors and ventilators. The first gusts of wind also drove the pups inside. They burst into the room and romped through the corridors, overturned chairs and tables as they scampered. After three sleepless nights, Executive Officer George Noville ordered a new tunnel dug and the pups chained up.

The grown huskies hated being confined. They gnawed away at their crates, hoping to gain some freedom beyond the limits of their neck chains. Once in a while a dog's efforts were rewarded, when his sharp teeth finally splintered the wood. But he never got far. As he moved through the tunnel he had to run the gauntlet of huskies still chained. They dove for the loose dog, reached out as far as their leashes allowed them. Snapping jaws found a leg or a shoulder, and within an instant the place was a bedlam of howls and snarls. The man on night watch would dash in, a lantern in one hand, a whip in the other. Charging down that narrow tunnel, shouting curses, he would beat the dogs off each other and tie up the escapee.

Thus far the dogs had been eating commercial dog food. Aboard ship the bags of food pellets were convenient if bulky. But for field work they took up too much space on the sledges. The expedition had some concentrated dog meal, which consisted of ground suet, meat meal, whole wheat, dried milk, wheat germ, cod liver oil, cooked barley groats, molasses, and hydrogenated soya bean oil. Such a diet was good enough for normal use, but on the trail, where temperatures dropped to 60 below zero — and sometimes lower — more substantial fare was needed. That meant killing seal, long a staple of Eskimos and polar explorers. The seal hunt was not a time for carelessness, as I learned to my chagrin. Once as I was driving my team homeward with two large seals lashed to the sledge, a fat Weddell seal popped up through a hole and flopped on the ice. The animal did not detect me or the dogs. Colt-45 in hand . . . it was a clean hit in the back of the head. I turned toward my team to bring the sledge over — and I couldn't believe my eyes. All I could see was the G (guide) pole of my sledge bouncing over the ice as the dogs, startled by the shot, raced pell-mell toward camp. I ran after them, damning them, but they were long gone. It was a lonely six mile walk back to Pressure Camp.

Despite such mishaps, the hunt went on, as there were great herds of seals in the area offering us easy targets. In a week or two, however, the seals would begin their northern migration. As soon as the ice formed solidly, they would follow the open water in pursuit of their main food supply, small shrimplike krill. These tiny morsels, abundant in Antarctic waters, also served as the major food source for whales and penguins.

Dug out of the snow a few feet from the tunnel was a chopping cave. Here the men hacked hundreds of frozen seal carcasses into pieces weighing about three to four pounds. One of these chunks of meat was fed to a dog every two days. Since the huskies weren't working — indeed, they got almost no exercises of any kind during the long winter night — they did not require a large ration.

On the trail it would be foolish if not impossible to carry enough four-pound slabs of seal meat for the dog team. When loading a sledge, especially for a long haul, every inch of space and ounce of weight had to be carefully allocated. Still, the dogs needed substantial food to pull sledges weighted down with half a ton (and even more) of supplies and equipment. The solution? seal oil.

A fire fed by "logs" of seal blubber roared under a 55-gallon drum. Into this cooker were dumped pieces of blubber from which the oil was rendered. Mixed with commercial dog meal and poured into molds, it hardened into cakes of dog pemmican, each one a full day's ration for a dog on the trail.

The smell of boiling seal blubber was unpleasantly pungent and penetrating. The odor stubbornly clung to a man. It got into his hair, his skin, his clothes. Some veterans swore that it even got into a man's soul — and that it stayed there, long after the last seal had been axed to pieces and the final drop of oil congealed into a cake of dog food.

◆ ◆ ◆

It was late on Saturday afternoon. My partner Albert Eilefsen and I returned from a long day of seal hunting, huddled on the sledge as the frigid southwest wind stung our faces. The sledge tracks from our outward journey that morning were clearly visible, which spared us the task of skiing ahead to break trail. The dogs, sensing that their day's work was about over, hurried homeward, anticipating the chunks of seal meat that would be thrown to them.

Our thin trail eventually merged with a much larger one — the "highway" that tractors used to haul equipment to Little America. Before long, a tractor appeared through the snowdrift. The curious dogs headed directly for it. As we drew nearer, the tractor stopped; and I noticed a mittened hand waving through the window. I halted my team and walked over to the tractor.

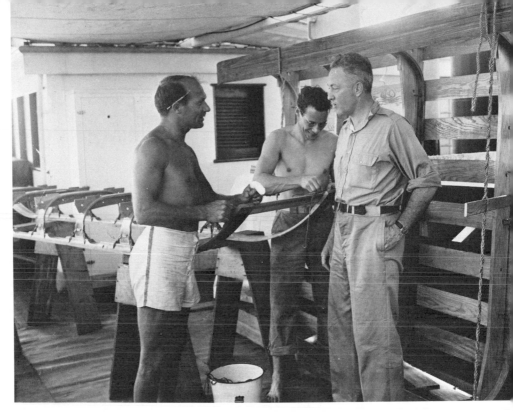

Finn Ronne, *left,* and associate lashing dog sledges onboard the *North Star,* en route to the Palmer Land station as Admiral Richard Byrd, *right,* stops for a morning visit.

About three or four steps away I recognized within the fur hood filling the window the tense face of Byrd, icy white with lips tight against his teeth. "Finn," he snapped, "I thought you had better sense than to sit on the sledge and let the dogs pull you, because we need to preserve all the pulling power we can. It should not be too much to ask you and your partner to run alongside. You know what I mean, don't you?"

I was stunned; for a moment I could not speak. Then swallowing my anger, I blurted "Yes, sir," turned and walked back to the sledge.

Byrd, cozy in his heated cabin, continued on to Little America where, with CBS announcer Charles J. V. Murphy, he would make the first radio broadcasts for Grape-Nuts. Albert and I, exhausted after 12 hours in raw weather with very little food and no heat, watched him out of sight. Then we climbed back on the sledge and rode the rest of the way to Pressure Camp.

CHAPTER 3

B YRD DECIDED TO SPEND most of the winter alone at an advance
base. A trail-breaking team would sledge about 400 miles inland to the foothills of the Queen Maud Mountains, depositing
food caches along the trail and marking it with orange flags. Tractors would follow with materials for the base. Preparations had to
be thorough but expeditious, for when the four-month-long winter
night closed in, travel would be impossible. Already the sun was
almost parallel with the horizon; soon it would not rise at all.

The men chosen to go were Allan Innes-Taylor, former Canadian Mountie and expert dog driver; Stu Paine, a college stu-
dent; Pete, the radio operator; and myself. As the expedition's ski
expert, I had the responsibility of breaking trail as well as driving
a dog team. Ed Moody, an expert dog driver, and young Dick
Russell, each with a team, were to support us for the first 100
miles or so, helping the main party advance supplies southward.

Shortly before we moved out, Pete got sick and had to be
replaced. Unfortunately, that was not easy, for good radio operators were in short supply down south. A surveyor — who shall be
nameless — mentioned that he had tinkered with radios; and
after John Dyer in the radio shack gave him a short refresher
course, he volunteered to take on the job.

The sledges were loaded with radio, hand-cranking generator,
tents, sleeping bags, cook stoves, fuel cans, and other gear. Food
supplies for 60 days accounted for over half the load. Pound-
and-a-half blocks of dog pemmican, frozen as solid as armor plate,
were stacked like brick.

We drivers had our own pemmican. Highly concentrated to furnish the nourishment needed on the trail, it consisted of dehydrated beef grits, bacon grits, whole milk, green pea meal, oatmeal, soybean grits, dehydrated celery, onions, tomatoes, dehydrated shreds of potato, synthetic lemon powder, juice enriched with ascorbic acid (vitamin C), paprika, cayenne, black pepper, and salt. The bacon grits had to be finely diced by hand since machine grinding robbed it of chewing value. The ingredients were measured carefully. The dry substances were mixed thoroughly; then the bacon grits, some beef tallow, and bacon fat were added. After the mixture was stirred for a few minutes, it was poured into 12-ounce molds and allowed to harden. The pemmican could be eaten raw, but it tasted better if shaved into hot water and made into a heavy, hearty soup.

We also took canned butter, peaches, bacon slices, tea, coffee, and biscuits. Besides providing us with carbohydrates, the biscuits gave us something solid to chew on. Polar explorers favored the "trail-biscuit" formula, consisting of oatmeal, whole wheat flour, shortening, whole milk powder, whole egg powder, honey syrup, baking powder, and salt. These ingredients were mixed with very little water, so that the biscuits did not freeze rock-hard in below-zero weather.

The individual foods were packed into marked bags. An assortment of these placed in a large burlap sack weighing about 70 pounds was enough to feed a man for a month, at the rate of 37 ounces of food — 5,500 calories — per day.

While every piece of equipment we took was important, nothing surpassed the Nansen cook stove. This kerosene cooker with double-wall construction was made in such a way that all the heat generated by the burner could be used. It had a ring pot into which lumps of ice were placed; when it melted, good fresh water came out of the spigots. It was a marvelously efficient burner, turning out a meal about half an hour or so after the pots were put on the fire.

Before the two support drivers turned back, it was time to give the surveyor a few pointers on breaking trail. Generally, with a man skiing in front, the party could travel faster, because the lead dog would follow the skier's track. I asked him to ski for awhile. When he had progressed about 100 yards, we turned the teams loose. He soon got onto the trick of lining up snow-features the same distance apart in order to ski straight. The teams quickly caught up with the man, who was already tired. In fact, they were right on his heels. Forced to slow down, they became entangled in the harness and began fighting. We worked for half an hour to quiet the huskies and get them back into their traces.

The number of feuds between dogs was truly amazing. Once two dogs got into a fight, they would remain bitter enemies and go at each other every time they met. I was sure some huskies carried grudges for months.

It was apparent that we would never make the mountains, still 450 miles south of us, if the surveyor continued in the lead. I decided to ski ahead from then on. He struggled not to be left behind, hung onto my sledge, adding to the dogs' burden.

Leading the dogs proved to be a monotonous chore. There was nothing to look at but the horizon, nothing whatsoever to hold the eyes. It was not until the third day that I decided to try an experiment with Power, my lead dog. He seemed to obey commands almost before they were given; he sensed exactly what to do. So, next morning I took up position alongside the lead sledge, my hand on the G pole. I shouted, "Power — Yake!" He moved ahead and the team followed him across the snowfields. He kept the gangline taut and broke trail like a veteran. With a mariner's compass mounted on the rear end of the sledge, all I had to do was call out an occasional "Gee" or "Haw" to keep us on course. It was no longer necessary for me to ski ahead of the teams.

The two teams supporting us dropped their last caches and turned back toward Little America. We, the four of us, continued on, carving a trail in an icescape that became increasingly more undulating due to the wind-carved ridges. The temperature fell to 65 below zero, with 20 mile-an-hour winds whipping out from the interior. It knifed through our clothing, exposing us to frostbite.

On this trip I learned first hand how much punishment the human body could endure. By necessity, our regime was pretty much the same every day. We arose about the same time every morning, rousting ourselves out of our sleeping-bag cocoons, pounding arms and stamping feet to stimulate circulation. Allan lighted the primus stove, and the snow that I put into the cooking pot the previous night began melting. He cooked oatmeal and mixed powdered milk with water. While we dipped our wooden spoons into the steaming cereal, he boiled powdered coffee and fried bacon strips. Trail biscuits were fried in the bacon fat. The colder the weather, the more we craved fatty foods.

After Allan washed the dishes, he filled the thermos bottles with hot chocolate, the other bottles with water. I rolled up the sleeping bags and passed them out the tent to Stu. Radio and food box followed. The last thing we did inside the tent was turn off the primus stove. We always let it burn until the last minute because the temperature usually hovered between 40 and 60 below zero. We ducked inside frequently to warm our hands over the flame.

With the primus and the kerosene cans packed, we took down the tent. This could be a difficult chore when the wind was gusting. The tent poles were slipped into sleeves sewn into the corners of the tent, the ropes coiled, then the entire tent roll lashed to the sledge.

The dogs began yelping and howling from the first moment they saw us. Eager to be off and pulling, they warmed up by snapping and nipping at each other. To prevent the sledge moving before we were ready, I drove an iron tipped hickory pole into the snow, between the crossbars. No matter how hard the dogs pulled, we stayed put. Power, the lead dog, was hitched up; then the other dogs, in tandem, were led into place and harnessed. I took my position at the G pole, jerked the arresting hickory staff out of the snow, and we were off. During the first minutes, the dogs usually set out at a gallop, but they soon throttled down to a steady pace. With a heavy load in tow, they averaged about four to five miles per hour.

The drivers were generally quiet on the trail, at least most of the time. The only loud sounds were commands from me or one of the other drivers. Skiing beside the sledge, my right hand on the G pole, I watched the dogs. When the tail traces attached to each dog hung slack, I knew that he wasn't pulling his share of the load. I bent down, picked up a small piece of ice and flung it at the lazy dog, at the same time calling: "Come on, you b . . . ." All the dogs turned to look at me and, trained to obey commands without hesitation, strained against their harness and pulled with spirit.

About every half-hour we stopped to give the dogs a rest. They stretched, lay down, maybe rolled in the snow. After about ten minutes they grew restless, and we hit the trail again. After four hours of steady going, we stopped for lunch — hot chocolate in the thermos, oatmeal biscuits, and cold pemmican. And water. We drank lots of water because of dehydration.

Our trail stops were always brief, even for lunch. As long as we kept moving, our body heat was sufficient to keep us warm; but when we stopped for any prolonged length of time, the chill due to the wind cut through clothing, and ski boots began to freeze solid.

The dogs generally told us when we had done enough sledging for one day. Their pace slowed from a trot to a walk in the late afternoon, and finally they stopped. In an emergency we could whip them on, but ordinarily there was no reason to push the dogs.

We quickly unloaded the sledges. The cook tent, the last item lashed on in the morning, was the first thing to be taken off. After it was set up, one of us carried the food box and primus stove inside. The cooking pot was filled with snow, and the stove lit.

Meanwhile, another man anchored two long poles in the snow, placing them about 40 feet apart. Between the poles he stretched a steel cable studded with small spools. From each of these, welded in place to prevent sliding, dangled a two-foot chain, which was snapped to a dog's collar. After the dogs were tethered out of reach of each other, we fed them. It was amazing to see them clamp their jaws around the frozen blocks of pemmican, each animal downing his ration in three or four savage bites. Then the huskies curled up to sleep, swishing their tails over their bodies and across their faces. Blowing snow often covered the dogs completely. Peering out of the tent in the morning, we saw nothing to betray their presence. The moment one of us stepped outside and made a noise, the snow erupted as furry heads popped through the white blanket.

By the time we made camp and crawled into the tent, our ski boots and gloves were frozen hard. After we struggled out of them, we put on dry woolen socks and sealskin mukluks, then stood and stamped our feet wildly, as though dancing some pagan ritual, until feeling returned. We strung a line overhead, between the tent poles, and hung up our frozen socks to dry.

Sledge party camped on the slopes of Mount Nilsen in the Rockefeller Mountains in King Edward's Land about 150 miles east of Little America.

The sledge dogs, tethered far enough apart to prevent fights, wait to be fed a pound of food after a 25 mile stretch of heavy pulling.

We constantly guarded against frostbite, especially of our feet. In the open, nose and chin were always vulnerable; and we frequently checked each other's faces for telltale white spots. When a frozen patch appeared, bare hands massaged the face to restore circulation.

All of us had difficulties with our sleeping bags. Early in the trip the zipper on mine broke, so that it could not be closed. I crawled in still wearing my fur clothing. During the night my body heat warmed the bag, and moisture formed inside it. When I emerged in the morning, the moisture condensed into ice crystals. I tried to "pump out" the bag — that is shake the warm air out. But it was no use. Before the trip ended, my sleeping bag collected 20 pounds of icy ballast.

As we continued to sledge toward that spot in the wasteland where Byrd intended to set up his lonely base, the cold deepened to a constant 50 below zero. Our kerosene turned syrupy. We burned some paper close to the vaporizing chamber of the primus stove, thawing the fuel enough to get a flame going. But that was a dangerous practice. Guess wrong, and you blew up the tent.

One evening, as we were sledging along, the very air seemed to shake, as if an avalanche was approaching. The dogs stopped in their tracks. We stood there spellbound. What was going on? Suddenly the crust beneath us quivered and fell about six inches. The frightened dogs lunged in all directions, and we had to struggle to keep them under control.

As quickly as it began, the snow quake ended. We suffered no damage, only momentary fright. Snow quakes, not unusual in the Antarctic, occurred when huge stretches of the barrier crust contracted, resulting in all that snow and ice settling to a new level.

At last we reached our destination, set up camp, and waited for the tractors to catch up with us. We were tired and hungry. Allan wasted no time preparing a pot of steaming pemmican. Now we faced the problem of what to do next. The surveyor, try as he would, could not make radio contact with Little America. For two days we huddled in our tents while shrieking winds clawed at our fragile shelters and threatened to rip them asunder. To pass the time, we sang songs like "I've been working on the Railroad." When the blizzard let up, we scanned down the trail and were relieved to find that our orange markers — some of them, at least, remained visible. The tractors eventually would catch up with us. But, without radio communication, we would not be sure of anything.

The radioman donned the headset and again tried the radio. Nothing. I asked Stu Paine to take a crack at it. He fooled around with the transmitter for a few minutes and, while I cranked the generator, tapped out Little America's call letter (KFZ). Morse-Code signals crackled immediately in the earphones. Stu had made contact. And in the nick of time. Those tractors we had been waiting for were not coming — not here, anyway. The message indicated that Byrd had again changed his mind about the location of his advance base. We were to backtrack about 90 miles, to 81 degrees south latitude. He decided there was not enough time to establish the base further south.

Reluctantly, we broke camp and loaded the sledges. It was tough to turn back after struggling to get this far, more than half-way to the Queen Maud Mountains, our original goal. We easily followed the trail flags we had planted, and at times, even the sledge-runner tracks could be seen. With Power unerringly finding the route back, the dogs moved faster, perhaps because the sledges were much lighter. But we had ample supplies. Coming south, we had built snow beacons — cairns about eight feet high with flags on top — and inside them cached food and other gear in case of an emergency.

The reading of the sledge meter told us we had covered the distance to the general area that Byrd had designated. But were there no tractors? Perhaps they were just beyond the ridge to the north silhouetted against the pale sky. The barrier surface here was not the smooth, unbroken plain one would imagine. It was more like the ocean, but its long waves were motionless, frozen in time. The distance between each crest was about quarter of a mile.

, We made camp as usual, then turned into our sleeping bags shortly after the evening meal. Our sleep was interrupted by horns blowing. The tractors were here.

Next morning we began building Byrd's hut. First a pit was dug — 15 feet long, 11 feet wide, and six feet deep. At the bottom we placed heavy-timbered support beams that formed the foundation. Sunk into the snow, the shack would be sheltered from the wind and remain free of snow drifts, which can cover almost anything when Antarctic blizzards blow. We assembled the structure quickly. The prefabricated walls were numbered, so there was no guesswork on where to fit the pieces. We laid the heavy timbered floor, then bolted walls and roof together. The sun shone for only several hours and we had to resort to pressure lanterns to see what we were doing. Then the temperature dropped to 61 below, the kerosene turned to mush, and we were in the dark. But not for long. The tractor party produced blow torches, enabling us to finish the job without having to grope our way.

All of us suffered from frostbite. Stu looked bad. His skin was deadly white, his nose swollen the size of a tennis ball, and his beard crusted with ice. My lips were cracked and bleeding; and I had no feeling in the right cheek. For six months afterward, whiskers would not grow on that side of the face.

On our second day at camp, Byrd's plane arrived. Bundled warmly in his fur parka, he jumped down, eager to inspect his new quarters. We unloaded bags and boxes from the Fairchild plane, its engine roaring impatiently. "Hurry up!" urged pilot Bill Bowlin. He was anxious to get back to Little America before dark. I couldn't blame him. Seconds after the last box was pitched out to the snow, he gunned the motor. "So long, Finn," Bill shouted, and the plane streaked across the snow and climbed into the cold sky, leaving a trail of white vapor.

Byrd's little cottage was nothing but a barren shell at this stage. The men quickly set up his bunk and fired up the potbellied stove. The place began to take on a homelike character. Snug in his bunk, Byrd got a good night's sleep. So did some of the men, stretched out on the floor in sleeping bags. But there wasn't room for everybody; we dog drivers shivered in our tents on top-side as the temperature plummeted to 65 below zero.

The next morning Byrd told me he went topside for a midnight stroll. "You were snoring like a good Norwegian, Finn, so I knew you were still alive." In my log book I wrote: "This was the chilliest night on the entire trip."

After we finished building the shack, tunnels were dug adjacent to the hut so that all the gear would be within easy reach of Byrd. Nothing he might need was more than a few steps away.

It was with mixed feelings that we geared up for our homeward journey. We were happy to have completed our mission, but somewhat apprehensive about leaving Byrd behind alone in that small hut buried in the snow. We wondered if he could last out the winter. He had plenty of food and a tank-farm of fuel drums, so I felt confident that he wouldn't starve to death or freeze. Still, I had doubts, especially after the special treat he had served us the night before, when he confessed that a bucket of raspberry gelatin was the first food he had ever prepared in his life. That stuff was as tough to eat as guttapercha.

Household chores would occupy part of his time. But his main task would include maintaining radio contact with Little America and keeping records of wind-direction and velocity, temperatures, barometric pressure, and humidity. He would not have to leave his warm quarters, since gauges were located at his working table. To while away the hours, the weeks, and the months — and perhaps the entire year — he brought his wind-up Victrola and stacks of records. "Carry me back to Old Virginny" seemed to be his favorite.

Topside, the view was one of utter desolation — a sea of blinding snow. Nevertheless, dwindling supplies indicated that we start back. Three of us, myself included, would drive the three dog teams.

The surveyor, who complained of a sore foot, hitched a ride on a tractor. He claimed that he had twisted his foot skiing . . .

Our return trip was a grueling seven days' struggle against the elements. My diary revealed a typical day:

> "Made only 12 miles . . . started snowing in afternoon with a southerly fierce wind and surface drifts . . . now storm has reached blizzard proportions . . . wondering how the dogs managed to stay alive out there in the open. It was tough going to get harnesses off and chaining the dogs to the tethering line. Could not use the fingers because leather gloves were as made of steel . . . wrist bleeding badly and blisters in the face . . . the temperature just now indicated 62 deg. below zero . . .

Most of the small trail flags were drifted over. The tractors had sped ahead, and their tread tracks were visible only occasionally. I trusted Power's ability to keep us on track, and he didn't disappoint me. Somehow that marvelous husky seemed to know the exact course to take. Only rarely did I have to check him on the magnetic compass.

All the huskies behaved magnificently. They were tired, and no wonder; it was rugged work pulling the sledges through the deep snow. They even seemed to eat more slowly than usual, a sure sign of extreme fatigue. Still, after a few hours sleep, they sprang to their feet when it was time to move out, shook off the snow, and strained to be off again.

As we neared Little America, Harold, one of my Manitoba dogs, suddenly keeled over. He was pulled back to his feet immediately, as his teammates tugged at his harness. We started again, but it was plain that something was wrong with Harold. He did not pull at all; his pulling trace was slack. I stopped the team. Harold slumped over dead. I removed the harness from his body and stood there, staring for a few moments at the still form, and I would never forget it.

The team started again, leaving Harold where he lay. In a few minutes the swirling snow would cover him completely.

Before nightfall, Alan and Stu were forced to kill two of their dogs. Totally exhausted, they couldn't stand up. Shooting the poor beasts was not quite the simple job it seemed. The revolver had to be thawed or it wouldn't fire, and the only way to do that was by holding it in our hands, inside our gloves. However, it had to be handled carefully or the cold metal would stick to the skin. We took turns thawing the weapon, a task lasting 15 to 20 minutes.

We also suffered. All three of us were thin and worn. Alan's eyes were puffy, his face drawn from lack of sleep. Stu's face was covered with frostbite sores and scabs. My feet felt frozen, and I thought they would have to be chiseled out of my boots. We moved slowly, almost drunkenly. It took much longer now to pitch the tent and get the primus stove going. We were rapidly nearing the end of our endurance.

The final day of the journey was clear and still. At noon the sun reached its highest — barely above the horizon. It was a bizarre sight, a dark red ball of fire that was less a dawning than a sunset. Tomorrow it would drop below the earth's rim, not to return for about four months. As I watched the ebbing sun, a reflection of its rays burst forth, casting weird shadows. Suddenly a mirage formed, looking something like an over-exposed photograph. And there, in the sky, we saw the barrier cliff, its blue edges disappearing into the water. We stood there transfixed, oblivious to everything but that shimmering image above us. Now I understood the claims of other explorers who had reported seeing land where there was no land. They, like us, saw mirages, the reflection of objects hundreds of miles distant.

Now we were almost home and the dogs seemed to sense that they would not have to pull the sledges much farther. The radio masts came into view; and soon we saw some of the men from the base coming out to meet us. Down the last hill, past the old emergency cache, we sledged, our bodies erect. The huskies sprinted toward Dogtown.

CHAPTER *4*

THE WINTER NIGHT NOW HAD Antarctica in its icy grip. All outdoor activities ceased. But underneath the snow there was a
bustling community of 55 men. We had much to do. To begin
with, there was the day-to-day maintenance of Little America's
population — household chores such as mess duty, caring for the
dogs, bringing in coal and stoking the potbellied stoves, clearing
the tunnels of snowdrifts, and filling the snow melter. Chief
among our tasks was the preparation of equipment for field operations when the sun returned. The airplanes and tractors got a
thorough going-over, but the sledges in particular demanded attention since most of them took a beating on the trail. It was my
responsibility to put them in first class shape. Albert helped.

The sledges had been stacked topside, and the rawhide lashings, frozen as hard as iron, had to be thawed before we could do
any work. We set up shop in the mess hall. When a sledge was
brought in, we lashed it tightly against the ceiling, where the air
was warmer. We cut new slats, renewed sprung lashings, replaced
worn bridges. After the sledges were repaired, we varnished them
to keep out moisture. The rawhide lashings, too, received a protective coating, to guard against the wet always present in summer.
The sun, even though the temperature might not be above zero,
still carried a solid punch of heat to melt snow around the runners.

Our sledges were patterned after the original Nansen design,
which he used when drifting across the Arctic Ocean in 1893–96.
This sledge features a single arched bridge sunk into longitudinal
grooves in the two 12-foot-long runners. The design provided

great strength and flexibility as the sledge slid over the wind-whipped sastrugi, those furrowed ridges on the snowy surface. Built of seasoned hickory, the sledge was held together with rawhide, so the joint would give but not snap under stress. A piece of rope strung in front between the runners served as a brake. When sliding down a steep slope, the dog driver dropped the rope ahead of the runners; the friction slowed the sledge.

Despite our efforts to keep busy, I volunteered to help the mail clerk sort and cancel letters — it was easy to become sullen and morose in our claustrophobic quarters. Hobbies such as wood carving and the diversions of reading, card playing, movies (westerns, most of them) only temporarily dispelled the gloom. But to go outside when a blizzard was raging was out of the question.

However, there were periods when a bright moon shone and the wind died down. At such times the more ambitious of us scrambled out of our surface home, strapped on skis, and skimmed over icy slopes with childlike abandon. Dyer and I built a ski jump. My best effort was 40 feet — an Antarctic record. But, I must admit, I was the only contestant.

Sometimes we witnessed glorious displays of the Aurora Australis. From fathomless darkness, colors broke across the sky, first of shimmering ribbons of white with great blushes of rose that glowed and receded. Then a vast curtain, almost directly overhead, seemed to part; and a mass of whirling fire lit up the heavens, a cyclone of colors so marvelous that we gasped in astonishment.

The Southern Lights vanished as suddenly as they appeared, and in the cruel darkness storms raged unseen. High in a radio mast we always kept a beacon light burning. It was the one light we could not allow to fail.

Despite the risks of being caught in the open I chose to spend much of my free time away from the main camp in a shack fabricated from a room-sized aviation crate. Here I could get away from the turmoil. I called my hideaway "Blubberheim," and with the help of a young radio operator, outfitted it with bunks, a small stove, working table, and radio. We strung an electric cable from my "Heim" to the generator at camp, about 75 yards away. Many a tough time I had to walk that distance when a blizzard was blowing.

One Saturday afternoon in July the unthinkable happened. As I headed toward the mess hall, the light in the tower suddenly blinked out. Plunged into total darkness, I quickly lost my sense of direction. For all I knew, each step I took might have been leading me farther from camp. Still, to have remained in one spot could mean certain death from freezing, since the temperature was more than 50 below zero. I had no light, no food, no shelter; soon my body warmth would be expended, even though I was fairly well dressed.

Grains of hard snow whipped by gale winds pelted my face, stinging like millions of needle points. In desperation I shouted for help, but my cries were shredded by the shrieking wind. I staggered and fell, struggling futilely against the ceaseless, invisible forces. Fighting fear, fighting panic, I crawled, groping in the dark, reaching out for something solid to touch. But I found only snow. I was lost.

The blizzard paused to catch its breath, and I lay down in the lee of a snow mound, listening, dreading the wind's shrill return. In the eerie quiet my raw senses played tricks. I closed my eyes, and brilliant lights flashed in my brain, mocking my blindness. I felt surprisingly warm, even comfortable, and I imagined I was in my bunk safe from the storm. I faintly heard the dogs barking . . . something must have aroused them . . . I thought I would close the door . . . In the half-dream I attempted to rise and pitched forward on my face. The impact shocked me back to reality, to my hopeless plight on the ice. I rolled on my back, stared into the black void, resigned to my fate. But again I heard the distant barking of dogs. Was I delirious? I covered my ears with mittened hands, and the barking sound faded. I pulled my hands away, and the sounds returned.

Jubilant, I struggled to my feet and strained to see and hear the search party coming for me. But there was no flash of lanterns, no voices calling my name. There was none of that; there was only the far-off yelping of dogs. But where? I peeled back the hood of my parka and pressed my head to the snow. That was where. The dogs were beneath me. I was standing on Dogtown!

"I'm coming, Power! I'm all right, Kim!" I dug into the snow, yelled into the snow, defying the snow that would have been my grave. "I'm safe! I'm coming!" I cried out in my joy. The barking

Gathered in the mess hall at Little America on June 22, 1934 to celebrate Mid-Winter Night — the longest and darkest night during the wintering period.

grew louder; the dogs must have heard me. Thank God I helped dig the tunnels. I visualized how they were laid out and where I might be. Following the beckoning din from below, I finally found the entrance and stumbled into the tunnel.

I passed a couple of men in the tunnel, but I said nothing. The experience had left me numb, speechless. I nodded and continued on toward the warmth and bounty of the mess hall. Albert poured me a cup of coffee. "Finn," he said, "you are late for supper."

In August the long night ended. After an absence of four months, the sun struggled to the horizon, hung suspended for a few minutes, then sank out of sight again. But each day the twilight hours lasted longer, crowding out the darkness until we beheld the midnight sun. Even so, the bitter cold lingered; not until the middle of September did it warm to 30 deg. below zero.

Anxious to get to work outside, we pulled the sledges to the surface and stretched out the gang lines with harnesses attached. Then we brought up the dogs. After being chained in the dark for so long, they almost went crazy when they saw the bright sunlight. It took two men to line up each dog and slip the harness over his head. The first team we hitched to a sledge for a practice run bolted and headed toward the bay. Three men chased the runaways, finally catching up with them about a mile or so away, at the pressure ridge. The need to release pent-up energy was apparent in both men and dogs. During the unloading of the ships, one man had lost control of his temper and had to be sent home. When his lead dog Weily did not immediately respond to his command, he beat the animal severely, and it ultimately died. Half a dozen men watched in disbelief. I could see that he was not a man to drive sledge dogs.

I was eager to try out my new team, which included Taku's seven pups, now almost full-grown huskies. I broke them in a few at a time, working them in with the veterans; Power I kept as a lead dog. Teaching the youngsters to pull together was no easy task. At my command "Yake," Power jumped forward; Ski, who had been born in Little America, and knew what it was all about, leaned into his harness like an old dray horse. The three pups in the nine dog team were pulled along, although they didn't like the idea. I nudged them with the tips of my skis when they hung back; sometimes I cracked the whip over their heads, and they moved right out.

Within two weeks my "puppy team" was pulling as well as any team in Little America. For dogs so young and inexperienced, they exhibited surprising strength and stamina. And speed. No other team would keep up with them.

I taught Power the command — "Steady" — meaning he should move straight ahead, following his nose, so to speak. The dog seemed to have a built-in direction finder. When I checked his course with the compass, I was amazed to find that he was never far off.

Since my team was the first in camp ready for work we were first to hit the trail, on the "Emergency Cache" mission. Before the winter night set in, a deep crack had formed in the barrier southeast of Little America. For awhile it was feared that we might find ourselves marooned on a tabular iceberg drifting out to sea if the patch of ice we called home split off from the barrier. Therefore, we established an emergency camp three miles south of Little America and stocked it with tents, sleeping bags, radios, food for men and dogs, and a galley stove with several tons of coal. Had the fissure in the ice widened, we would have holed up there and waited for the ships to return from New Zealand in the spring. However, the crack closed, and we didn't have to move. Now, with plenty of light and good weather, my team set out to transport the emergency cache back to the main camp. At first I gave my dogs light loads — 600 or 700 pounds — but I increased the weight on each trip. Finally they were pulling 1,650 pounds without difficulty. I was very pleased with my puppy team.

◆ ◆ ◆

Our performance did not go unnoticed by Dr. Thomas Poulter, second in command and chief of the scientific staff. At the end of the winter night, he asked me to join his seismic party working the area of the Bay of Whales. I jumped at the chance to escape the tensions in camp where, after months of close confinement, personalities were beginning to clash. Some men were as bad as the huskies.

Early one October morning Dr. Poulter awakened me. The only other person up was the night watch, stoking the galley range. I soon learned that Dr. Poulter was not the sort to have a hearty breakfast, smoke a pipe, then go to work. When I reached the galley, all that he had on the table was bread and butter. Coffee, of course, was always there. Seeing this was the only food he had provided to start the day on, I fetched some cheese and orange juice. I asked Poulter if we would be returning for lunch. He said that we wouldn't; he already had something for us to eat on the sledge.

The party moved out in bright sunshine, my team leading the

way. About four miles from camp, on top of the Ross Ice Shelf, Poulter decided to make the first seismic sounding. My job was to dig five holes in the snow with an auger; into these, spaced about 100 feet apart, I placed phones linked to a cable that led to the recording instruments on my sledge. A second sledge, towed by the cable, stopped a quarter mile astern, where a hole was dug for a dynamite charge. Raising an orange flag, Poulter signaled for the charge to be set off. Then he fed a sensitized paper strip through the seismic instrument, recording the results of the shots. It took about 25 minutes for him to get a reading, Moving five to ten miles after every shot, we kept busy the entire day. Our seismic soundings told us we were floating on relatively thin ice — less than a thousand feet thick. Inland it was two miles thick and more.

Lunch time was about two o'clock, and we were curious to find out what Dr. Poulter had prepared for us. To our dismay we discovered that it consisted of two frozen loaves of bread, two chunks of frozen butter, a hunk of frozen cheese, and two thermos bottles of black coffee. Next time, I told him, I would prepare the lunch.

In early October, Pilot Bill Bowlin flew to Advance Base and brought Byrd back from his lonely vigil. He looked pale and thin walking from the plane over to Noville's shack, where a bunk was ready for him. His stay was cut short, it was reported, because a faulty kerosene stove almost did him in. But another view was that Byrd, a Virginia gentleman, was simply unable to cope with the demands of living alone in an isolated environment. He was unaccustomed to doing things for himself. Quipped one observer: "He would starve to death camped in the middle of a grocery store."

I once fitted Byrd with skis and boots; he never took to them, nor did he desire ski instructions I offered. As for trail experience, he wasn't interested in knowing how to fix a sleeping bag or pre-pare trail food in the open; sleeping in a tent wasn't his cup of tea either. He didn't have to, of course. But without such experience, he was deprived of survival knowledge that he would have found useful at Advance Base the five months he was there alone.

After the first few weeks there, he failed to keep regular

radio contact with Little America. We had brief, intermittent contacts, then long periods of silence. Occasionally Byrd acknowledged receiving blind voice transmission by tapping "r" (received). Naturally we became worried. Finally, Tom Poulter decided to lead a tractor party to Advance Base. It was a hazardous undertaking during the darkest and coldest months. By ingenious navigating across treacherous terrain, Poulter and two companions reached him after five attempts.

As suspected, food had been the problem; Byrd was weak from undernourishment, and his shack was a mess. During his stay, the electric generator conked out, the radio transmitter didn't work right, and fumes leaked from the kerosene stove.

It was foolish for Byrd to stay alone, of course. A few of us had offered to spend the winter with him, but he declined. He was determined to pull off his stunt — probably for the publicity he knew it would generate.

Poulter's party stayed with him for two months, nursing him to health, before he could be flown back.

◆ ◆ ◆

Trail rations typically included concentrated food, meat, pemmican, biscuits, cocoa, and water. That was the menu for my sledging trip to the South Polar Plateau. We were part of a major exploratory and scientific effort designed during the winter. Plans called for three dog teams and a tractor group to fan out from Little America. One sledge party was for geological purposes; another would move toward Marie Byrd Land; the third would go south across the Ross Ice Shelf to the polar plateau. The tractors would travel east to monitor the movement of the glacial ice.

I headed the transportation of the Plateau Party, which included seismologist Gill Morgan, physicist Irwin Bramhall, and Albert Eilefsen.

Excellent skier, master mariner, veteran of sealing expeditions to the Arctic, Albert drove a dog team the way Alaskan sourdoughs did. When he barked a command to the dogs, they obeyed. If they didn't respond fast enough to suit him, he didn't hesitate to swing his 12-foot whip and crack it over their heads. His huskies learned right away who was boss.

Gill and Bram had never driven a dog team before, nor had they ever strapped a pair of skis on their feet before they came on

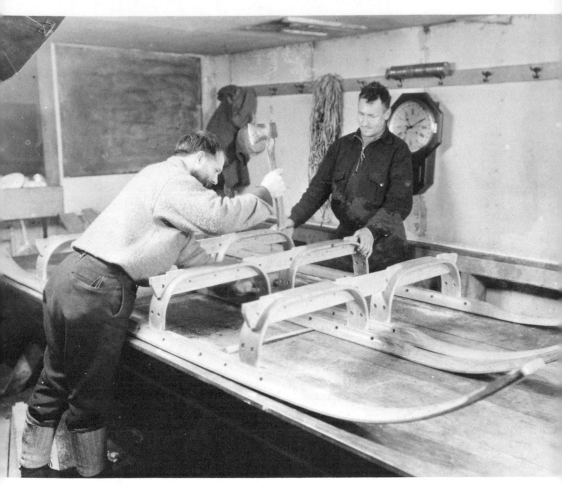

Finn Ronne, *left,* and Albert Eilefsen repairing dog sledges during the winter for use the following summer.

the expedition. It was up to Albert and me to teach them. The scientists tried hard, but they couldn't get the hang of it. Albert didn't hide his disappointment. At the end of a day of instruction he sat on his bunk and, shaking his head, muttered, "no good, no good." But I told him to be patient; they would improve because they were determined to get to the polar plateau.

The Plateau and Geological parties started off together, heading across the Ross Ice Shelf toward the mountains that surrounded the polar plateau. Gill and Bram fell behind the first hour; we had to stop frequently so they could catch up. But I could not fault them; they had come to Antarctica to study rocks and ice, not to drive a dog team. Gill, an expert in oil exploration with years of experience in the Texas oil fields, had come with us to examine the possibility of discovering oil in this land of snow and ice. Such a thing was unheard of, but he had a hunch. Bram, quiet and studious — he always beat me at chess — was to take magnetic readings along our route to the plateau. He also had instruments to measure variations in gravity as we approached the Geographical South Pole.

With each passing day the sun became more intense, and temperatures zoomed to 20 above zero, occasionally almost to the melting point. We peeled off our heavy parkas and worked in shirt sleeves. The heat wave did not last long, however. Within a few hours the temperature again dived below zero.

Only once did the huskies cause trouble. While breaking camp one morning, a dog managed to tear loose from the harness. She bounded away, eluding our efforts to capture her. Finally we gave up, proceeding without her. But the wily husky followed at a distance. Hoping she would see the error of her ways, we tossed her a ration of pemmican. She greedily accepted the handout, but did not venture closer. We could not afford to waste food on a dog that didn't work; however, if we stopped leaving food for her, she would starve. There was nothing in the snowy waste for a dog to kill and eat; shore-hugging penguins and seals being miles behind us.

After playing the husky's game for four days, I decided to try once more to capture her. I rigged a trap of radio-antenna wire, baiting the noose with a half-ration of dog pemmican. Then I retreated about 30 yards and waited, holding the end of the wire in my outstretched hand. The hungry husky, eyeing me warily, approached the food and sniffed it. Standing behind the sledge, I pretended to take no notice. The instant the dog stepped into the noose and seized the bait, I yanked the wire, catching her tightly by a forepaw. She struggled and howled, but it was no use. Once she was tethered, I gave her a light lashing to reestablish authority; sparing the whip could have jeopardized her survival. Then I gave her a cake of food.

I had learned a lot about my puppy team since I first broke them to harness. Wray, for example, was an excellent worker, sprightly, with a very serious nature. Sometimes she noticed that her larger sister Mascara was not pulling her share of the load. But the lazy dog did not get away with it. Wray jumped over the gang line, bit Mascara on the ear, then jumped back into place before Mascara knew what happened. At the same time I called out sharply to Mascara and picked up a piece of packed snow and threw it at her. For hours afterward Mascara worked hard, but there was a puzzled look in her eyes.

Keeping to a course due south, we reached the Advance Base where the leader spent five months alone. We made camp there for the night. Fortunately for us, when the base was evacuated, a half year's supplies had been left behind. In the food tunnel I had helped build we discovered a welcome respite to our pemmican rations. That evening we dined on cooked ham, sweet potatoes, canned vegetables, tomato juice, with English plum pudding for dessert.

The temperature dropped steadily as we progressed inland, and we pulled on heavy furs. About 50 miles south of the camp we entered an area crisscrossed by dangerous crevasses. Gaping, bottomless cracks in the ice were everywhere; some of them covered by bridges of snow waiting to booby-trap the unwary. Bram's trailer-sled slid into one of them. Bram narrowly missed falling into the same crevasse. By then, he was across on solid surface. After that close call, we probed every step of the way with a long iron bar, testing the trail before moving the sledges across. It was slow and painstaking work, but we didn't complain; no one was anxious to step off the edge. After about ten miles we found the surface more stable; we resumed our normal pace and continued on course.

Operating the radio — a skill I perfected during the winter — I learned that the tractors were experiencing rough going. One message halted us in our tracks; we were instructed to turn back and help the vehicles cross the crevassed area we just passed.

Retracing our track northward, we encountered the tractors after a 20-mile run. One of the machines had fallen into a crevasse. Luckily no one was hurt, but the tractor was lost. Nose-down in the fissure, it was impossible to winch it up without heavy equipment. Still, we tried. Hooking up a tow chain, we attempted to pull the tractor free with the other machine, but all we got was a lot of smoke and noise. The only thing we could do

A Citroën snow mobile caught in a crevasse during the 1933–1935 Byrd expedition. It took a crew three days to bring the vehicle back to the surface.

was unload the tractor — a ticklish task — and abandon it. If the other tractors were to reach the Polar Plateau, a safe passage through the crevasses had to be found. Hastily we organized two exploring parties. One group sledged southwest. My group angled toward the southeast.

My party covered about five miles, over an area that struck me as too risky for the tractors to chance. I stopped to talk over the situation with my partners. Picking at the snow with my ski pole, I was startled to see the surface collapse — almost beneath my feet. A hidden snow bridge had given way, leaving Pete Demas and me on one side of the chasm, Richard Russell on the other. All of us were thinking the same thing: Had we been standing a few inches closer, we would have plunged hundreds of feet to certain death.

When we returned to the tractors, Albert was there waiting. His luck was no better than ours. The only alternate was for the tractor to back out of here and explore eastward. We radioed Little America, where all field operations were coordinated. After several hours of consultation, it was agreed that the original program had to be scrapped and the parties reorganized. The Plateau Party was dissolved, with Gill and Bram joining the redirected tractor contingent. I volunteered to provide support to the geological party, aiming south for the Queen Maud Mountain Range. I asked Albert to join me.

Crevasses again took their toll. Geologist Blackburn narrowly escaped a fatal fall down a chasm; and two sledges, loaded with scientific gear, dangled over the side while the dogs struggled for solid footing. Hours of hard work by men swinging from ropes retrieved the supplies, and the sledges were hauled up. At the 83rd Parallel, about 420 miles from the South Pole, Albert and I, having completed our obligations to the geologists, turned back. Testing each other on skis, and with those magnificent pups catching the spirit, we averaged 38.3 miles per day. From the Advance Base to Little America, a distance of 123 miles, we almost sprouted wings, averaging 61.5 miles per day. All of this was accomplished with a cargo of gear weighing about 650 pounds.

Although we didn't realize it at the time, we had made one of the fastest Polar sledge trips ever recorded. Even Amundsen's spectacular return from the South Pole — an average of 31.5 miles per day was eclipsed.

When we arrived at Little America, only the night watchman was awake to greet us. Seeing two haggard figures burned by wind and sun, frostbitten, unshaven, badly needing a bath, he remarked: "You two look like a pair of turkey buzzards."

CHAPTER 5

THE CHRISTMAS SEASON WAS AT HAND. Even in Antarctica there would be celebrating with a special holiday dinner and gifts from home saved for the occasion. The Christmas spirit boosted morale. God knew we needed it.

Refusing to engage in petty squabbles, common in a polar camp, I retreated to tranquil Blubberheim. There I quietly prepared myself for the challenge in the field. Such a test was not long in coming.

It was a Saturday evening — just finished my sponge bath. While I was heating water for tea, the trap door to my little bungalow opened and a hooded figure dropped in. It was Byrd. He had not exactly brought me a Christmas present. I handed him a mug of tea and, between sips, he told me that I was needed for a rescue mission. He had just received a radio message from the tractor party of Gill and Bram. One machine was so badly damaged it had to be abandoned. The other tractor couldn't move until repairs were made. Byrd wanted me to sledge 150 miles eastward with needed spare parts. It meant I would miss the Christmas feast, but so would the men stranded on the ice. "Sure I'll go," I told him. "Who shall I take with me?" He told me I could chose any man in camp.

I decided to take the surveyor. True, he couldn't ski well and couldn't drive dogs, but he had a humorous nature and tried to be friendly. Besides, I felt a little sorry for him. Since his last trip, no sledge party would take a chance on him; he was left out when rosters were made up. He had not had the chance to use a surveyor's transit yet. But this was a short trip — no more than 300 miles to get there and back — and I could compensate for his lack of skills. I wouldn't rely on him to keep us in radio contact with the base, since I polished my operating proficiency during the winter — one of the dividends of time spent at Blubberheim, where I copied radio newscasts from the *New York Times*.

The weather forecast was unfavorable, but Byrd was anxious I start immediately. Barely six miles from Little America we ran into a woolley fog that made it impossible for us to go on. Visibility was less than ten feet, and I couldn't see Power, my lead dog. Reluctantly we pitched camp, which made us feel rather foolish since we were almost within shouting distance of the base. Worse, we were stuck in that one spot for three days. Finally the fog lifted, and we moved on. It was Christmas Eve, and the sun was bright and high in the sky.

I skied ahead, but the dogs were so spirited after their long rest I had to push myself to stay well in front of them. The surveyor, as might be expected, again was pulled along by the team. I told him to pull his own weight. The surface was good; the skis glided smoothly; he should have no trouble keeping up.

North of our trail the black outcrops of the Rockefeller Mountains came into view. I checked the sledge meter and estimated we were still about 40 miles short of our destination. On the eve of the 28th, we topped a ridge and saw the tractors in the distance.

No Santa Claus with a bag full of gifts could have been more welcome to these men, marooned for two weeks. Mechanic Joe Hill, anticipating our arrival, already had started working on the engine of the disabled tractor. After handing him the spare parts, which he immediately began installing, it struck me as silly that we should have to spend eight days delivering a package that weighed less than five pounds. The parts — pan gasket and small rocker arm — should have been carried as spares on the tractor in the first place. But since they were not, why was not one of our small airplanes used to deliver them? The task would have taken no more than three hours, and the men could have made it back to Little America in time for Christmas. But that was Byrd's decision.

The Rockefeller Mountains looked inviting, especially the tallest — Mount Nilsen. It was named for my father's friend, Captain Oscar Nilsen, whose whaling ship *C.A. Larsen* carried supplies for Byrd's first expedition in 1928. I tapped out a radio message requesting an OK to detour to the mountains. Back came the answer: "OK. Suggest you look for nests of snowy petrels."

Gill Morgan joined us. He and the surveyor, skiing side by side, held onto a rope attached to my sledge, enabling them to keep up. We headed straight for the mountains nearest us. The team was going at a good speed when the two let go the tow line and waved me on, yelling that they would catch up later. I doubted if they could, but I did not pause to argue the point, and drove on. From time to time I looked back and noticed the distance between us increasing. Before long they were out of sight.

I had on my sledge all the necessities for making camp — sleeping bags, tent cooker, food for men and dogs, radio equipment, and each man's bag containing extra clothing. For about three hours I kept up the pace, recording the distance covered — 18 miles — on the sledge meter. I decided it was time to stop and wait for the others to catch up. An hour passed, and no skiers appeared. Could something have happened to them? I doubted it. The weather was good; the surface was safe, with no crevasses to impede their progress.

Too impatient to wait longer, I fired up the primus stove and melted snow for hot chocolate. After munching a couple of trail biscuits and downing a mug of the beverage, I filled the thermos bottles and wrapped half a dozen of the biscuits in a canvas bag, which I placed on a snow cairn about three feet high. It was so conspicuous that I was satisfied Gill and companion would see it. To the food bag I pinned a note stating that I hoped they would enjoy a little light exercise before partaking of the evening meal that would be awaiting them at the mountain. "Back in Norway," I added, "I used to ski 30 miles four times a week to see a girl friend on the other side of the mountain."

The dogs still had plenty of life, so as soon as I stowed the cooking gear on the sledge, I was off again. At the mountain two miles away, I found the wreckage of an airplane from Byrd's first expedition. It was a sobering sight, a grim reminder of what could happen in this hostile environment. At the first outcrops the dogs started acting strangely, refusing to pay attention to my commands. At first their behavior puzzled me. Then it dawned on me that these animals, born in Little America, had seen nothing in their white world except men's boots, sledges, tents, and the chunks of seal meat thrown to them. Understandably, their curiosity had gotten the better of them. They wouldn't leave until they had sniffed every piece of rock within reach.

I finally got them pulling again, and in a few minutes we reached the foothills of Mt. Martha Washington. I pitched two tents and placed all the sleeping gear inside, hitched the dogs to the tethering line, and set up the radio for transmission. Then I lit the primus and began preparing the evening meal. The menu consisted of steaming pemmican, hot tea, milk, biscuits, and canned peaches cooked in fruit juice. I expected my two dinner guests any minute. I had a long wait; they didn't show up for three hours. When they did arrive, they were snorting mad at me for — as they contended — running off and leaving them. On the other hand, I was tempted to admonish them for not maintaining a better pace. Instead, I calmed them with helpings of hot food, hoping all the while that they had learned a valuable survival lesson on the trail.

Having covered more than 40 miles during the day, we slept soundly, not waking until late the next morning. After a hasty breakfast, we headed toward the mountain peak. At the highest point we had a breathtaking view of Scott's Nunataks to the north, an isolated group of peaks visited by three of Amundsen's men in 1911.

Crawling over slippery rocks, I came upon a small nest occupied by a snowy petrel. I reached for the bird, and it spat at me a foul-smelling orange-colored liquid — obviously the bird's defense against intruders. Undaunted I reached into the nest of rocks and pebbles and found two small eggs. After showing them to Gill, coming up behind me, I carefully replaced the eggs and got another splat from mother petrel for my efforts.

Our next objective was to climb Mount Nilsen, about 12 miles northward. We skied down the slope to our tent camp, hurriedly hitched up the dogs, and sledged up a valley of ice to a higher plateau. In a couple of hours we were standing in the shadow of Mount Nilsen. Anxious to begin climbing the 3,000-foot peak covered with broken boulders, we wasted little time setting up camp. In little more than an hour we scrambled to the top.

In an atmosphere unsullied by haze, we looked out across snowy wastes to sharply etched horizons more than a hundred miles distant. Hungrily I drank in the magnificent view to the east, gazing out upon lands never before seen by the human eye. While standing atop Mount Nilsen, the highest elevation in the area, I vowed to have my own expedition to Antarctica some day. I would sledge across from the other side of the continent and explore the empty vastness before me.

On a piece of paper torn from my log book I wrote a message of this first ascent of Mount Nilsen, listing the names of my companions and the date and purpose of our mission. I sealed the note in a small can, which I carried in my knapsack, and buried it inside an eight-foot stone cairn the three of us erected on top of the mountain.

As we moved down the slope, I saw dark clouds to the east approaching rapidly. A sudden rise in temperature and a dead calm with gathering clouds indicated that a storm would break soon. Racing against what could be a disaster in our exposed position we scurried back to camp. Bone-tired, we crawled into our sleeping bags without bothering to fix a meal.

I awoke an hour later for my scheduled radio transmission to Little America, but it was impossible to leave the tent. A howling blizzard threatened to demolish the tents and blow us off the mountain. The radio set on the sledge was already under several feet of snow.

For a full day we remained in our tents while the storm raged. Although to venture outside in the 60-mile-an-hour wind risked being blown off our feet, I felt we could not afford to remain in our exposed position any longer. We had to brave the blizzard and break camp. For two hours we dug out, defying the fury of the wind. Then we hitched the dogs and started down the mountains.

We struggled to control the dogs on the glassy surface. It slipped down rapidly, and the dogs had to zigzag repeatedly to avoid being overrun. Sometimes the whole team slid sideway. What a wild trip!

Finally we reached the leeward side of the mountain where the winds could not reach us. How different here, so safe and snug, while above us the storm continued unabated. We pitched camp to rest and get our bearings; then established radio contact with Little America. I learned that the sailing ship *Bear* had left New Zealand and would arrive at the Bay of Whales in two weeks. The time for us to leave Antarctica was drawing near.

Back in Little America, waiting on the *Bear*, I reflected on the sledge-trips I had made across hundreds of frozen miles. Dogs had been my constant companions since the sun's rays first beamed over the northern horizon in late September. Now the red glow was fading! Soon another Antarctic night would again engulf the continent.

My seismic sounding activities with Dr. Poulter had been a relief from the daily drive to make miles on the sledge meter. Then I had returned to the field and traveled to the edge of the unknown, to my resolution made on top of Mount Nilsen, where the challenge of discovery forecast my future.

Byrd's second expedition had combined exploration with science as its major objectives, although most of the publicity sent out was about his experience at Advance Base. More important, the geological party of three men had investigated a remote sector of the southeast area of the Ross Ice Shelf and made important discoveries. They located a coal-seam more than 15 feet thick in mountains close to the South Pole. Significant work was also accomplished at the wintering base, where synoptic weather observations had been taken on a regular basis. These recordings formed a link in the worldwide network of recordings under the auspices of the U.S. Weather Bureau.

Science was well served by Dr. Bramhall's recordings of magnetic variations on the Ross Ice Shelf and at Little America. A series of cosmic ray measurements also enhanced the scientific program.

When *Bear* arrived at the Bay of Whales, we all had a day off to read our mail. Within a week's time I was aboard ship heading for home. We had a rough stretch of ocean to cross up to New Zealand, and many of those men who had wintered over became seasick as soon as we rounded West Cape in the Bay of Whales. I saw few men in the mess hall at mealtime for the next several days.

Our first stop was Dunedin, on the South Island of New Zealand, where family and friends had come to greet us. It was a thrill to become familiar with fruits and vegetables again and to meet these friendly people "down-under." The first dish I ordered at a restaurant was fresh strawberries with whipped cream.

It took us 49 days to steam from Dunedin to Panama because *Ruppert* was making only about five knots. I could have walked as fast. The slow pace was an attempt to save bunker oil. We heard upon arrival at Balboa, Panama, that no funds were available to buy enough fuel to get us back home. The National Geographical Society learned of our predicament and wired the expedition $10,000. Thus we were able to keep our schedule, arriving in Washington, D.C. on Friday, May 10, 1935. President Franklin D. Roosevelt was on the dock at the Washington Navy Yard to greet us. A police escort led us to the Willard Hotel, near the White House. After a splendid dinner, we attended a reception and were introduced at Constitution Hall to an audience gathered to honor Byrd and expedition members.

Two days later I took a taxi to Quantico, Virginia, where *Bear* had docked. Along the road I saw expedition members hitchhiking — quite a come-down for recently honored guests of the National Geographical Society. I picked up several shipmates in the taxi.

I paid the driver with a five dollar bill which I had recently received in a novel way. In Balboa, Panama, when *Ruppert* was docked, all hands had been summoned to the bridge-deck, outside Byrd's quarters. The sun had set, making it difficult to see; so I was startled to hear Byrd say: "Finn, is that you?" I replied affirmatively, and he whispered: "Let me have your hand." As our palms met, I felt a crisp wad of paper. Money! I couldn't wait until I got to my bunk down below and switched on the light. The taxi driver would have been amazed to know that I had paid him with my entire wages for 19 months' work on the Second Byrd Expedition. Oh well, easy come, easy go — .

CHAPTER 6

ANTARCTICA AND U.S. COMPARATIVE SIZE

A NTARCTICA IS A HOSTILE LAND. With its towering walls of ice, bitter winters, and hurricane winds that scream down out of the interior highlands, it has time and again frustrated frail human encroachments upon its solitude. It has beaten back all but the most daring invaders, taking its toll in unfathomable crevasses, savage seas, and the frigid windswept plains where death waits silently with the soft caress of sleep. It is a mighty land of towering mountains, infinite distances, awesome silences, and furious thundering sounds. It is a weirdly beautiful land where the pulsing glow of Aurora Australis backlights gleaming sculpture of moving ice, twisted and contorted by its own incalculable weight.

Ice! The Antarctic continent is covered from shore to shore with a perpetual mantle of ice thousands of feet deep. Ice is the patron sovereign of this glacial land, shielding it in elemental isolation from the teeming disturbance of living things. It is the cosmic cooler of the southern hemisphere, furiously exhaling its frigid breath out over the oceans, driving before it pieces and islands and mountains of floating ice, and inhaling from the spray of cold seas the moisture with which to renew itself.

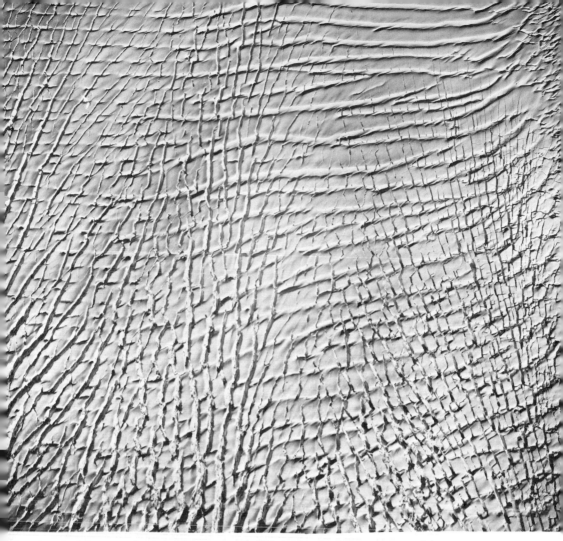

Aerial view of a heavily crevassed glacier on the Palmer Peninsula as seen from 10,000 feet. Some of the crevasses measured 250 feet deep and 40 feet across at the top surface.

Antarctica's 5,100,000 square miles equals the area of the United States and Mexico combined. Its coastline stretches 14,000 miles. Nearly the entire surface of the continent is covered with a mantle of ice and snow averaging 8,000 feet in thickness; in some areas ice almost three miles deep. No other place on earth registers such cold temperatures — well in excess of minus 120 degrees. Winds often exceed 200 miles per hour.

The tremendous layer of ice, accumulated over many thousands of winters, is constantly moving, pushed into motion by its own ponderous weight. Glaciers, mighty rivers of ice, inch down out of the highlands, flow onto the coastal plains, and break off into the sea.

If the enormous layer of ice could be removed from the continent, a large mass of land separated by ice-filled straits would emerge. Otto Nordenskjold, the Swedish scientist and explorer, first noted differences in 1901 between what he called "East and West Antarctica." East Antarctica is larger. In many ways it is like the mountain formation of Australia. Smaller West Antarctica extends roughly from the area around the Ross Sea to the tip of the Antarctic Peninsula, across the Drake Passage from Cape Horn. The terrain is generally similar to the tall, jagged mountains of the South Atlantic islands and the towering Andes of South America.

◆　◆　◆

Geographers supposed the existence of a southern continent centuries before any means were devised for reaching it. Ptolemy, in the second century A.D., conceived of both an Antarctic Circle and a Terra Incognita. By the beginning of the 16th century the existence of a southern continent had become a dominant theory. In 1505 Vespucci published *De Ora Antarctica,* describing the discovery in 1502 of a considerable landfall far south of the Atlantic, which he conjectured was the Antarctic continent.

Magellan in 1520 mistook Tierra del Fuego for the Unknown Land. Sixty years later Sir Francis Drake, the first Englishman to sail the lower latitudes, proved Tierra del Fuego to be the southern tip of South America. Other mariners were drawn further south by violent storms raging off Cape Horn. In 1599 one of them, Dutch Captain Dirck Cherritz, sighted mountainous snow-covered land south of 61 degrees south latitude. But his accounts were of little value since he wasn't sure exactly what he had seen. Gradually the belief grew that there were no lands of any consequence to be found below Tierra del Fuego. This storm-racked archipelago, therefore, was thought of as "Ultima Thule"—the end of the earth. Yet, throughout the 17th and 18th centuries, there were more sightings of other outposts in the sub-Antarctic. Such intrepid mariners as Lozier Bouvet, Marion-Dufresne, and Yves de Kerguelen-Tremarco kept thrusting southward, voyaging over vast stretches of uncharted oceans. During this time Marion Island and the Crozet Islands were discovered in the south Indian Ocean. Kerguelen, who had been blown off course by a terrible storm, glimpsed a forbidding mountainous, ice-sheeted land even farther south, near the 50th parallel. He returned a year later for a better look. His "Land of Desolation," as he dubbed it, is known today as the Kerguelen Island.

Of these early voyagers, Captain James Cook made the deepest southern penetration. On January 30, 1774, two years after Kerguelen's discovery, Cook sailed to within a thousand miles of the South Pole; a huge ice field halting his progress at 71 deg. 10 min. south latitude, 107 deg. west longitude. It was not until 1934 — 160 years later — that the ship I was aboard, *Jacob Ruppert*, of Byrd's second Antarctic expedition, pushed farther south in that sector of the Pacific.

Captain Cook conceded the probability of a southern continent; however, he wrote, "I make bold to declare that the world will derive no benefit from it." Besides, why risk crews and ships against the terrifying pack ice. In the area *Ruppert* entered we encountered no less than 5,000 icebergs in a single week. "Devil's Graveyard" we called the place.

It was in an area south of Cape Horn, South America where the sighting of the Antarctic continent was first made in 1821. This area, across the Drake Passage which is the most stormful stretch of ocean water in the world, juts northward — like the handle of a dipper and pointing in a northeasterly direction.

But despite ever present dangers from ice and storm, sea captains ventured into the waters of the Antarctic, lured by rich rewards from the fur trade. Seal hunters ranged ever deeper, slaughtering entire herds, reducing the seal population by perhaps one-half in fifty years. To protect their interests, mariners kept secret the islands they saw. It is probable that men first caught sight of the Antarctic mainland in the early part of the 19th century, when British and American crews armed with clubs and knives swarmed over the islands to butcher millions of seals and, not infrequenty, to battle each other.

In 1820 and 1821 four voyages are known to have passed close enough to the Antarctic Peninsula to have seen the dark lofty peaks of the mainland. The largest of these expeditions, under Russian Admiral Thadius von Bellingshausen, discovered two islands at high latitudes; but the Russians presumed that what they had seen was part of the continent, and they dutifully christened it Alexander I Land, in honor of the czar. (It was my good fortune 120 years later to sledge into that area and disprove the Russian claim.) Captain Edward Bransfield, commanding the brig *Williams,* sighted a mountainous coast he named Trinity Land. The British were cheered by "the idea that this might be the long-sought Southern Continent." But the claim was disputed, the Americans believing that Bransfield had actually discovered a large island. Within the same year, two American sealing captains, Nathaniel Brown Palmer and Christopher Burdick, sailed close to the mainland.

In the sloop *Hero,* a mere 47 feet long and of 45 tons burden, the 21-year-old Palmer sailed south through the strait between Snow Island and Livingston Island and discovered Deception Island. The crater rim of an extinct volcano, it was a pleasant deception, since the island provided a landlocked anchorage free of ice. Palmer, seeking new hunting grounds, not a continent, scanned from the top of the island one exceptionally clear day and sighted a mountainous coast to the south. Palmer's log, in the Library of Congress, details his observations with entries such as this of November 17, 1820: "Bore away to the Northern & saw 2 small islands and the (mainland) shore where Perpendicular . . . ." There is no doubt that Palmer saw and subsequently sailed along the mainland, because in January, 1959, when on a cruise to visit bases on an expedition with the Argentine Navy, I stood on the same high crater rim and viewed exactly the same mountains he had seen. I can therefore safety state: "there is no doubt that Palmer saw the mountains of the mainland — 50 miles away." Sailing farther south to Trinity Island, he again saw the mainland, this time only ten miles off, but ice prevented his reaching it.

After returning briefly to Friesland Island, Palmer sailed south along the west coast of the peninsula. This time he passed through De Gerlache Strait and the Grandidier Channel, which separates the peninsula from the Briscoe and Adelaide Islands — to Marguerite Bay in Latitude 68 deg. South. On his way back to the South Shetlands he was becalmed in a fog, and when the fog lifted, he was surprised to find his little ship between a frigate and a sloop-of-war. He instantly ran up the American flag, to which the other ships answered with Russian colors.

A boat came over from the frigate with an invitation for Palmer to come aboard. He accepted, and found that the ships comprised an expedition sent out by Czar Alexander I under Commander Thadius von Bellingshausen. The Russians had already circumnavigated the continent and discovered Alexander I Island which I proved on my sledge-journey in 1940 to be an island. They were thus the first to navigate the sea formed by the western angle between the Antarctic Peninsula and the coast of the continent proper — called Bellingshausen Sea after their intrepid commanding officer.

When Palmer told von Bellingshausen about the South Shetlands and his own discoveries of the past few weeks, ending with an offer to pilot the Russians to Deception Island, von Bellingshausen wrote in astonishment:

"Previous to our being enveloped in fog, we saw those islands, and concluded we had made a discovery; but behold, when the fog lifted, to my great surprise, here is an American vessel apparently in as fine order as if it were but yesterday she had left the United States. Not only this, but her master is ready to pilot my vessel into port!" He forthwith named the mountainous land seen by Palmer to the south, "Palmer's Land."

◆ ◆ ◆

As the demand for seal hides continued to grow, seamen probed ever deeper into southern latitudes. A former merchant mariner named James Weddell ventured farther east into unknown waters. In January 1823 — summer in the Antarctic — he sailed through wide leads, zigzagging between ice floes. Once he almost lost his ship as gale winds pushed it toward towering icebergs. Finally Weddell was stopped by solid pack ice. But he had sailed 240 miles beyond the southernmost point reached by Captain Cook, although he was in a different area. At first Weddell thought the waters were another ocean, and he named it for King George IV. Later the name was changed to Weddell Sea, to honor the man who discovered it. (The full shoreline of the Weddell Sea was not charted until November, 1947, when my own expedition mapped it and took aerial photographs of the coast to its southernmost limits).

Weddell's findings signaled other sea captains to follow him into the Antarctic. The voyages of John Briscoe in 1830–1832 circumsailed the continent and penetrated the pack ice to the west of the Antarctic Peninsula. He sighted and named Adelaide Island, although Palmer undoubtedly had already sailed past it. Briscoe continued past what are now known as the Briscoe Islands, and later he went ashore on another island he thought was the mainland. To this he gave the name Graham Land, in honor of the First Lord of the British Admiralty, triggering another dispute among mapmakers.

With the continent's discovery, there began the nibbling away at isolated points along the fourteen thousand miles of coastline, until its configuration became fairly well known. The French scientist Jules Sebastian Dumont D'Urville, sailed Antarctic waters for the second time in 1840, and discovered and named Adelie Land after his wife. The species of little penguins he saw on a rocky island were henceforth known as Adelie penguins.

The seal hunters of the early 19th century undoubtedly made other discoveries, but their locations were kept secret so that other sealers would not poach on their finds. If nations had been interested in animal conservation in those days, and if they had freely proclaimed their discoveries, the maps of the Antarctic probably would have been drawn many years earlier.

Oddly enough, even the discoveries and sightings that were reported to the world were not put together on a single map. The idea simply didn't occur to anyone for a long time. And, incredulously, no nation seemed to be concerned with the location of the South Pole. Perhaps most thought the Pole would be located in the middle of a frozen sea, among daunted icebergs and ice floes. The Pole's location within a continental land mass was determined by a lieutenant in the United States Navy. His name was Charles Wilkes, and he was 40 years old when appointed leader of the first United States expedition exploring into the Antarctic.

The Wilkes expedition sailed in August 1838. Never was any flotilla more poorly outfitted. The ships were in bad condition, the men had little warm clothing, and the food was awful. The crews endured one hardship after another. One of the ships, *Peacock*, was almost lost and had to return to Sydney, Australia. Wilkes pressed on. Sighting land on January 19, 1840, skirting the ice-bound edges of his discovery, he continued westward for almost 1,500 miles, threading his way through waters studded with ice floes and huge bergs, some of which drifted perilously close to his fragile craft.

The beauty of the ice formations overwhelmed Wilkes. He wrote: "If an immense city of ruined alabaster palaces can be imagined, of every variety and shape and tint, and composed of huge piles of buildings grouped together, with long lanes of streets winding through them, some faint idea may be formed of the grandeur and beauty of the spectacles."

Wilkes had no doubts in his mind that he was viewing a continent. He followed the heights along the shore, where the ice came down to the water as a steep white cliff. Nowhere could he find a bay or a cove or any kind of inlet. Wilkes saw that it would be impossible to put a landing party ashore anywhere. No one else could either — not for 60 years.

Even with his crude instruments, Wilkes was able to fix some coastal features. He was also able to make some ocean soundings, and found a shallow continental shelf off the coast. In some ways Charles Wilkes was a peculiar man. A stern Captain, he did not get along well with his crew, including his fellow officers. Wilkes had few friends. Yet, he could be very courteous toward another captain on a mission of exploration. Unfortunately, his courtesy brought him to grief.

Wilkes stopped in Australia to rest his men and refit his ships; James Clark Ross was there too, as commander of a British expedition into the Antarctic. Trying to be helpful, although under orders not to divulge any of his possible discoveries, Wilkes furnished Ross with several of his charts, which included locations of certain lands he had discovered plus description of the ice, winds, currents, and other dangers Ross could expect to encounter. The charts were also flawed by a few errors, which were not entirely Wilkes's fault.

On one chart Wilkes indicated land that he named Cape Hudson. Later, other sea captains sailing over Wilkes's route found no trace of the cape. Thus, because of this and several other mistakes, all the rest of Wilkes's sightings were dismissed as false. Even worse, Ross, upon returning to England, passed some of the American navigator's findings as his own.

His expedition dogged by misfortune — one ship lost, others damaged, more than a hundred desertions, Wilkes returned home to face the disgrace of a court-martial. In a more enlightened time he would have been acclaimed a hero, and presidents and kings might have pinned medals on his chest; for it was this irascible naval officer who was first to establish that Antarctica was more than a string of islands in a frozen sea. His findings, he wrote, should "leave no doubt in any unprejudiced mind of the correctness of the assertion that we have discovered a vast continent." Above all, he desired "to maintain the truth in relation to a claim that is indisputable."

But what about the errors? How can they be explained and still maintain the truth? To begin with, Wilkes did not have reliable navigational equipment. Understandably, he made honest mistakes; but they were not too difficult to correct, since often it was only a matter of a few miles one way or another. However, the case of vanishing Cape Hudson was not so easily resolved.

In 1915, about three-quarters of a century after Wilkes's discoveries, Captain J. B. Stenhouse, commanding the Australian ship *Aurora* of Douglas Mawson's expedition, sailed to a point near the area where Cape Hudson had been located. And sure enough, there was the land exactly as Wilkes had sketched it. One of the officers aboard *Aurora* made a similar sketch. "No wonder Wilkes reported land," Captain Stenhouse wrote in his log. The next day Cape Hudson had disappeared.

What Wilkes and Stenhouse had seen was a polar mirage. The refraction of light in polar (and in desert) areas can play strange tricks with objects. Wilkes and Stenhouse *had* seen land — but it was Cape Freshfield, about 230 miles away, as it appeared to both captains.

The same kind of deception fooled other notable explorers, including Ross. When he sailed into that body of water later named the Ross Sea, he reported a range of mountains some 25 miles distant. He was so certain that he had seen them that he gave them a name — Parry Mountains. More than half a century later, the explorer Robert Scott went over the same area on foot, but he saw no mountains, only a huge floating ice shelf. There was, however, a mountain range exactly as Ross had described — except that it was 275 miles away.

Using Wilkes's discoveries as a foundation for his own expeditions, Ross began searching for the south magnetic pole in 1841. But he became instead the first to point the way for the attainment of the south geographical pole. Because of Wilkes' information, Ross knew in which direction *not* to sail; as a result, his name is associated with two of the largest features of Antarctica.

With the two strongest ships yet to sail into Antarctic waters, the *Erebus* of 370 tons and the *Terror* of 340 tons, Ross succeeded in crashing through the ice pack and, helped by a wind from the north, kept slicing through the ice until he emerged into what is now called the Ross Sea. He thought the way was open for him to sail directly to the South Pole. But his hopes were dashed at the sight of a huge barrier cliff — Ross Ice Shelf — towering 150 feet high and stretching to the east for more than 400 miles. As Ross sailed along the barrier, he witnessed one of nature's anomalies — a volcano spewing fire and smoke in a land of ice and snow. He named it Mount Erebus. A nearby inactive volcano he called Mount Terror. These were the names of his two ships.

The next half-century saw little exploratory activity in the Antarctic. Then, in 1892 Norwegian sealing Captain Carl Anton Larsen discovered Oscar II Coast and Foyn Coast on the eastern side of the Antarctic Peninsula. On Seymour Island off the northeast coast he collected the first fossils found in the Antarctic. January 1, 1895, Norwegian whaling Captain Leonard Kristensen and Carsten Egeberg Borchgrevink landed on the Antarctic continent. For years it was believed that they were the first to set foot on the mainland; but the discovery of a ship's log has since revealed that an American, John Davis, on the Antarctic Peninsula, February 7, 1821 was the first. He was captain of the sealer *Huron*. It is not inconceivable that others more secretive might have preceded him.

In 1898 an expedition under Belgian Adrien de Gerlache sailed into the Antarctic to perform geological exploration of the area south of Cape Horn. Aboard were two young men destined to leave their names in polar annals: Roald Amundsen, who served as second mate, and Frederick Cook, ship's surgeon. Suffering through "a night of 1,600 hours" — as de Gerlache phrased it — the crew of *Belgica* fought in vain to free their ship from the pack ice. Channels laboriously opened with dynamite explosions and ice saws quickly froze over. Drifting aimlessly for more than a year, the men, ill-prepared for winter and short of food, became sick in mind as well as body. Amundsen, who had spent months aboard a small sealing ship in the Arctic before joining de Gerlache, knew the value of fresh meat in fighting scurvy. He and

Dr. Cook did heroic work tending the sick, providing fresh seal meat and penguin meat, encouraging the men to fight lassitude by forced activity. A walk on the ice around the ship was labeled "madhouse promenade." To Amundsen, Cook was "the one man of unfaltering courage, unfailing hope, endless cheerfulness and universal kindness." Although the young doctor from Brooklyn was later discredited as an explorer and spent time in prison in connection with oil leases, the Norwegian never turned his back on him.

For the second time in 1898–1900 Borchgrevink, Norwegian leader of the Scottish expedition on the *Southern Cross*, was the first to winter on the mainland, at Cape Adare, western entrance to the Ross Sea. One man that winter gained the dubious distinction of being the first to die on the continent. At the end of the winter night Borchgrevink sailed south. Stopped by the Ross Ice Shelf, he cruised easterly, parallelling the ice wall until he came to a broad identation in the barrier. A party landed and sledged inland — the first to do so — from the Bay of Whales, foothold for Amundsen a decade later.

◆ ◆ ◆

After the turn of the century began the so-called "Golden Age of Exploration." Questing for the poles — and for the glory of being first to reach those imaginative points — many nations sent out expeditions. The first to accomplish anything on the continent of Antarctica itself was Scott's expedition of 1901–1903. The British naval officer sledged beyond the 82nd parallel to set a new record in southing. In 1901 Swedish Professor Otto Nordenskjold led a scientific expedition in the ship *Antarctic*, under the command of C. A. Larsen, who had seen service in this sector ten years earlier. Unable to penetrate the Weddell Sea, they established a wintering base on Snow Hill Island to the north, and scientific investigations began. Despite the ship being wrecked and parties being marooned, the expedition survived two winters before an Argentine ship rescued the doughty Swedes and Norwegians. They had used their time well, carrying on scientific missions in the face of adversity. Nordenskjold had made a sledge journey south to Oscar II Land, collecting fossils and geological specimens.

From now on, scientists were included on all polar expeditions. No longer was geographical discovery sufficient to justify the risks and expense; the quest for knowledge had become a prime motivator. From 1901 to 1903 the German scientist Erich von Drygalski, in his ship *Gauss*, led an expedition to Kemps and Knox Land, from where he made a sledge journey inland. At about the same time the Scottish *Scotia* expedition, organized and led by Dr. W. S. Bruce, attempted to penetrate the Weddell Sea but was turned back by heavy pack ice. After wintering in the South Orkneys, Bruce's party returned in March 1904 to discover Coats Land in the southeastern part of the Weddell Sea.

The French physician and scientist Jean Charcot began his expeditions in 1903. He intended to head for the Weddell Sea but, after learning of Nordenskjöld's difficulties there, swung to the west and aimed for the Bellingshausen Sea. After wintering on Wandel Island, north of the Antarctic Circle, he sailed south and sighted Alexander Island, where his ship *Français* was damaged. Though forced to retreat after his first experience in polar exploration, he returned to the Antarctic in January 1908. Excellently equipped in his new ship *Pourquoi-Pas?* Charcot found ice conditions to the south better than before. He explored the extent of Adelaide Island, renamed Loubet Coast on the mainland, and continued to push south until he found and named Marguerite Bay. Here, where the Antarctic Peninsula joins the mainland, were vistas I would come to know well in the 1940's. It is likely that Palmer reached Marguerite Bay long before Charcot, but the American, searching for seals, apparently took little note of it. Charcot found the bay filled with ice and sailed on to within two miles of Alexander Island — or Alexander Land, as it was known then. To the southwest he sighted the three peaks of a new island, known today as Charcot Island. It remained an elusive place until Sir Hubert Wilkins spotted it from the air in 1929. In 1947 I made the first landing on the island and took a series of sun lines to establish the location of the three peaks that dominate the lonely snow-covered terrain.

◆ ◆ ◆

In 1907 Irish-born Henry Shackleton, a member of Scott's party in 1902, declared that his goal was to reach the South Pole, the first to make such a statement. He had little difficulty recruiting a crew. Tall, broad-shouldered, strong as a bull, he was a born leader. Men followed him willingly because they believed in him.

Shackleton set sail in a 40-year-old reconditioned Norwegian sealer named *Nimrod*. The passage across howling Antarctic seas to the pack ice was a rough one for the overloaded ship. Decks were awash constantly; and the Siberian ponies tethered in stalls on deck often lost their footing. One pony was so badly injured it had to be shot.

Fortunately the winds slackened and sailing conditions improved. Shackleton planned to winter at Balloon Bight — later renamed the Bay of Whales — which Borchgrevink had discovered in 1898, but found the face of the barrier changed considerably since his first visit here with Scott. Deciding that it was too risky to winter there, he pushed on to McMurdo Sound and built his hut at Cape Royds on Ross Island, about forty miles from where Scott had stayed at Hut Point.

Shackleton's wintering party was only a few miles below Mount Erebus. After the base camp was constructed, a party climbed to the top of the volcano, the only men to have done that until an American helicopter landed scientists at the rim of the crater during the International Geophysical Year of 1957–1958.

When the long winter night finally turned to spring light, Shackleton and his men struck out for the Pole. Using the tough Siberian ponies to pull the loaded sledges, the four-man party left camp November 3, 1908. Before them lay 800 miles of storm-swept wilderness encased in ice and numbed by 7-below-zero temperatures.

At first they averaged about 15 miles per day. On Christmas, after more than 50 days of hard sledging, they reached the edge of the polar plateau, having climbed the vast Beardmore Glacier and seen, in Shackleton's words: "the play of nature in her grandest moods." The South Pole was still 300 miles away.

By that time they were man-hauling their sledges. The ponies were gone, the last one having been lost in a crevasse, yet the men moved ahead, planting one foot in front of the other with a dogged determination. On January 9, 1909, in the icy desert, with only a few biscuits and chocolate bars in their pockets, they marched south for five hours. Finally they could go no farther. They were then at an altitude over 9,000 feet, where every breath knifed into their lungs. In his log Shackleton wrote: "Our last day outwards. We have shot our bolt, and the tale is latitude 88 degrees 23 min. South, longitude 162 East . . . . . Whatever regrets may be, we have done our best." They were then 97 miles short of their goal.

Shackleton did not hesitate to turn back. Later he said that he could have walked to the Pole, but he never would have returned to tell about it. Although desperately short of food and fuel, the men dragged the sledges back to camp more than 700 miles away.

Shackleton deliberately turned his back on success, for the lives of his men came first. And they followed him without question, even when victory was very close.

CHAPTER 7

In 1911 Norwegian Roald Amundsen, German Wilhelm Filchner, British Robert Scott, Australian Douglas Mawson, and Japanese Choku Shirase were in the field, each with the South Pole as his goal. Amundsen left Norway aboard *Fram* in June 1910, having previously announced that he was headed for the North Pole via Cape Horn and the Bering Strait. Robert E. Peary's claimed attainment of the North Pole on April 6, 1909, short-circuited Amundsen's plans. When the Norwegian reached Funchal, Madeira Island, he telegraphed Scott, ready to sail on *Terra Nova* from New Zealand, that he was going south.

Fram headed into the South Atlantic and almost circumsailed the Antarctic continent before reaching the Ross Sea. Amundsen had no intention of using any of Scott's previous routes in his polar dash. Explorers are a peculiar breed, very strong-minded, each an individual to himself. In Amundsen's mind, the McMurdo area where Scott intended to winter was British, and he was bound to respect it. Therefore, Amundsen pointed *Fram* for the Bay of Whales, where he built a wintering base and named it *Framheim* — "forward home" — a modest hut 26 feet long and 14 feet wide. Significantly, it was 80 miles closer to the Pole than Scott's hut at McMurdo Sound.

There was one opportunity where Scott and Amundsen might have met, but it never happened. Scott had remained at his McMurdo base when *Terra Nova,* returning from a short cruise to King Edward VII Land, sailed into the Bay of Whales and tied up about a hundred yards from *Fram.* The British came aboard the Norwegian ship, where my father met them. Afterwards the English officers were given a sledge ride to Amundsen's winter quarters, about three miles south.

The British were astonished at the way the huskies pulled heavy loads and at the speed of the dogs. They intended to use Siberian ponies on their southward trek. Amundsen, on the other hand, had taken the good advice of his friend Fritjof Nansen. When Nansen returned from his unsuccessful attempt to reach the North Pole aboard *Fram* he paid tribute to his husky dogs, calling them "the infantry of polar exploration." Amundsen had used huskies to pull his sledges when he discovered the Northwest Passage, from 1903 to 1906.

Amundsen offered the British half of his sledge dogs if Scott wanted them. He also invited a couple of the British officers to spend the winter with him. But his offers were politely rejected. Amundsen could never understand why Scott preferred ponies to dogs. Had Scott accepted the huskies, perhaps one of polar exploration's greatest tragedies might have been avoided — although I doubt it. Scott, for all his courage, was a rigid, unyielding naval officer, unwilling to bend to the exigencies of cruel circumstances. Bound by his adherance to the infallibility of rank, driven by a misplaced sense of personal and national honor, he was, in retrospect, programmed for heroic failure.

Amundsen by contrast, was ever the pragmatist, always seeking to turn the odds in his favor. Methodically he thought everything through to the smallest detail before he took his course of action. Instead of freezing his ship into the ice for the winter as Scott had done ten years earlier, Amundsen decided to send *Fram* to Buenos Aires to spend part of the winter.

Soon after the last load of cargo had been unloaded at his wintering hut, *Framheim*, and the 100 or so huskies tethered to stakes inside eight pyramid-shaped canvas tents, mooring lines were cast off and *Fram* set a course northeasterly for Argentina. Amundsen's second-in-command, Lieut. Thorvald Nilsen headed the "sea-group" of nine men which included my father. These men were to return a year later to pick up the "land-party," which also consisted of nine men. They would winter on the ice, beginning in the early austral spring, then sledge to reach the South Pole.

After a few weeks rest in Buenos Aires, the sea-group embarked on a three-month oceanographic cruise, crisscrossing the

The Fram

South Atlantic and the Antarctic Oceans. Samples of water were collected at various depths, water temperatures recorded, and salinity content measured on a continuing basis.

The skeleton crew, standing three watches while constantly under sail, had a rough time going through the "Roaring Forties" and crossing the Drake Passage. At the designated time, without radio communication, *Fram* rounded the West Cape of the Bay of Whales. The crew of the ship was overjoyed to learn that the land-party had attained the South Pole as planned.

When *Fram* departed for Buenos Aires, Amundsen had eight men with him, and all except the cook were expert skiers. Before winter set in, they made a series of trips to the south, putting down food caches for the use of men and dogs on their return journey from the Pole.

These relatively short trips taught Amundsen and his men a good deal about their equipment. For example, they found that their sledges were much too heavy. They tinkered with the design, cutting down slats and bridges and removing steel plating from the runners. Although the weight of a sledge was reduced by half, it still operated quite well. The alterations meant that the dogs would not have to work so hard and would thus have staying power over the long pull.

Amundsen decided that he would take only four men with him. On October 20th, 1911, he with Helmer Hansen, Olav Bjaaland, Sverre Hassel, and Oscar Wisting set out on their historic trek from the base. Later Kristian Prestrud, Hjalmar Johansen and Jørgen Stubberud sledged to King Edward VII Land. The cook, Adolph Lindstrom, stayed behind alone.

Amundsen's party had a comparatively easy time of it. The weather was clear and mild, the winds not too strong. On the 18th day they crossed the smooth Ross Ice Shelf and reached the mountains. There they climbed to the plateau, up Axel Heiberg Glacier. It was not as long or as wide as Beardmore Glacier, but it had many more dangerous crevasses. At one place, which Amundsen named Devil's Ballroom, his men experienced the eerie sensation of sledging across a sheet of hollow ice. As they snaked their sledges onto the plateau, weird, echoing sounds reverberated underneath them. They were 10,000 feet high and breathing heavily; still they continued despite the discomfort. Two years earlier, Shackleton and his party suffered greatly at that altitude when they strapped themselves in harness and pulled sledges. Amundsen's dogs were able to pull in the rarified air, but even they had a hard time of it.

When he was only 23 miles from the Pole, Amundsen wrote in his log, "It seemed to me as if we slept a shorter time, and we ate breakfast in greater haste, and we started out earlier this morning than on previous days. As heretofore, we had clear bright weather, beautiful sunshine, and only a very light breeze. We advanced well. Not much was said. I think that each one of us was occupied with his own thoughts. Probably only one thought dominated us all, a thought which caused us to look eagerly to the south, scan the horizon of this unlimited plateau."

"Were we the first, or. . . ."

Yes, Amundsen was worried. What if Scott had beaten him to the Pole? He knew that Scott was a determined man, that the British officer had months of experience from his expedition to the

Antarctic eight years earlier. Scott had the advantage. Amundsen had to blaze new trails.

On December 14, 1911, Amundsen and his men finally stood at the geographical end of the earth. He wrote, "Our goal has been reached. Quietly, in absolute silence, the mighty plateau stretched out before us. No man had ever yet stood on it. In no direction was there a sign to be seen. It was indeed a solemn moment when, each of us grasping the flagpole, we hoisted the flag of our country over the geographical South Pole, on King Haakon VII Plateau."

Amundsen and his group remained at the Pole until the 17th of December. Using an artificial horizon and mariner's sextant, they took sun sights around the clock, in order to pinpoint the exact location of the Pole. Amundsen then bracketed the area to make sure, sending skiers out in three different directions to a distance of 12 miles; the fourth direction had been covered in reaching the Pole.

The party left the Norwegian flag flying atop a small tent — which Amundsen dubbed "Polheim" — pitched over the geographic South Pole. Amundsen wrote that the tent was made by my father Martin Ronne. He had fashioned it of light, windproof material during the time *Fram* was sailing from Madeira Island to the Bay of Whales.

In his book *The South Pole,* Amundsen mentions that his men went into the tent one by one to sign their names on a plaque lashed to the tent pole. He left a letter addressed to King Haakon, "giving information of what we had accomplished. . . . Besides this letter, I wrote a short epistle to Captain Scott, who, I assumed, would be the first to find the tent." On straps of leather sewed to the tent Amundsen found my father's prescient message of *"Good luck on the trip and welcome to the South Pole"* as well as the names of Martin Ronne's wife and children. So, I can say with pride that my name went to the South Pole, with Amundsen; but, of course, I knew nothing of this until years later.

With two sledges and 16 dogs, Amundsen and his party turned north, moving down the steep glaciers they had climbed so cautiously. Back they went, through the crevassed ice fields, across the 400-mile barrier to Framheim. The return journey was not difficult, for the many snow beacons they had built on the outward march led them true along their tracks. They came back with only two sledges and 11 dogs, the other sledges having been abandoned along the way. The trip had taken 99 days, and they had averaged about 15 miles per day.

Fram, with the victorious men aboard, left the Bay of Whales on January 30th, 1912, and arrived at Hobart, Tasmania, on March 7th. From there the historic words flashed across the world: "The South Pole reached December 14–17, 1911. All well. Roald Amundsen."

And what of Scott? His foremost thought was to carry out orders and bring glory to his country and himself. He had been selected to lead the expedition mostly because he and his family were friendly with some very important people, for Scott was then not noted for his ability as an explorer. But he was a hardy man, dedicated, unswerving in his devotion to duty. Why did he fail?

It seems that there were a number of reasons for Scott's downfall. He never did learn how to plan an expedition properly. And Scott was a stubborn man. He seldom listened to good advice, preferring to "go by the book." Nansen had cautioned him to forget about Siberian ponies and to rely instead on huskies, as the Eskimos had for centuries. Sir Hubert Wilkins later described how stubborn Scott could be. During the winter, when preparations were being made for the polar march, Petty Officer Edgar Evans pointed out that the mountain rations in the packets did not contain enough food for each man. Scott retorted, "You Evans, you should speak only when spoken to!"

When the main party reached the edge of the polar plateau, where the last group of support sledges and men were to turn back, Scott decided at the last minute that one more man should take part in the final dash to the Pole. The man he chose was Evans. And Evans was right about the small amount of food in the packets. But being right did not save his life.

Sir Hubert learned that the rations were supposed to be adequate for an average man doing a full day's work hauling sledges. But Scott did not take into account the fact that different men required different amounts of food. Evans, for example, was much taller and heavier than the others, so Scott expected him to pull heavier loads. Yet Evans was not given any additional food, which his body required.

It is clear that Scott did not know how to handle men. In fact he knew hardly anything at all about his crew. All good officers learn that when a mission is dangerous, the men must depend on each other for survival. But Scott had almost nothing to do with his enlisted men. While the officers and civilians lived in the main hut, the enlisted men bunked at the rear of the hut in a lean-to shelter. So Scott was never really sure what his crew was capable of doing.

Amundsen, on the other hand, knew everything about his crew. He knew their weaknesses and their strengths. For example, he was positive that they would perform well when the time came for their long journey south. Bjaaland had just won the international ski races at Chamonix, France. Hansen had spent three years with him during the Northwest Passage expedition and was an expert dog driver and navigator. Hassel had been a dog driver with Otto Sverdrup on his Arctic expedition. Wisting, an all-around handy man, was an excellent skier. This was the kind of crew Amundsen could depend on in any emergency.

But Amundsen was not without his personnel difficulties. Hjalmar Johansen, who had been with Nansen in the Arctic 15 years earlier, criticized Amundsen's leadership on a depot-laying sledge trip in late fall and Amundsen subsequently eliminated Johansen from the polar party. A feud developed because of it. Upon the expedition's arrival at Hobart, Tasmania, Johansen was dismissed and forced to return to Norway by working as a fireman on a British ship. Feeling that he had been disgraced, he eventually committed suicide. As I have learned from experience, polar isolation does not lend itself to harmony. Scott knew this all too well. But in fairness to him, some of his equipment had never been tested under severe polar conditions. For example, when returning from the Pole, Scott discovered that kerosene had leaked out of the fuel containers. Thus he and his men did not have sufficient fuel to prepare hot food, just when they needed it most of all. It was not until years later that explorers found that regular soldering turns powdery when exposed to temperatures under 45 degrees below zero.

Scott had encountered difficulties from the outset. Sailing from Port Chalmers, New Zealand on November 29, 1910, *Terra Nova* met more pack ice than had been expected. It took three weeks to reach open water in the Ross Sea. (Amundsen reached open water in four days.) Thus, Scott was late in starting his dash for 90 deg. South. By far the greatest disaster was the failure of the Siberian ponies to endure the long march. The last one was killed when the party reached the mountains, and from that point on the sledges had to be man-hauled. Scott had counted heavily on the ponies, and it must have been heart-breaking to realize they were a total loss. Yet it was his own fault, he should have known better. Shackleton had used Siberian ponies and they had failed him; Scott knew that.

On the final leg of the march, the polar party consisted of Scott, Dr. Wilson (who had been with him on the *Discovery* expedition), Captain Oates, Lieut. Bowers, and Petty Officer Evans. They were all as tense as Amundsen had been. They saw no sign of the Norwegians until they passed the farthest point reached by Shackleton, then they came upon some ski tracks, dog tracks, and the remains of a camp.

Scott's diary had the notation, "The worst had happened . . . Bowers' sharp eyes detected a black speck ahead, and found that it was a black flag tied to a ski runner. This told us the whole story. The Norwegians had forestalled us and are first to the Pole. It is a terrible disappointment, and I am sorry for my loyal companions . . . "

". . . . Great God! This is an awful place and terrible enough for us to have laboured to it without the reward of priority . . . Now for the run home and a desperate struggle. I wonder if we can do it."

On January 17th, 1912, a full month after Amundsen had left the Pole and started back to Framheim, Scott arrived at 90 deg. South. There he found the tent my father had made, and inside was a message from Amundsen:

Polheim, 15 Dec. 1911

Dear Captain Scott,

As you are probably the first to reach this area after us, I will ask you kindly to forward this letter to King Haakon VII. If you can use any of the articles left in this tent, please do not hesitate to do so.

The sledge left outside may be of use to you. With best regards, I wish you a safe return.

Signed: Yours truly,
ROALD AMUNDSEN

Sick at heart, hungry, cold, and almost exhausted, they took some sun observations to check on the accuracy of Amundsen's determination of the Pole's location. This they found to be accurate. Then they unfurled the Union Jack, lined up for a picture of the entire group, pulled a string to trip the camera shutter and packed their gear. They began the long march back to McMurdo Sound, 800 miles away.

And what were their thoughts as they plunged across the eternally wind-blown surface snow? What would any man think of a journey that had begun with such promise and ended with the bitter taste of defeat. Somehow, Scott found the words and noted in his diary:

"We have turned our backs now on the goal of our ambition, and goodbye to most of our daydreams."

When Amundsen was making the outward march, he had erected many snow cairns, short distances apart, so that he could find his way back across the unmarked wasteland of Antarctica. Scott depended on his own sledge tracks to mark the route. But, in many places the tracks had drifted over, and he kept losing his way. Day after tortuous day, as the men pulled their sledges across the plateau and down the glaciers, it became glaringly evident that they had not spent enough time in planning and preparation. There began a chain of events which proved disastrous and led to the downfall of the entire polar party.

First, the weather was bad. The skies were overcast and the temperature dropped lower and lower. Amundsen had gotten out in time. Now the summer season at this high elevation, close to the center of the continent, was drawing to a close. The sun had dipped close to the horizon. Soon it would be a land of darkness and bitter cold — and death.

Second, they found themselves short of fuel, which limited the number of hot meals so necessary to keep the men moving. This lowered their spirits further. Dragging the sledges became almost unbearable.

Third, they encountered numerous crevasses, many more than on the southern leg of the journey. They had been losing their way almost continuously.

The men were so frostbitten that they were unable to pull the sledges for more than a short time, and then they had to rest,

Robert Falcon Scott

to try getting some warmth back into their hands and feet. But they couldn't get rid of the numbness.

As the temperature dropped to 37 degrees below zero, Scott wrote, "Sunday, March 11 — Titus Oates is very near the end, one feels . . . it must be near the end, but a pretty merciful one . . . must fight it out to the last biscuit."

Evans, the strongest man in the party, was the first to die. Scott's rations were never sufficient for man-hauling sledges, and Evans, a big man, required more food than his companions. He had worn himself out while the party was still on the plateau; as the men came down the glacier toward the Ross Ice Shelf, his condition worsened, Evans became weakened, then somewhat dazed. Later he was found crawling on his hands and knees with a wild look in his eyes. The others pulled him to his feet but soon he sank again. Evans died quietly that night. The others did not leave him until two hours after his death.

Titus Oates was next. Gangrene was attacking his frostbitten feet; Oates realized he was slowing the party. "I am just going outside and may be some time," he said simply. With his final crumb of strength, he left the tent and stepped out into the storm, never to return.

Onward staggered the remnants of Scott's polar party. They were finished and they knew it. On March 29th, while pinned down in the tent by a violent blizzard, Scott wrote:

"Since the 21st we have had a continuous gale from WSW and SW. Every day we have been ready to start for our depot eleven miles away, but outside the door of the tent it remains a scene of whirling drift. I do not think we can hope for better things now; it seems a pity, but I do not think I can write more. R. Scott."

The end of his note read, "For God's sake look after our people."

It was not until November 11th, six months later, that Scott's tent was found by a search party, led by Charles Wright. Except for the very top, the tent was covered with drifting snow. Inside were the bodies of Scott, Wilson, and Bowers. Apsley Cherry-Garrard, who was in the search party, described the scene movingly:

". . . We with the dogs had seen Wright turn away from the course by himself, and the mule party swerved to the right ahead of us. He had seen what he thought was a cairn, and something that looked black by its side. We halted . . . Wright cried, 'It is a tent!' I do not know how he knew. Just a waste of snow . . . we walked up to it. We brushed the snow away and the green flap of the ventilator appeared. We knew that the door was below . . ."

Having read this account and studied all the writings about the Scott expedition, I was fortunate to hear the details related to me, personally, by the man who first spied the tent.

On April 5th, 1968, I had the pleasure of meeting Sir Charles Wright, expedition physicist. The occasion was the annual dinner of the Explorers' Club in New York City. Since both of us were veterans of Antarctic sledge trips, we had much past history to discuss. It was then that he told me, in great detail, about finding Scott and the last two men in his party. And I could see the tears welling up in this gray-haired gentleman's light blue eyes, as he told of that sad day in the history of Antarctic adventure.

Digging around the tent, the rescuers came upon the sledge used by Scott, and some odds and ends — the meteorological log, and the geological specimens, 30 pounds of them, all of great importance. The rocks, as much as anything else, showed the kind of men Scott chose for his crew. These brave men, teetering on the brink of death, clung to them until the very end!

Inside the tent were three bodies. Bowers and Wilson were in their sleeping bags. Scott had thrown back the flaps of his bag, and his left hand was stretched out over Wilson, his life-long friend. Beneath the head of Scott's bag, between it and the floor cloth, were the diaries and some letters. Everything was tidy. There was no snow in the tent's inner lining. These conditions, and several other aspects of the tent's appearance, led the rescue party to believe that Scott was the last to die.

Cherry-Garrard's description continued:

". . . Somehow we learned that Amundsen had been to the Pole, and they, too had been to the Pole, and both items of news seemed to be of no importance whatsoever. There was a letter there from Amundsen to King Haakon."

What a perfect example of the courtesy and respect of one great explorer for another. Scott had taken the letter from the tent at the South Pole, just as Amundsen had requested. And this was the perfect proof that they had *both* reached the South Pole.

"Hour after hour," Cherry-Garrard went on, "or so it seemed, Atkinson sat in his tent and read. The finder was to read the diary and then it was to be brought home. Those were Scott's instructions written on the cover. But Atkinson said he was only going to read sufficient to know what had happened, and after that they were brought home unopened and unread . . ."

Having learned from the diary what had happened, the rescue party marched south, hoping to locate the body of Oates, who had walked out of the tent eleven miles south of the death camp. But the search was in vain; drifting snow had obliterated any trace of him. At the eleven-mile mark the searchers built a snow cairn, then trudged back.

Cherry-Garrard concluded:

"We never moved the men. We took the bamboos of the tent away, and the tent itself covered them. And over them we built the cairn.

". . . I do not know how long we were there, but when all was finished and the Chapter of Corinthians had been read, it was midnight of the same day. The sun was dipping low over the South Pole. The Barrier was almost in shadow. And the sky was blazing — sheets and sheets of irridescent clouds. The cairn and the cross stood dark against a glory of burnished gold."

There is one other incident that should be mentioned: Scott and the remainder of his party were almost saved. A reinforcement party under the leadership of Cherry-Garrard, had sledged to a spot known as "One Ton Depot," which had been set up the year before, while Scott was making preparations for his Polar dash. It was so named because it contained a ton of food and supplies. This was the depot Scott and the remainder of his party were struggling to reach; they would come within 11 miles of it before being marooned in their death tent. When Cherry-Garrard reached One Ton Depot, Scott was still 55 miles away. The rescue team wanted to go farther for a day or two, but bad weather forced them back.

◆ ◆ ◆

In 1911 Wilhelm Filchner's ship *Deutschland* became the first to reach the head of the Weddell Sea approaching from its eastern side. Filchner's party landed and attempted to build a base on the ice in Vahsel Bay. During the erection of buildings, the ice suddenly broke loose and drifted northward. The men were trapped aboard their ship, locked in the moving ice. Not until almost a year later, after drifting a thousand miles, did the German expedition ship reach open water.

Japan's Lieut. Shirase visited the Bay of Whales in 1912 and made a short sledge trip on the Ross Ice Shelf. From 1911 to 1914 Australia's Douglas Mawson — a member of Shackleton's group that ascended Mount Erebus — commanded his own expedition to unexplored regions along the Adelie Coast. For his discoveries and scientific work, he was knighted.

In 1914, just as World War I started, Shackleton set sail on the Norwegian barquentine *Endurance* with another party of daring men. This time he brought dog teams instead of ponies. He was determined to sledge inland from the Weddell Sea to the South Pole and continue all the way across the continent to the Ross Sea. On the final leg of the traverse he intended to follow Scott's ill-fated route of 1912.

This attempt was doomed from the start. The ship was caught in the Weddell Sea and crushed. After drifting for 9 months, Shackleton and his crew abandoned the wreck, hauled small boats onto an ice floe, and continued to drift north for another six months. Many dogs had to be killed — really acts of mercy — for the men did not know if any of them would ever see land again. When the floe began to break apart, they piled into life boats and continued to drift for months. Finally after a harrowing 458 days, they pulled themselves ashore at bleak, deserted Elephant Island. While most of the crew were left to fend for themselves as best they could, living under an overturned boat with a tarpaulin on top, and eating raw seal and penguin meat, Shackleton and four men set out in an open boat, the larger of the two they saved from the ship, to seek help. At last they reached South Georgia, but unfortunately on the wrong side of the island. In a grueling display of courage, three of the five desperate men clawed their way over 3,000-foot mountains to reach a Norwegian whaling station on the other side. Those left behind on the opposite side of the island were soon rescued, but it was not until the following spring, some five months later, that a Chilean steamer could break through the ice to Elephant Island. Miraculously, Shackleton's men were still alive, huddled under their boat shelter. "We knew that somehow Shacky would make it," one of them said. But the ordeal had taken its toll; Shackleton's hair had turned from black to snow-white.

In 1921 Shackleton again sailed south, this time from South Georgia aboard the research ship *Quest*. While at sea working, he died quite suddenly.

His death, at age 49, greatly saddened Sir Hubert Wilkins, who had signed on the expedition as a naturalist. Years later he told me how Shackleton could effortlessly recite poetry while standing watch at the wheel. Yet, the Irishman was a troubled man, plagued by bad luck, haunted by failure. Albeit a magnificent one.

"There seems to be no need to inquire into the cause of Shackleton's death," stated historian J. Gordon Hays in *Antarc-*

tica. It was given as angina pectoris, caused by, or accentuated by, his strenuous Antarctic journeys.

Shackleton's body was placed on board a ship for Montevideo, thence ostensibly to England. A radio message to Lady Shackleton was sent, informing her of her husband's death and requesting instruction for burial. While the ship was enroute to Montevideo, she replied that she wished him buried in South Georgia.

The ship returned to Grytviken, where Shackleton was buried in a small cemetery for Norwegian whalers. His grave lies on a rocky ledge facing south, overlooking the storm-filled Antarctic sea. Beyond stretches the Antarctic continent, whose endless snow fields and glaciers beckoned him to return again and again, until the day he died.

◆ ◆ ◆

The advent of the airplane ushered in a new era of polar exploration. It was first introduced into the Antarctic regions, over the Antarctic Peninsula, by Australian explorer Sir Hubert Wilkins. He was the first man in history to use an airplane to discover new land. Up until this time, some exploration had been carried out on both the east and west coasts of the peninsula, but no one had actually crossed it. Based at Deception Island in the South Shetland group, Sir Hubert, who had been to the Antarctic briefly twice before, made his historic flight on December 20, 1928. He discovered the high Antarctic Peninsula Plateau, which proved to run the length of the Peninsula north and south. Six to eight thousand feet high, the plateau was flat on top with steep sides. Wilkins flew along the east coast of the peninsula, discovering and naming many new features. He added thousands of square miles to the known Antarctic. Wilkins led a second expedition in 1929 and established the outlines of Charcot Island.

Sir Hubert was a most remarkable man. I first met him at radio station KDKA, Pittsburgh, in the summer of 1929. He had come from New York to relay a message to Byrd who was wintering in Little America. Wilkins, at the time, planned to explore the Pacific quadrant of Antarctica by ship and plane, and hoped to reach Byrd's base, where his ship would locate him and his pilot. Wilkins wanted to discuss with Byrd where a food cache might

Sir Hubert Wilkins, *left,* and Finn Ronne at the 1958 annual dinner of the Explorers Club in New York a few months before Wilkins' death.

be placed for his return in case of emergency, but Byrd never replied.

As a regular guest on these Saturday evening broadcasts to the Arctic and Antarctic, I spoke to Norwegian and Danish trappers in the Far North and sent greetings to my father with Byrd. I was a design engineer with Westinghouse, that operated the first radio broadcasting station in the world at that time.

Years later, it was my good fortune to work closely with Wilkins in the office of the Quartermaster General of the Army. We had desks next to each other and made Arctic field trips together testing clothing and all type of polar, or cold weather equipment.

Born and raised in Australia, he joined a Canadian expedition under Vilhjalmur Stefansson in 1913; was onboard the *Quest* in 1922 when Shackleton died off South Georgia; flew with pilot Ben Eielsen and landed on the pack ice hundreds of miles from shore, north of Alaska, and walked back to civilization after their airplane was wrecked. In 1928 he crossed the north polar basin from

Alaska to Spitsbergen in a single engine plane, a distance of 2,500 miles, without landing. For this daring flight he was knighted by the King of England. In 1931 Sir Hubert proved the feasibility of using submarines under the polar ice pack. He had the unique distinction of having spent more time in the polar areas than any other man. We remained close friends until his untimely death of a stroke in 1958.

In 1928–30 Commander Richard E. Byrd established Little America close to Amundsen's old base Framheim in the Bay of Whales. My father, who had also known Framheim, now estimated the old base was covered by 50 feet of drifting snow and ice. On November 28 and 29, 1929 — with pilot Bernt Balchen at the controls — air photo reconnaissance mapping was performed by the first flight to penetrate the interior. King Haakon VII Polar Plateau was attained.

When Byrd returned to Little America in 1934, I was along — the first to step ashore. Be that as it may, that first step marked the beginning of my love affair with Antarctica that would span four decades.

CHAPTER 8

I FELT LUCKY WHEN BYRD CHOSE ME for his 1933 expedition. It completely changed my path in life — from design engineer with Westinghouse in Pittsburgh to polar explorer in the Antarctic. Since returning from the expedition, my thoughts often dwelt on the 15 months I had spent inside the Antarctic Circle. I had wintered on the continent in four months of complete darkness, had fought below zero temperatures and sledged over ice fields through snowy desert, tracking into the unknown. I had raced screaming blizzards in their eternal chase to obliterate the trail impressions the dogs and I left in our wake. At times I had been blinded, frostbitten, lost, and helpless; the shrieking wind penetrated my very soul and made me wonder what this was all about. I had fallen into treacherous crevasses and climbed unfriendly mountains. But in that cruel land of eternal ice, I beheld an unimaginable crystalline beauty; and I felt myself a part of a surrealistic scene as I stood transfixed while the aurora australis washed over me.

I reflected on my experiences with satisfaction and yearning. Antarctica was my destiny; of that I was certain. I knew that I would return to the ice-locked continent. But when? I recalled that New Year's Day when I stood at the summit of Mount Nilsen in the Rockefeller Mountains. I had scanned eastward to the horizon with my field glasses; beyond, I knew, lay unknown land. I dared to dream that some day I would lead my own expedition over that distant horizon. Perhaps, I thought, I might find there a mountain range to rival the Himalayas. I might even find an active volcano to add to the one Sir James Clark Ross sighted in 1841. The dream was persistent and became a part of my reality.

Upon the return of the Byrd expedition in May, 1935, I assumed my old job with Westinghouse. Even so, my heart was in Antarctica. More than ever, I was determined to launch my own expedition; and I was busy night and day devising plans. One day I drove up to New Hampshire to the Chinook Kennels, where I had first encountered husky dogs. Milton Seeley, the owner, assured me that he could supply all the dogs I would need. Next I contacted whaling companies in Norway. With their support — their ships operated in Antarctic waters every year — I could land a small party on Charcot Island, stepping stone to the Antarctic Peninsula and the unknown land to the south. Here I would build my base. My expedition would have constant radio contact with the whalers during our crossing westward to the Bay of Whales. Riiser-Larsen, when put ashore at Cape Norvegia for his island sledge journey in 1929–30, had set up a similar arrangement. It proved its worth, eventually saving the lives of three men adrift on ice floes.

Charcot Island was first sighted by Jean Charcot in 1908. Sir Hubert Wilkins flew over it in 1929 and made aerial photographs. The island was completely surrounded by sea ice, thus was not accessible from the sea. However, from Wilkins' photographs, it seemed feasible that a landing could be made in front of the island on what appeared to be sea ice.

I had lined up a couple of prospective dog drivers to go with me. Eager for the experience and adventure, these young men were even willing to help shoulder expenses. Despite financial handicaps, my plans for a Ronne expedition to the Antarctic proceeded undaunted. My aim was to get off in October 1937. Already I had acquired 30 sledge dogs, now kenneled at my friend Adolph Dupre's winter resort at Seven Springs, near Somerset, Pennsylvania.

I discussed my plans with the surveyor I had taken with me to the Rockefeller Mountains in 1934. He expressed enthusiasm for my project and quickly offered his services. I had thought he might. But, remembering his ineptness as a radio operator, I urged him to improve his skill in that capacity, so that he would be more useful in the field. At the same time I asked him to check out the latest radio equipment, and inform me of the result.

At that time he was a field representative with the Department of Interior. He wrote me from Honolulu that he had discussed my expedition plans with his chief, Dr. Ernest Gruening, telling him of my arrangements with Norwegian whaling interests. He explained to his boss that although I was born in Norway, I was then an American citizen, and had been so for over 10 years.

The upshot of it was that Dr. Gruening became interested in the idea of an American expedition and promised to take it up with officials in Washington. This he did — and with no less an official than the President, Franklin D. Roosevelt.

The President thought an American expedition was an excellent idea. However, he did not see why Norwegians would be needed to supply ship transportation when a U.S. Coast Guard cutter could do the job. Furthermore, the President expressed the belief that the United States Government should take a more active part in Antarctic exploration. After all, there had not been an official American expedition to the Antarctic since Lieut. Charles Wilkes sailed in 1840. The President also proposed that Admiral Byrd and Lincoln Ellsworth be called to Washington to organize the expedition. Byrd came, of course. Ellsworth would have nothing to do with it.

Before I could discern exactly what was happening, I lost control of my own expedition. From the bureaucratic whirlwind, the United States Antarctic Service Expedition emerged. Its purpose: Explore unknown territory and conduct scientific research from two bases 1,500 miles apart.

A request for an appropriation of $435,000 was drawn up by the Dept. of Interior. But even before the appropriation was submitted to Congress, Byrd wrote me from Boston that he was planning a privately financed expedition in the event that government funds were not forthcoming. He asked me to join him, cautioning me "not to tell anybody, that means no one."

Byrd's plans were dashed when Congress voted to fund the expedition. This did not displease me, for I expected to be given a leading role, inasmuch as my initiative triggered the entire operation. That presumption was naive. When I came to Washington early in July 1939, I learned that my erstwhile friend and protege, the surveyor, had preceded me. As is so often the case when ambition outpaces ability, influence was the determinant. He was named leader of the east base. Byrd picked Paul Siple to head the west base. Siple, it might be remembered, first went to the Antarctic with Byrd as a twenty-year-old boy scout. Despite the fact that the core of my idea had been appropriated by others, I did not lose sight of my goal — to return to Antarctica.

"The thing is," Byrd told me, "that the surveyor has gotten himself well on the inside with the Interior Department through his boss Dr. Gruening. Otherwise, he would not have been the designated leader of east base. That was a position I thought you would be worthy of; but as it stands now, I cannot do anything." I thought back to our conversation a few months earlier in the Willard Hotel, when Byrd came to Washington and said that he was backing me as leader of east base. Now he was asking me which man I wished to serve with — Siple or the surveyor.

It was not whom I wanted to work with, but where I desired to go that determined my decision; I had been with both men in the Antarctic and knew their limitations. I told Byrd that I preferred to be where I could make a sledge journey westward of Charcot Island, as I had originally planned. "That you will be able to do," Byrd assured me; "furthermore you will be second in command at the base. The surveyor will need you."

It was decided that the expedition should sail from Boston, Byrd's hometown. I rented quarters there to work in the Navy Yard, where we maintained an office; but I also spent much of my time in New Hampshire, where the sledge dogs were assembled, dog drivers trained, and equipment tested. During this period we contracted for sledges, harnesses, ski boots, trail food, and a thousand other items vital to the expedition.

Byrd in a business suit — rather than a fur-lined parka — showed his true ability. Dealing with company executives or government officials, he more often than not got his way. Men were added to the expedition daily, and the mountain of supplies seemed to double in size overnight. Every day brought something new. The latest acquisition was the tanklike "snow-cruiser," ordered from the Armour Research Foundation in Chicago. Although many of the men selected to go on the expedition had no polar experience, they did not hesitate to tell newspapers all the grand things they were going to accomplish. When the reporters interviewed me, I told them to wait until we returned and then write about what we did; not now, when nothing had been done.

Actually, the only legitimate news item about our preparations concerned the snow cruiser, a monstrous contraption weighing about 40 tons, with a width of 12 feet and a length of 55 feet.

Unloading supplies and equipment from the *North Star* on the bay ice in the Bay of Whales during the U.S. Antarctic Service Expedition of 1939–1941.

On its journey to Boston, highways had to be widened, bridges taken down and police escorts provided.

The cruiser was loaded onto *North Star*, the Department of Interior ship used regularly off the coast of Alaska. The other ship assigned to the expedition was the *Bear*, used in 1933–35 on my first trip south. The U.S. Navy refurbished the old ship, replaced her reciprocating steam engine and boiler with an 800-horse-power diesel at a cost of $150,000. Byrd, now the owner of the ship, received a rental fee of $235 per month while *Bear* remained in service to the Navy. The officers and the crew were, of course, military personnel on active duty. Ironically the ship did not carry an ounce of the expedition's cargo. Nor were there any civilians onboard. What purpose, then, did the ship serve? It served as the Admiral's flagship, even though the admiral wasn't on board. He, like the rest of the expedition, embarked on the *North Star*.

Byrd enjoyed the cruise as much as anyone. I had meals with him often during the two months he was a passenger. He liked to spend time on the boat deck watching dog sledges being assembled. The runners, bridges and crosspieces, made of hickory, were lashed together with rawhide. The sledges were quite flexible, enabling the runners to conform to the surface of the ice. Sixty sledges, each weighing about 75 pounds, were assembled during the passage across the Pacific.

After brief stops at Wellington and Dunedin, we soon felt the rough seas of the Antarctic Ocean. The topside weight of the snow cruiser made the ship roll more than usual; for several days some of the men were too seasick to get out of their bunks. We penetrated the pack ice to the open water of the Ross Sea, then headed for the Bay of Whales.

About a mile from where the *North Star* was moored, a site was selected for West Base. We immediately started unloading because the ship was scheduled to sail for Valparaiso, Chile, and pick up 600 tons of supplies for the east base.

The greatest problem confronting us in the Bay of Whales was the unloading of the snow cruiser. Dr Poulter, in charge of the project, had a landing ramp constructed. About 80 feet long, it would serve as a bridge from the main deck of the ship to the floating ice. Just as we gathered to watch the cruiser roll down the ramp, *Bear* sailed into the bay. We had parted company in Panama. Her tremendous cruising radius enabled her to sail directly without calling at any port to refuel. She arrived just in time to witness Dr. Poulter's operation.

Slowly the cruiser moved down the ramp. Suddenly there were creaking and popping sounds as the front wheels broke through cross timbers. The ponderous vehicle came to a dead stop, poised over several hundred fathoms of water. At any moment we onlookers expected to see the $150,000 monster plunge through the ice to the bottom of the Ross Sea. Dr. Poulter in the driver's seat had other ideas. Abandoning caution, he gunned the motors. The mammoth van groaned and shuddered and, miraculously, pulled itself free; then inched down the ramp to the solid bay ice. At the moment of safe arrival we all gave a cheer. On top of the cruiser was Byrd, hanging onto a piece of rope.

I skied alongside as the cruiser moved inland three miles, to a small inlet off the Bay of Whales. But there she stopped; a slight grade from the bay ice to the permanent barrier proved to be too steep for the vehicle to negotiate. The huge wheels, powered by electric motors in each hub would not turn. It soon became apparent that the trouble stemmed from an engineering miscalculation; power had been sacrificed for speed in the gear reduction unit. We had a white elephant on our hands.

Although the snow cruiser never moved another inch forward, she was not a total loss. Several men from West Base made the stranded vehicle their sleeping quarters.

We worked 12-hour shifts — 7 to 7. Since I was officer in charge of surface transportation, I elected to work at night and let the newcomers have the easier daytime shift. One morning after breakfast I heard someone say that killer whales were swimming near the ship. Postponing sleep, I instead pulled on my parka, grabbed my motion-picture camera, and hurried out on deck to shoot pictures of the whales. Clinging to the railing for support, I got beautiful close-ups of them breaching and sliding into the cold water below me. In a few minutes Byrd strolled by. I turned and said, "Good morning, Admiral." He walked on without uttering a word; perhaps he had not heard me.

The giant snow cruiser on the bay ice in the Bay of Whales shortly after arrival in January 1940.

I continued photographing whales until they swam out of sight, then returned to my cabin on the main deck. A short while later, as I stretched out to get some sleep, my roommate came in and told me that Byrd was upset with me. Why? Because I was taking pictures when there was much work to be done. My roommate said he explained that I had been working all night and was off duty at the time, that I had, in fact, borrowed from my sleep to film the whales. Byrd's curt answer was that no one should sleep until the ship was unloaded.

I was amused. The only time I had ever seen the admiral do anything to speed up unloading was in 1934, when Paramount newsreel photographers set up their cameras next to a mountain of food crates on the ice. As dog teams swung between the stacks of crates and hauled loaded sledges up onto the barrier about four miles away, Byrd in his Teddy-bear suit picked up a carton of corn flakes weighing about eight pounds and placed it on my sledge. The camera men cranked furiously to capture the admiral at work. He hefted two more boxes, then retreated to his cabin on the bridge.

After *North Star* was unloaded, we headed out to sea bound for Valparaiso, Chile. We parted from *Bear* again, and this time Byrd was on board. His ship would follow the periphery of the coast from the Ross Sea to the Antarctic Peninsula, while we sailed the stormy South Pacific.

About halfway to Valparaiso, *North Star*'s surgeon recommended an operation for Power, my lead dog and companion for seven years. The doctor assured me that the operation — for a urinary infection — was not serious. "You can assist me, if you wish," he said. We walked aft to the well deck, where a wide plank between the hatch and the railing served as an operating table.

I helped strap Power to the table, then the doctor sprinkled ether on some cotton in a paper funnel placed over the dog's nose. As the doctor started cutting, he instructed me to apply more of the anesthesia. Suddenly Power's heart stopped beating. The doctor tried to massage it back to life, but it was no use. Power was gone.

I felt very sad. Never again, I vowed, would I become so closely attached to an animal. That evening when Power was thrown overboard, my eyes were wet with tears. I was not ashamed. "A man who doesn't have tears has no heart," a trapper in the "Far North" once told me.

From Valparaiso — a pleasant if busy two weeks respite — we steamed south to Punta Arenas on the Strait of Magellan. We stayed here five days while we reloaded the crowded ship, then challenged notorious Drake Passage, south of Cape Horn, where ships have gone down without leaving a trace. Tremendous waves tested the ship, but *North Star* rode them like a cork; very little water spilled on her decks. That was fortunate for the 76 huskies chained topside. By this time, the howling dogs had been on board for about three months without exercise. Finally we reached the pack ice, and the constant rolling of the ship ceased as she plowed through the slush. The dogs quieted down.

We entered Marguerite Bay in ice-free waters. To the east loomed the backbone of the Antarctic Peninsula, a high ridge stretching from the northernmost tip for about 1,000 miles south to the interior of the continent. Anchored at Horseshoe Island was *Bear*. After leaving West Base, she had skirted the fringes of the continent for 1,500 miles.

For a week the two ships drifted aimlessly in the bay. No effort was made to locate a suitable site for East Base. There was not even much communication between the two ships. I did not understand the lethargic attitude. If a decision were not made soon, the establishment of a base there would have to be scrubbed. It was not the simple task one might expect, for certain requirements had to be met. Foremost, it was essential that the base have an access route to the interior of the continent, so that we could get the dog teams and sledges in the field for geographical exploration.

Unable to remain passive about our situation, I took the initiative and suggested that a few of us go ashore and examine a snowy plain I had spied; it might prove to be an adequate location for our base. In a few minutes a motor boat landed us on a pebbled beach. We climbed to the top of the ridge, where I clamped on skis and took a short run to the opposite side. I found that although a base on this level plateau would give access to the interior, it was inaccessible to the ship; hauling the Curtis Condor plane up the steep slope would be an almost impossible task.

When we returned to the ship, we noticed activities on board

Bear. A hydroplane was lowered into the water with Byrd in it. Our little jaunt had apparently stirred him out of his reverie. The plane was soon airborne, cruising low between the small islands. It was the first of several flights made that day, but unfortunately none of them located an adequate site for a base.

That evening the boat party set out again. Our destination: a squat, partly snow-covered island off to the southeast. (Later it was named Stonington Island, after Stonington, Connecticut, home port of Nathaniel Palmer, who first sighted the Antarctic mainland.) Standing in the bow of the boat, I jumped ashore and headed for a snowy ramp leading to the high ice tongue of a glacier. Here I saw a reasonable level area free of large stones, an ideal spot for setting up base buildings. The snowy ramp, which connected the island to the mainland would also provide an avenue to the interior for our dog teams.

But where would we park the Curtis Condor? Ashley Snow, the aptly named Navy pilot who was to winter with us, was satisfied with the landing strip I proposed — the back bay. After it froze, planes would be able to land and take off within a few feet of the base compound.

In high spirit we returned to the ship. News of our successful homesteading spread quickly among the men, all eager to get started. Next morning at daybreak the ship moved close to shore on the western side of the island and unloading commenced. I was in charge of constructing the base, because of past experience. My assistant was rangy Glenn Dyer, a cadastral engineer with the U.S. Land Office of the Department of Interior. With carpenter Charbonneau, we measured and marked where the supporting posts of the buildings were to be located, then the carpenter sawed the 12″ x 12″ beams by hand. The buildings would go up quickly once the floor, wall, and roof panels were brought ashore. Meanwhile, we set up a couple of tents for sleeping quarters, another for cooking. During the next ten days we roughed it outdoors while the buildings were erected.

Strong winds frequently sprang up from the southeast, hampering our work. On a number of occasions *Bear* was forced to seek safe anchorage at Horseshoe Island. Finally, on the morning of March 21, the last of the cargo was unloaded from the *North Star.* Now the two ships made ready to sail for South America — and on to Boston.

The night before they departed, Byrd requested that East Base personnel come to his cabin one by one. Presumably, he wished to give each of us a pep talk, remind us of our responsibilities, that sort of thing. But that was so out of character for Byrd; he was not a loquacious person. When my turn came to enter his private sanctuary aft on the *Bear*, he seated me so that a bright light shone directly in my face. It was most blinding. Straining to see through the glare, I noticed that his lips were tight, his eyes hard and flinty. I did not understand why I was being subjected to these third-degree dramatics. Was that some kind of joke? Had I done something wrong? Was Byrd well?

Finally he spoke, his Virginia drawl unable to mask the coolness in his voice. He had heard rumors that I expressed displeasure when we were drifting aimlessly around Marguerite Bay. "Yes," I told him, I was disappointed to see us laying to for so long, without getting on with the job." He answered that we had lots of time and that he did not wish to be criticized by anybody. Next he questioned me about the pictures I had taken at the Bay of Whales. When we docked in Valparaiso I had mailed the exposed film to New York for processing. He said I broke the rules, that a letter sent to him by President Roosevelt prohibited expedition members from taking pictures without official clearance from him. I reminded him that a protest had been lodged against that order; besides, my purpose in mailing the film was to determine whether or not I was using the right lens setting for color photography.

After listening to more of Byrd's petty criticism, I decided I had had enough: "Admiral, if you wish, I shall be happy to go back with you on the *Bear* right now." Byrd changed his tone immediately: "No, I want you to stay and carry through your plans for a long sledge journey." He then started telling me how much he had liked my father, how great a man he was, how valuable his work had been on his 1928 expedition. We shook hands, and I wished him good sailing back to the States.

I should note here that Byrd did not come down to Antarctica the second season. He stayed in Boston the entire year. I remember a radio broadcast beamed to us on June 22, midwinter's day, when the sun was at its lowest. The Governor of Massachusetts spoke to us by shortwave: "Greetings to you, Admiral Byrd, and your men at Little America . . ." He did not know that Byrd was in Boston, only a couple of blocks from the studio. Although the press and radio referred to this as a Byrd expedition, he had nothing to do with its creation, its financing, or its administration. He did give advice from time to time.

During the building of the base we did not see much of the surveyor either. He spent much of the time in the sleeping tent playing with a small kitten he had picked up in Punta Arenas. It was plain that he was no leader of men. But since we had been friends for a long time, I gave him all the assistance I could.

The Army construction corps had designed the three pre-fabricated buildings — the combination bunkhouse and mess hall, the machine shop and the science building.

The bunkhouse had five two-man cubicles on each side against the outer walls. Two dining tables occupied the center aisle. The galley was at one end and sick bay was at the other — so if the cook poisoned us we didn't have far to go. I had my own 12′ x 12′ building with a storage shed attached. I invited Arthur Carroll, a Navy photographer to be my hut companion. He turned out to be the best choice of the 25 men. With a small pot-bellied stove to provide heat, we had a very pleasant, comfortable set up.

On the 9th of April, the radio operator came to me with the news that Norway had been invaded by the Germans. I was concerned for the safety of my three brothers and sisters and their families. Their welfare was very much in my thoughts.

There were 26 men in the wintering group, with 21 men housed in the buildings; the cook had a bunk in the galley. The remaining three men slept in the radio shack and meteorological section.

Once when I came into the meteorological office, I found one man (let me call him Ralph) working with the met-men instead of on the outdoor job I had assigned him. "The surveyer gave me permission to work here!" he said. I told him to go back to the work *I* had assigned. Then I marched over to see the surveyor. Ralph followed, flaming mad. He was taller than I and rather slender. During the heated conversation, he brought his mittened fist close to my face in a threatening pose. I stayed cool, watching every move he made. Suddenly he swung. Anticipating the attack, I avoided him and stepped in with a right that landed flush on his chin, knocking him out cold. He remained that way for half an hour or more, and I was momentarily concerned that

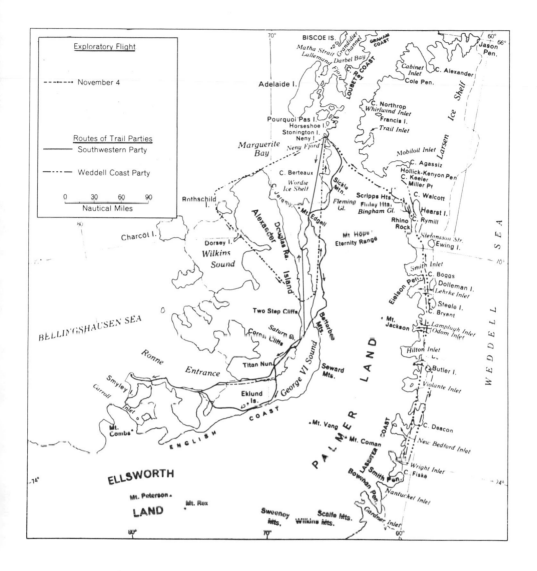

I might have severely hurt him. But after the doctor examined him, I was assured that Ralph would be all right. Turning to the surveyor I said: "I wish you would not interfere with my planning of the men's work. If you do, you can have the job yourself and go to hell." I walked over to my own hut, disgusted with the sour turn of events. Later that evening he came over to apologize. Within the week, Ralph too apologized. From that time on, everyone would know who ran East Base. It was either that or chaos.

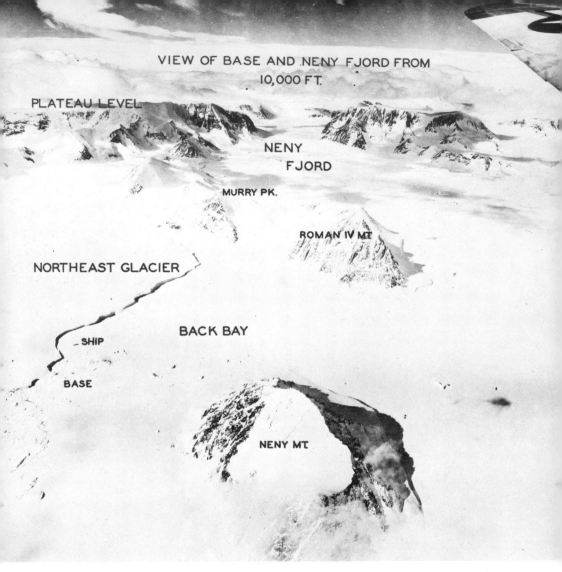

VIEW OF BASE AND NENY FJORD FROM 10,000 FT.

PLATEAU LEVEL

NENY FJORD

MURRY PK.

ROMAN IV MT

NORTHEAST GLACIER

SHIP

BACK BAY

BASE

NENY MT

Aerial view of the entire area where the Ronne Antarctic Research Expedition wintered, 1946–1948. The expedition ship, *Port of Beaumont, left center,* is frozen into the ice in the Back Bay.

Major construction work was completed by the end of April. The aviation gang then began work on the twin-engine Curtis Condor plane. It was brought ashore on a raft of lifeboats. Normally we had overcast weather with high winds; but during a day when good weather prevailed, the wings were attached and the motors tuned. Several weeks later, we made a reconnaissance flight south. We followed the west side to scout for possible sledge

Members of the Main Southern Party. *Left to right:* Finn Ronne, leader; Carl Eklund, biologist; Lytton Musselman, dog driver; Paul Knowles, geologist; Joseph Healy, dog driver; Donald Hilton, surveyor; J. Glenn Dyer, surveyor.

routes. I determined that it should lead from Neny Fjord, where a smooth glacier ended as a new trough began. Farther on, in the central area of the planned route, I suggested placing a food cache, where there was an easy entree down the slopes onto George VI Sound. It was exactly the situation I had hoped for.

The following day, May 21, we flew a cache of man food and kerosene to the smooth area I had spotted. The location was fixed by our surveyor Donald Hilton with a series of sights to prominent mountain peaks surrounding the area, and marked with a beacon of snow blocks about ten feet high topped with an orange flag. Despite these precautions, we later failed to find the cache.

My main southern sledge party consisted of three units. Paul Knowles, geologist, and Donald Hilton, surveyor, were to support me for a week only. This party would then return to base in order to start their own Weddell Sea party. Glenn Dyer, surveyor, Lytton Musselman and Joseph Healy, dog drivers, would support me as long as I deemed it necessary, but for no more than three additional weeks. Carl Eklund, biologist with the Fish and Wildlife

Service would be with me the entire time — an estimated three months. The other men would return to base after the caches were laid.

The men chosen to go into the field spent a busy winter night preparing sledges, tents, sleeping bags and making trail markers. The man-food rations were prepared, weighed, and packed in canvas bags, each weighing 75 pounds and sufficient to feed one man for thirty days. A total of 64 such bags were prepared for use on the trail. This project took place in my own small shack, which resembled an overstocked grocery store. The assembled bags were stored in a lean-to alongside my building.

As daylight gradually returned in August, 1940, we turned our attention to outdoor activities. Non-skiers practiced on a slope next to the base. The dogs were harnessed in teams and trained to pull heavy loads. As usual, they created a great stir, howling and barking 24 hours a day. We trained them on the sloping glacier that entered the island close to the base buildings and led to the high plateau beyond.

On top of the 6,000-foot-high plateau, we decided to set up a weather station. A party of ten men and 64 dogs lined up to cross the glacier to the eastern mountains. As we tackled the steep slopes, slashed with crevasses, I asked the men to follow my trail; to deviate might prove disastrous.

The teams followed my ski tracks until we came to a dangerous crevassed area. Then I scouted ahead alone, making herring-bone tracks in the snow. I found many extremely dangerous cracks in the surface; some open, others covered with a thin layer of snow. Before my companions followed, I suggested that we take off our skis and put on crampons. On ledges of solid ice we made a snaking trail, ugly black holes on either side. Some of them must have been 80 feet deep or more.

It was getting late, and darkness soon engulfed us. Clambering up the steep slope, we finally found a level area large enough to set up the tents and cook our first meal on the primus cooker. I was amazed — and relieved — that no one had dropped into a crevasse.

Next morning the overcast drifted away. After breakfast, all hands were eager to climb the rest of the distance to the elevation where we intended to set up the weather station. The view from this height was breath-taking. We clearly saw mountains on Alexander I Land, with glaciers flowing seaward between rocky ridges to an ice escarpment. We leisurely pitched our tents in calm weather, staked out the dogs, prepared our meals, and enjoyed our accomplishment.

About 6:30 in the evening, a hurricane-force wind struck the camp. It continued for two days and nights. When I crawled outside my tent to check on the men in the other tents, I found them in surprisingly good spirits. Some of them were singing — even at three o'clock in the morning. Ignorance truly was bliss. I was fearful that we might be blown off the top. The wind had undercut the surface around the tents, and some of the tent pegs were dangling in the air. I crawled through snow drifts to the sledge and, with the aid of a flashlight, rummaged in a canvas bag for replacement pegs. Although the wind was blinding me, I managed to feel my way around and spike them into the ice, anchoring the tents more securely.

In the early morning hours, the wind died down. Heading toward a snowy mound where the dog teams were supposed to be, I called the name of a dog. He poked his head through the crust, as did the others soon after. The huskies had survived the storm without any harm.

We took down the tents and loaded the sledges. By the end of the day we had covered the 17 miles back to base. We licked our wounds and prepared to tackle the next set of problems.

The Curtis Condor became an invaluable aid. Twice in September, I participated in flights to locate safe return routes to base. I also made several reconnaissance flights, the one on November 4 taking us across Marguerite Bay to the northern tip of Alexander I Island. 150 miles south of the tip, we turned east, crossing George VI Sound, and followed the mountain ridge back to base. Our longest flight, it was the prelude to our most ambitious undertaking — a sledge journey from East Base to explore the regions south and southwest of Alexander I Island, continuing westerly to determine the delineation of the coastline in the Pacific quadrant of the continent. That was the plan that had first begun to take shape six years earlier, when I stood on Mount Nilsen and looked eastward into the unknown. I was elated at the prospect.

CHAPTER 9

THE EVENING BEFORE DEPARTURE, Dyer came into my quarters for a chat and expressed deep concern at not having been assigned to any field party to do survey work, which was his profession. The Department of Interior sent him with us to perform exactly such work. If he could join us, he promised to do the menial tasks required on the trail by all hands, no matter what their rank, responsibility, or position. So, I agreed to take him on condition that he would return to base at my discretion. Adding a man required a realignment of sledges, food, tenting, and loads to go on the sledges. But we set to work, tired as we were, and made the last-minute changes. Glen Dyer was a happy man. I thought it only fair to give him the chance.

In the forenoon of November 6, 1940, the seven of us moved down onto the bay ice, setting a course for Cape Berteaux. It was a bleak day, with low clouds, poor visibility, and a slow surface of heavy, wet snow. We first sledged over the sea ice in Marguerite Bay, encountering a number of open leads. Carl's lead dog fell in one. Other dogs became scared, so we had to drag them across. For three days we traveled on the smooth bay surface to Wordie Ice Shelf. After spending a couple of hours to locate a sloping surface leading to the 400-foot-high ice cliff, we labored until late in the evening to get the sledges up, pulling each one with two teams of dogs.

After chow, I took Knowles, a geologist, with me to scout for a safe route through the heavily crevassed area ahead. It looked hopeless. By the time we returned several of the men were already in their sleeping bags, though it was early evening. Pushing sledges and dragging dogs around were strength-sapping tasks, especially for personnel new to the trail.

Next morning we started through the crevassed glacier. I, leading the caravan, skied ahead. As as safety measure, I snapped an alpine line to my webbed belt, the other end of the rope I attached to the main gang line of Carl's dog team that followed me. On a couple of occasions I fell through the surface, but the line held. I yelled, and Carl halted his team, skied forward, and pulled me back on top.

By late afternoon, we had passed the worst area. It was the most dangerous area that, I believe, can ever be encountered on the Antarctic continent. Huge open crevasses, over which we crossed on narrow snow-bridges, were most common; but the hidden crevasses were also numerous, and they caused us great concern. Four dogs were once hanging in their lines ten feet down, but were easily pulled up to safety.

On smooth level surface I headed for the location of a cache deposited by plane before the real winter started. Hilton set up his transit and took a series of bearings. With these as guidelines, we moved around for more than two hours without finding any trace of the ten-foot snow beacon with a 12-foot-high flagpole on top.

I was unable to learn the reason for not locating the cache. Either Hilton had a different magnetic variation from the one used when the cache was laid down, or the snowfalls in this areas were so heavy that they buried the cache completely.

Next morning on the regular radio schedule, I explained the situation to the base and requested that the plane fly out additional supplies for another emergency cache, before we continued sledging south.

The evening we arrived at the Wordie location, I decided to send Dyer back to base with Knowles and Hilton, who had performed exceedingly well supporting us. Glenn came over to me and asked that he be allowed to continue with us a little longer. I discussed the situation with Carl, and we came to an understanding. Dyer could join the second supporting party; and the three men would mess together, independent of Carl and myself.

◆ ◆ ◆

It was not until late in the evening of November 16 that the weather started to clear. The base had radioed us that the plane would take off at midnight. An hour and a half later it landed close to our camp. We unloaded the cache items, then built a 12-foot beacon with a 20-foot bamboo pole, an orange colored flag at its tip. Next morning early we were on our way. My four companions sledged behind me, with Grub, Carl's lead dog, right on the heels of my skis. In deep, soft snow, we traveled slowly southward, following the center ridge of the high plateau. Visibility was almost zero. As I broke trail, wind-driven snow hit me straight on. It was a cruel way to travel. I had to face downward and watch the needle of the Brunton-compass in order to keep a steady heading. We kept on sledging in this manner until the evening of November 20. At times there was a continuous white-out — like skiing into white cotton.

On November 20, after a good night's rest, we awoke to find a clear sky with good visibility over a mountainous scenery to the south and west. From our high elevation of 7,000 feet, Alexander Land could be seen to the west. The aerial photographs delivered to me by the plane crew at Wordie, enabled me to place our location, named "Plateau Camp" on top of a long glacier free of crevasses.

With a clear and seemingly smooth route ahead, I was satisfied to release Musselman, Healy, and Dyer. The supplies they brought this far would enable us to extend our stay in the field. I designated Dyer as leader of the supporting party returning to East Base. They all had done a good job in assisting us. Before Carl and I continued on our own, five of the weakest dogs were shot. They had served as well.

We started off with 15 dogs and enough supplies to stay in the field for 74 days. Moving quickly down the glacier to the valley running north and south, Eklund and I began our program to explore the completely unknown land-area south and west of Alexander Land, and to determine the continental coastline. Sledging was good on the hard surface in the long valley shadowed with high mountains on both sides. We headed for a cache laid down by airplane at the Batterbee Mountains. On the morning of December 3, our field glasses picked out the long bamboo pole with its orange colored marker. After spending a day reloading sledges and discarding unnecessary gear, we headed for a table-shaped, stratified mountain toward the southwest.

We now entered an entirely unexplored area. No surface party had ever sledged that far south in the whole of West Antarctica. Nineteen miles from Batterbee cache, we were greatly surprised to find pressure ice extending beyond the horizon in a southeasterly direction. By the water's salty taste, which we sampled in an open lead, we concluded that the sea extended this far into the sound. The pressure ice here was badly broken, and it took us some time to find a passage through. On a steep side bank, the lead-sledge skidded and tipped over into the open water. After retrieving it, we pitched camp to dry our gear. Then again we began climbing gradually, sledging on smooth surface. At the table mountain we found a fresh-water lake and found a passage along the shore that had a rock-strewn slope. I noticed a peculiar-looking boulder and stopped for a closer look. Hefting the heavy rock, I saw embedded in it a foot-long piece of petrified wood about 9 inches in diameter, the texture of the bark was unmistakable. With the tip of my G pole I chipped off several pieces and put them in my knapsack. Now I had proof that trees once grew on this barren continent. I then took a series of sun observations for a fix and made a photographic record of it, so that a complete outline of this new area was well determined.

On December 7 we headed due south in order to locate the extension of the southern shore line of Alexander Land. In two steps, one mile apart, we dropped down to the sound-level of 150 feet and crossed over the King George VI Sound's southern shore. The continental coastline stretched in an east-west direction, and its bank to the sound was heavily crevassed. Due south, about 50 miles away, could be seen a high mountain whose height we estimated to be 6,000 to 8,000 feet. Its western slopes were partly covered with snow.

Sledging was good on the hard snow, along the continental coast westward. The surface at some places was of a rolling nature; undoubtedly open water was in the many crevasses we crossed. Snowy petrels with the perfect camouflage of pure white were numerous here. On a rock nunatak, about 1,000 feet in height, we built a stone beacon. Inside it, in a small tin can I deposited one of the claim-sheets issued by the Department of

State: ". . . Sledging with dog-team in company with Carl Eklund — came upon this rock-outcrop (nunatak) which apparently is an island in King George VI Sound. The peak of this nunatak was ascended today." The brief note in the rock cairn claimed the land in the name of the United States.

On December 17, we reached an area where the surface was wavy; finally coming to a lower level with leads of open water. No bottom could be found with our 170-foot line. This, as well as the saltiness of the water samples collected, told us that we were now on sea-ice.

On December 20th, my birthday, using the handcrank generator I tapped off a message to base asking that a telegram be sent to Washington, to Secretary of the Navy Frank Knox, advising him of my desire to apply for a commission in the United States Naval Reserve. I had been listening to shortwave broadcasts coming from India about the battles going on in North Africa between Rommel and Montgomery. I had a feeling that America would be involved in the war before long, and if so, I would like to have a role in it.

Ice pressures impossible to penetrate stopped us December 21, as we headed for a cape in the distance. From a small embayment, we located a slope leading to higher elevation. We climbed to about a thousand feet and followed the crest in a northerly direction. A most unexpected sight opened before us. In an arch from 300 degrees true, clockwise to 100 deg. true was a sea entirely free from land. Only a few large icebergs broke the blueness of the water. We scanned the horizon with field glasses for mountains or islands, but none appeared. Now for the first time I considered the possibility that Alexander I Land was not connected to the mainland; but instead, was actually an island surrounded by water. The southern and eastern shores of this newly discovered area are separated from the continent by George VI Sound with the smooth, solid ice sheet bordering east and south.

Two days were spent here on top of this promontory to obtain a fixed position and survey different capes and bays surrounding us. As this would be our farthest westing, a 12-foot beacon was built, with a claim-sheet and a report of our discoveries. The lateness in this summer season, and our distance from base prevented us from continuing our westerly exploration, although, in returning, we headed due west for a while along a high ice cliff to determine its extent. The land west of us was of higher elevation, and to the south could be seen three mountain peaks surrounded by clouds in a belt located in the center, half the distance to the top.

Since we left the supporting party's camp where they started on their return back to base, our trail radio had been working irregularly. Many times the base was unable to hear us clearly. Connections and brushes were checked a number of times, but to no avail. Despite the static, our radio schedules with base were kept every day.

As we camped on the shelf ice one day for lunch, a savage dog-fight erupted. Mike, one of the few dogs left from my puppy team born in Little America, was badly cut; his left paw was mangled. To aid his recovery, I let him sit for four days on top of the sledge being pulled by the team. He seemed to enjoy the ride. One evening I did not tie him to the tethering line, since I thought his injured foot would prevent him from running away. As usual, he received his quota of pemmican at the end of the sledge, where he always sat. Then we went about our regular camping chores, setting up the sleeping and cooking tents, feeding the dogs, bringing sleeping bags into the tent. I also stretched out the radio antenna on the surface, then entered the tent to begin preparing our evening meal. I didn't think any more about Mike.

Next morning when I came out, I noticed he was missing. He had just walked a short distance, I thought. But there was no response to our calls, and we could see no trace of him. Reluctantly, we sledged on. Late that afternoon, as the sun was getting close to the horizon, after having covered about 15 miles, I found the track of Mike's foot-pads across our direction of travel. Evidently, he must have lost his direction, for we never saw him again.

Our sledge track led to a two-peaked nunatak. Here our return course turned northward, to locate and survey the shores of what we now called Alexander I *Island*.

By this time the surface was getting bad. In the daytime it was made soft and slushy by the intense heat from the sun. The dogs had tough going in this icy mess, and ice crystals cut their feet badly. Night travel was not much better, for the surface then was just like broken glass. Within four days we had to shoot six dogs. There was nothing we could do to stop their paws from bleeding. Two of the best and heaviest dogs we hauled on the sledges for days, hoping to be able to save them, but ultimately we had to dispose of them. It was a pity to have to go to such measures, but there was no other way out, since weights, distances, etc., were so closely figured. We could not permit ourselves to make frequent stops for dogs' feet to heal. Our best procedure was to reach the Batterbee Cache with whatever dogs were left, there to make use of the supplies deposited for such an emergency. In our great struggle to keep the teams moving, we unfortunately lost contact with the base, so that further explanation of our condition was not conveyed to them before we reached the cache. By that time only seven of our dogs were left. While passing the stratified mountains and the last southeastern nunatuk on Alexander Island, we collected rocks containing fossils and some lichens; eggs from a snowy petrel rookery were also collected.

At the Batterbee Cache, a message was sent to the base telling about the condition of the dogs' feet and of our intention to stay there for at least two weeks so that the injuries could heal. We stayed there for ten days, and the dogs improved rapidly. Our last radio contact with the base was January 7, 1941, after which our generator or transmitter failed to function. But our receiver continued to work properly, and by listening on regular and emergency schedules, we were able to hear bulletins regarding plans for a flight to Batterbee Cache to pick up our party.

On January 16, just before midnight, we loaded essential equipment and food for men and dogs, abandoned all unnecessary gear and extra supplies, and started to travel rapidly toward the Wordie Cache. Special canvas boots we made helped the dogs tolerate the icy crust. A great variety of surfaces were encountered, such as shallow lakes with fresh water a foot deep, soft wet snow, and the worst of them all — crystals, which formed during the night. In four days of traveling on the sound, we covered a total of 101 miles.

At our last camp on the sound we heard over the radio that the airplane had fallen into a crevasse, damaging a ski and the propeller. It made us uneasy to listen to broadcasts from the base expressing concern for our safety and making desperate plans for our "rescue." Here we were sitting in the tent listening to one emergency after the other, but with no way of telling the worried base personnel that we were absolutely safe.

Back on the trail, we had only a few crevasses to cross in

order to reach the high elevation leading to Wordie Ice Shelf cache. The surface here was better, and the dogs' feet improved, healing from the cuts received when sledging on the sound during the nights.

The heat from the sun opened new crevasses, and snow bridges we previously crossed had now collapsed. Without too much difficulty, we crossed to the lower side of the Wordie Glacier and headed for Sickle Mountain. From there I contemplated taking a new inland route back to base. Since no living person would know where we had been since the last radio contact many weeks ago, we built snow beacons at every prominent spot with notes enclosed for any party coming out to meet us.

A heavily crevassed area extending downhill in front of Sickle Mountain slowed our progress. It took us three hours to cover a distance of only a mile. Our course from here ran almost due north, straight across the Antarctic Peninsula. From the high elevation we could see far out over the Weddell Sea. Approaching a small isolated nunatak in a depressed area on our course, we found the surface to be extremely soft and fluffy snow. Without skis on I sank down almost to my hips, and the dogs, of course seemed to be crawling on their stomachs. It was a slow progress. Luckily terrain conditions improved not far off. Again at the end of the nunatak we built a beacon with a note inside for a possible rescue party.

Carl, the most pleasant sledging companion I ever had through more than six thousand miles of surface travel over the Antarctic, was constantly "on the go," collecting geological rock samples for Knowles and studying the birds nesting in most of the mountains we visited. He also did practically all the camp work with the dogs. hitching and unhitching as well as feeding them each evening. Our trail work was pretty much evenly divided between us. While I navigated, conducted the land-survey work, and prepared all the meals, we both operated the radio, taking turns at cranking the generator. Not one cross word ever passed between us — although there were a few humorous ones. Carl had a shipload of Olaf and Sven stories, made funnier by his imitation Swedish accent. I found it impossible to keep a straight face at mealtime, when he would express a desire for some yam or yelly to spread on his bisquits.

From the nunatak to where the trough leads to Neny Fjord,

the terrain was level, and we had no problem picking our route. Up the glacier we sledged for six miles and then made camp. Clouds started to form; it was cold during the night, and visibility was reduced to almost zero when we were ready to start the next morning on January 27. Later a strong surface wind caused drift. This did not bother us since the area now was free of the deadly crevasses. Determined that this would be the next to the last day on the trail, we pushed up the trough and finally reached the crest after 11 miles of travel. With breaks in the clouds, we recognized the mountains overlooking Neny valley. Down the slope, towards the fjord, we met a sledging party of four men, 22 miles from base. We were traveling in the center of the valley, making good time down grade with a splendid panoramic view when they were about a mile to the north coming over a crest. The surveyor was one of the party. He felt relieved that their planned journey ended so quickly.

After depositing all the dog food and man-food rations in a well-marked cache, four dog teams and six men headed for base without setting up another camp for the night. It was a speedy trip down the glacier, arriving at about three o'clock in the morning. Carl and I had had a long day and travelled about 34 miles the last day on January 28, 1941.

During the 84 days in the field we travelled a total of 1,264 miles. I had established 34 astronomical fixes with 12 principal control stations. At these stations, complete photographic circles were taken at 30 deg. change in azimuths, thereby identifying features that were shown on aerial photographs taken over some of the regions during later flights. From these control stations and intersection stations the positions of 320 major mountain peaks and nunataks were determined.

A new coastline extending 500 miles was discovered and surveyed on this journey, thus eliminating the supposition that the Russian Admiral von Bellingshausen had ever sighted the mainland of the Antarctic when he charted the northernmost cape of this 300-mile-long island stretching in a north-south direction. I had determined by surveying that what is called King George VI Sound trended south and west, and terminated into an open sea as a branch of the South Pacific Ocean. This proved Alexander I Land to be an island.

CHAPTER *10*

THE ICE STILL HELD AROUND Stonington Island, where the base was located. The barquentine *Bear*, outside the pack ice, couldn't reach us. Eventually the ship had to return to Punta Arenas for refueling. Meanwhile, at the base we were pummeled by storms, and faced the prospect of a second unplanned wintering. Since there was not sufficient food for all 26 men and the coal for heating the buildings was running low, the situation became more serious with every passing day. Finally, the problem was resolved when *Bear* broke through to Mikkelsen Island. Getting there wasn't easy, but in two heart-stopping flights, the old base was evacuated. From the glacier flight strip on Stonington we headed directly for Adelie Island, skimming pretty low over the dense pack ice. Pilot Ashley Snow just barely got the overloaded Condor high enough to cross Adelie and make his approach to Mikkelsen. The area for landing was no more than three-quarters of a mile in length.

Men from the ship had climbed to the top of the dome on the island and set up flares so we would know the wind-direction before coming in for a landing. These men had also stretched ropes at the most difficult spots to cross over to reach the motor-sailor waiting for us.

We were not slow in getting out of the plane, taking a few personal and scientific records with us. To my suprise, some of the men started cutting out pieces of the covering on the fuselage and wings — for souvenirs. In minutes the Condor was little more than a skeleton.

The base at Stonington Island.

We loaded belongings on a small hand-drawn sledge and started down a steep slope. All hands hung on to slow the descent. I was on skis with a rucksack on my back. The heavy pack and steep slope sent me hurtling down at a greater speed than I anticipated. As I neared the 500-foot cliff, I almost lost my balance. Had that happened, I would have rolled down to the cliff and fallen into the water. But just short of the brink I was able to make a quick turn — pivoting sharply — and come to a stop. One of the sledges did fall over the cliff. Seeing rock exposures farther down, I took my skis off and walked the rest of the way, digging my heels into the hard snow.

It was delightful to have the deck on the *Bear* under our feet once again. At sunset we got underway for Cape Horn. Our course led across Drake Passage, probably the most turbulent stretch of water in the world. During the night I was awakened by the squeaking sound of the old timbers in the hull of this ship, built in Scotland in 1874. A glorious day lay ahead of us. With all sails set, we made good headway and passed the Horn to enter the Straits of Magellan from the east. Two days later we tied up at Punta Arenas. *North Star* was already there, having sailed into port directly from the Bay of Whales. After three days of leave, we boarded that ship and headed for Valparaiso, Chile, the Panama Canal, and Boston.

On May 10, 1941, we landed in Boston without fanfare. No one met us officially. This was in great contrast to the last time I returned from the Antarctic in 1935, when *Bear* sailed into the Navy Yard in Washington, D.C. There we had been met on the dock by no less than the President of the United States, Franklin Roosevelt. Now in Boston the reception was zero. The reason for this, of course, was that Byrd did not favor an official reception. This was a government sponsored undertaking in which he was not the central hero. He was not even on the dock when we tied up. He had not been with us over the winter, but stayed quietly somewhere in the U.S.A. while we were wintering.

Since arrangements had been made for me to prepare a detailed record of my geographical discoveries, I headed directly for Washington and reported to the Division of Territories and Island Possessions of the Department of Interior. My second day at work, a young lieutenant for the Bureau of Navigation handed me a letter. It contained orders for me to report to the Medical Department at the Washington Navy Yard for a medical examination and stated that "if found physically fit for active duty," I should report to the Chief, Bureau of Ships in Washington, D.C.

These orders were complied with, I was found fit in all ways, and on May 28, 1941 I reported for active duty.

In the Navy, I served as desk-officer in charge of all types of tenders for submarines, destroyers and repair ships. This was exactly in line with my experience and education as a naval architect and marine engineer. I was also engaged in a number of interesting activities related to the Arctic and Antarctic. The Navy, in fact, appointed me a member of a coordinating committee for the Development of the Arctic. Another activity was my work with the "Place-name Committee" under the U.S. Board on Geographic Names which was under the jurisdiction of the Department of Interior.

I was often in consultation with Lieut. Comdr. Robert A. J. English, who had been the skipper of *Bear* on Byrd's Second Expedition. He had also served as Executive Secretary of the United States Antarctic Service while we were down south conducting geographical and scientific investigations. Now, English was assigned to write the history of the Antarctic in a volume entitled *Sailing Directions of the Antarctic* for the Navy's Hydrographic Office. I was often in consultation with him in his office in the Main Navy Building on Constitution Avenue in Washington.

As such I came in contact with many individuals and assisted in settling some of the problems that spring up from nowhere. Some of them could be rather ticklish, as is related here in detail in order to let the reader in on back-stage activities. It also indicates the thoroughness necessary, specifically when it pertains to the United States Government's activities.

One day Admiral Byrd came down and joined us in discussing names of recent discoveries to be listed in Bob English's publication. Bob English had read him what had been written about Byrd's famous flight from Little America on the 29th of November, 1929. After having read the short chapter once, Byrd read it the second time. I noticed his lips tighten. Soon a little heated discussion was underway. Byrd did not agree with the wording describing his flight to the South Pole that bright November day 14 years earlier. Bob English had written:

> "On November 28, 1929, Byrd with pilots Balchen and June, and photographer McKinley, flew southward over the Liv Glacier to the polar plateau. The homeward flight course was over the Axel Heiberg Glacier."

That sounded very good to me, and for a while I could not understand why the Admiral objected to the statement. He was upset because it did not have anything about him having flown to the South Pole. Byrd wanted the paragraph changed to:

"On November 28, 1929, Byrd with pilots Balchen and June, and photographer McKinley, flew southward over the Liv Glacier to the polar plateau and on to the South Pole, making a 12-mile circle. The homeward flight course was over Axel Heiberg Glacier."

Bob English stated: "Admiral, I shall be happy to change the wording as you suggest provided you give me evidence to prove that you flew over the South Pole." He said it should include sun observations taken, times and distances flown as well as wind velocities and directions.

Byrd's comment was: "English! that is none of your business! You do as I tell you!"

English replied, "No Sir— Admiral. I have the responsibility to write these sailing directions on orders from the Navy Hydrographer. Nothing will go under my name unless I have some evidence that it is correct!"

Byrd, still determined to have things his own way, threatened: "You do as I tell you! If not I shall have you court-martialed."

After that statement, I noticed that Bob English was getting hot under the collar. Clearly and distinctly he said: "Admiral, nothing would please me more than if you would proceed as suggested because I would welcome the opportunity for a court-martial to clarify some points."

Byrd, ashen-white, his lips tight, stared Bob English straight in the face. Then, without saying another word, he turned around, walked to the door, opened it slowly, and left.

English would not be intimidated. He never changed a word.

Byrd usually got what he wanted. As a result of his 1928–30 expedition, special Congressional medals were authorized by Congress. Similarly, medals were again struck to honor the Second Byrd Expedition. But after the return of the United States Government Expedition, no attempt was made to gain recognition for its members. At an Explorers Club meeting one evening, Senator Shipstead of Minnesota questioned me on why no attempt had been made in Congress to give members of the most recent expedition recognition. I replied that it would have been up to Byrd to initiate such action since he had been appointed by the President of the United States to head up the expedition. The Senator thought that Byrd was not interested since it was not his own private expedition. I was asked to send him a memorandum, stating in detail all of the circumstances surrounding this official exploration of the Antarctic. He wanted to know the number of people involved, and what was accomplished.

I did as the Senator had suggested. He introduced a bill; it passed the House and Senate, and was signed by the President. A medal was struck, to be presented in the office of the Secretary of the Navy, James Forrestal. Present at the ceremony were about 30 of the recipients, plus friends and relatives. Forrestal, who had been pressed into doing the presentation, agreed to pin medals on only three persons during the gathering — Siple, representing West Base, Cruzen for the sea-going forces and myself on behalf of the personnel for East Base.

After the presentation ceremony, I noticed a number of medals still lying on a small table. One I saw was for Richard Byrd. I stuck it in my pocket and walked out into the corridor where Byrd was talking to a group of expedition men. I joined them. Moments later Byrd asked if anyone had seen his medal on the table. Smiling, I said: "Yes" and passed it on.

In early 1946 I planned and organized the Navy's "Operation Nanook" to the Arctic — until it was determined that my active-duty rank precluded my taking command of the activities. Co-sponsor was Captain Clifford MacGregor, of the Naval Weather Service, who soon went on inactive status. I recommended Captains Cruzen and George Dufek be called to Washington to conduct this operation, which departed north on five ships, on July 1, 1946. I was asked to participate in an advisory capacity, which I did for about three months.

We entered Lancaster Sound and stopped at Devon Island before crossing over Baffin Bay to Thule and Kane Basin. A weather station was erected in cooperation with the Danish government, and the first airstrip was built at Thule, in northwest Greenland. This base, once manned by 16,000 men, played a significant part in the cold war, serving as an important outpost in the defense of our northern frontiers.

After almost three months with the Navy in the Arctic, I received word that President Harry Truman had signed into law a Congressional bill authorizing the Secretary of the Navy to lend me a ship suitable for my own expedition. I hurried back to Washington to tackle the tremendous task of getting ready for the Antarctic.

From the early part of September, I worked 14 to 18 hours a day. My wife Jackie assisted me by writing dozens of letters a day for the ordering of equipment and supplies, selecting personnel, and a thousand other things that had to be completed before sailing.

One evening in the fall of 1940, I received a phone call at our small apartment on F Street in Washington from an old friend from high school days in Horten, Norway. Kristian Ostby, Captain in the Norwegian Navy and Naval Attache and Air Attache with the Norwegian Embassy in Washington, was laughing when I answered the phone. Recognizing his voice immediately, I asked what was so funny. After he stopped laughing, he told me he had a couple of fellows in his office. "You know, Finn," he said, "they want to drift on a raft across the Pacific. They are *splinta galne* (completely crazy). They are here trying to get some help from the American government, but I do not even know where to start. Do you think you could help them?" I suggested that Kristian bring them to my apartment, so I could at least have a look at them. He said that he would bring them down right away. He gave me their names — Herman Watzinger and Thor Heyerdahl.

My wife, who was in the apartment at the time, recognized the name of Heyerdahl immediately. She recalled that while on our honeymoon at Stowe, Vermont, in the month of March, less than two years before, we had met a Mrs. Heyerdahl, who with her husband had spent some time on the Marquesan Islands in the Pacific.

In bringing the Pacific raft-explorers to my attention, Kristian knew that I had been successful in obtaining most of the equipment I needed for my Antarctic expedition. It had only been a month or so since Army Chief of Staff George C. Marshall had authorized me to draw from the Quartermaster Corps anything I needed of equipment — airplanes, weasels, clothing, food, camping equipment, and thousands of other items. Through General Curtis LeMay, my expedition would be entrusted with the testing of all military items under extreme Antarctic temperatures. It struck me as appropriate that some of the items that I already had could also be tested on the ocean, under conditions of high humidity and high temperatures. Therefore, by the time my friend Kristian and the two men arrived, I had a pretty good idea that the Army would be able to use their services to test tropical-food rations, water-condensing gadgets, radio equipment, etc.

As with all Norwegian households (although my wife was not Norwegian, I being the first Norwegian she had ever laid her eyes on) we started with cake and coffee, gradually working in to the real purpose of the visit. I outlined for them the procedure I had used in obtaining help, specifically which items of military equipment I knew were in surplus. I also offered to make calls the next morning to help them get supplies. Mr. Heyerdahl also stressed they were short of funds. I suggested he contact the North American Newspaper Alliance. I had just obtained $15,000 from the syndicate for rights to news accounts of my forthcoming expedition, so perhaps NANA would be interested in backing another adventurous undertaking. I recommended that the two men go to the Times Building in New York and speak directly with John B. Wheeler, president of the syndicate. This, I learned, they did, and with favorable results. So, both the suggestions I gave the pair proved fruitful. The story of them obtaining Army support is well written up in Heyerdahl's book *Kon Tiki.*

CHAPTER 11

B Y THE TIME WORLD WAR II ENDED, most of the earth had been
explored and mapped. Men had trekked into the most remote
regions, the murky jungles of the Amazon, the frozen Arctic
Ocean, the tundras and ice fields. Only one section of our planet
remained a mystery: the Antarctic. Of the continent's five million
square miles, only one fourth had been explored. There was still
much to learn about the vast area at the southern end of the earth.
For example, many geographers were not sure whether Antarctica
was one continent or two. Some thought that there might be an
ice-filled strait running from the Weddell Sea, bordering the
Atlantic Ocean, to the Ross Sea, bordering the Pacific. If there was
such a strait, it would cut the continent in half.

Perhaps that might seem unimportant. After all, what differ-
ence does it make if there is a narrow line of water separating the
"two" Antarcticas? Especially since it is always covered with ice
and snow anyway. But such things can be very important, not
only to mapmakers but to nations. In 1820, a German naval officer
named Thadius von Bellingshausen, in the service of the Russian
Czar, sailed into the Atlantic, across the sea which now bears his
name. As previously mentioned he sighted and marked a strip of
coastal area which he called Alexander Land. He thought it was
part of the Antarctic mainland. For almost 120 years, no one disputed von Bellingshausen's sighting. Then, during the American
government expedition, as Carl Eklund and I moved down the
western edge of the Palmer Peninsula, we could see that Alexander
Land was separated from the peninsula by George VI Sound. At

that time no one knew how far the sound stretched. Sooner or later we expected to come upon the end of the Sound and find where Alexander Land connected with the mainland of Antarctica. Instead, we reached open water. We had proved that Alexander Land was an island, not part of the Antarctic mainland.

New maps had to be made, to show that George VI Sound ended in an open bay connected to the ocean. Later, the Department of the Interior named that open body of water Ronne Bay, in honor of my father. A small island in the sound was named Eklund Island, in honor of my companion.

Eklund and I had sledged along the western edge of the peninsula, but not much was known about the rest of it. That was where I wanted to take my expedition — to the Antarctic Peninsula.

The Peninsula lies almost due south of Cape Horn. It is an icy and mountainous finger of land, poking up between the Bellingshausen Sea and the Weddell Sea. The drifting fog, blinding blizzards, and the constantly blowing winds make it one of the stormiest places on earth. Only for short periods of time is it safe to fly over the peninsula.

The Weddell Sea, which borders the Peninsula on the east, is sometimes referred to as "The hell-hole of the Antarctic." Because of extreme cold weather, strong winds, and powerful ocean currents, the Weddell Sea is usually choked with pack ice and ice floes. Even today, modern Navy ice-breakers find it difficult to slice through the pack ice, and ships from the past found it all but impossible. For that reason, even as late as 1945, no one had been able to make an exact map of the Peninsula coastline where it bordered the Weddell Sea, although many explorers had tried. That 500-mile stretch of shore was the last unexplored coastline in the world.

Running up and down the Peninsula is a mountain range. For some time geologists had suspected that these mountains were really an extension of the Andes. They ran down the western part of South America, continued on under the sea south of Cape Horn, then rose up again on the Peninsula. But, how far south did those mountains continue? Did they join the Queen Maud mountain range which lay to the south of the peninsula? No one knew, for the land between the ranges was still unexplored.

The main objective of my expedition was to trace the true coastline of the Peninsula where it met the Weddell Sea and thus

Penetrating the 200 foot high Weddell Sea ice pack.

determine whether Antarctica was actually one continent. My expedition would also conduct many scientific experiments. We would study weather and wind conditions, the cosmic rays of the Antarctic, earthquake tremors, oceanography, and geology. We would test cold weather equipment used by America's military forces.

I hoped to raise about $150,000, and thought that my mission could be accomplished with about 20 men or so. I needed a ship, large enough to carry the men and equipment, airplanes to fly over the unexplored regions, and cameras to take aerial photography. Also, tractors, food, clothing, coal, tents, stoves, sleeping bags, skis, sledges, husky dogs, radios, film and developer, cooking gear, compasses, gasoline, medical supplies, scientific equipment for our experiments — in all, thousands of items.

Part of the gear could be obtained from army-navy surplus. There was an incredible amount of equipment choking the military warehouses, which could no longer be used now that the war was over. It could be bought cheaply.

I hoped to get the loan of a ship from the government. Because of my naval assignment during the war, I knew which ships were not being used and which type would be most suitable for my purpose. I selected an ocean-going tugboat, which had a wooden hull; it was 183 feet long, boasted two strong diesel engines, and had ample cargo space.

But when I made my request, both the Chief of Naval Operations and the Secretary of the Navy said they could not help me. According to the law, the navy was not permitted to lend a ship to a private individual or organization, no matter how worthy the cause. In order to get the ship, Congress had to pass special legislation. How strange! The ship I wanted was headed for the scrap heap or surplus sale, but the Navy could not lend it to anyone.

However, because of the Navy's interest in my expedition, the legal branch of the Navy had a bill introduced in Congress for authorization to lend me the ship I had already selected. At the hearings, I was called upon to testify before the Naval Affairs Committees in the House of Representatives and Senate. Here I was well received and complimented by some of the legislative members for my initiative and incentive to pursue Antarctic interests for my adopted country. The bill was passed and President Harry Truman signed it.

To acquire the airplanes, I spoke with General Curtis LeMay, chief of the Air Corps Office of Research and Development. I presented him with a plan in which I offered to test military equipment in the cold climate of Antarctica. He was interested and agreed to help. Within a couple of months I had three airplanes, plus additional equipment.

Other help came from the United States Weather Bureau, the Office of Naval Research, and from North American Newspaper Alliance, a syndicate that agreed to buy the stories I would send from the Antarctic. A number of my friends and several private organizations also contributed some money. I raised $47,000, less than a third of my goal. But that didn't deter me. I was determined to make do with what I had.

It was surprisingly easy to enlist men for the expedition. While Congress was debating whether or not to give me a ship, the newspapers had published some stories about my proposed trip to the Antarctic. Before long I had received several hundred applications. They came from men in all walks of life, from all over the country. One of the first to volunteer was the surveyor, of all people, who had known of my determination to return to the Antarctic. In a letter to me in 1942 he said: "Finn, the NEXT expedition will be different. How about it? When will you be ready to go? I don't mean perhaps, after the war. And will we hand-pick our party? Yes."

It was a presumption I did not share. Because of insinuating himself into my plans, I had lost control of one expedition. No, I would not make the same mistake twice. I never bothered to answer his letter.

During this time in Washington, I struggled to gain support for my expedition from private as well as government agencies. I was always on the go with barely more than four or five hours sleep a night. Byrd lived a block away from me, and I saw him often. He always asked about my expedition plans.

Once he requested a copy of my operational plan with the remark that he might possibly be able to help me. I gave it to him, but nothing ever happened. That fall of 1946 Operation Highjump was suddenly launched under Admiral Richard Cruzen with Byrd representing the Office of the Chief of Naval Operations. In Cruzen's office one day, I was shown a copy of his operational plan. To my surprise I found that the eastern group had the area south and west of the Weddell Sea as a "Priority One" (marked in red). This was exactly the main geographical objective of my own expedition. It had been copied almost verbatim from my plan.

It would appear that I had a powerful opponent, one determined to thwart my interests in the U.S.'s role of discovery and exploration of the southern continent. Although I was an emigrant from Norway with no American family ties or powerful connections, my interests were similar to Byrd's, and I had a similarly strong desire to further them. Collision, I suppose, was inevitable. Byrd thought he owned the Antarctic. Now he sensed he had competition. But I wasn't a complete pushover. My hereditary background provided me with certain capabilities in the field of polar exploration that couldn't be underestimated. Unfortu-

Finn Ronne in 1946.

nately for me, our encounters were invariably politically weighted, therefore rarely to my advantage. It took courage to stand up to such overpowering odds, and, in retrospect, I suppose I was often too naive to realize my opposition's strength.

It was when seeking active support that these points became most visible in my negotiations with the Office of Naval Research. A research contract was held up for about three months due to Byrd's unwillingness to give a yes or no answer to my scientific research proposal. Eventually, when being pressed to make a decision, he did so, but not until he had forced the reduction of the financial worth of the work I proposed to perform for the Navy, to less than one-third of the original estimate.

It is important to remember that I could not pay the men I selected any salary for their services, and they knew it. In fact, some of the men offered to give me money if I would take them along. But, I wanted men who could help me sail the ship into the Antarctic, in addition to carrying on their duties on the ice. The Navy did not offer me a crew, only the ship. After studying applications and giving interviews, I chose 21 men from several hundred applicants — all eagerly seeking adventure.

Some of these volunteers had seen service in cold climates before. Commander Isaac "Ike" Schlossbach, who had been one of the Navy's first dive-bomber pilots, was a magnificent navigator. In 1931, when the great polar explorer Sir Hubert Wilkins led a submarine expedition under the ice-filled Arctic Ocean, Ike was the sub's navigator. He became skipper of my ship and second-in-command of my expedition.

Captain James Lassiter, who had been a pilot in India during the war, knew what it was like to fly over high mountains and the frozen wasteland. Another pilot was Lieutenant Charles Adams, of the Air Force as was Lassiter. Jim Robertson was the expert aviation mechanic. Sig Gutenko, the cook, had tended ship's galleys during voyages to the Antarctic and to Greenland.

There were also a number of scientists in the group, including Bob Nichols and Bob Dodson, who were geologists; and Andrew Thompson and Harries-Clichy Peterson, who had degrees in physics. Bill Latady knew just about everything there was to know about photography. Walter Smith was an outstanding seaman, having served as a deck officer and navigator aboard many ships in the Atlantic during the war. All the time I was planning the expedition, my wife Jackie wrote and answered letters, made telephone calls, helped in the purchase of supplies, and performed many other duties to make my work easier.

Finally, my ship had been refitted to my specifications for Antarctic service at a shipyard in Beaumont, Texas. I renamed the ship *Port of Beaumont* in appreciation for the support of its citizens. The entire crew assembled in Beaumont to help load supplies. Even Sir Hubert Wilkins came there to see that I got a good start. Airplanes were lashed to the deck and heavy tractors were loaded on board, along with drums of gasoline and oil, and finally the husky dogs and the sledges they would pull. In all, we had the necessities of life for a year in the Antarctic.

Meanwhile, I had added another member to the expedition, 18-year-old Arthur Owen, an Eagle Scout from Beaumont. He had won the opportunity to become an Antarctic explorer in a statewide competition. Events were to prove that I couldn't have made a finer selection.

At last, in January 1947, the mooring lines were cast off.

Slowly, we moved down the Neches River to Port Arthur where we topped off the ship's fuel tanks with diesel oil.

Just as Byrd embarked on the command ship *Mt. Olympus* — "Operation-Highjump" for the Antarctic, he sent me a radio message:

"Congratulations and good luck on your expedition. We must continue to cooperate in the future as we have done in the past. Richard E. Byrd"

This was really more than I expected, but it pleased me to get his blessing.

Up to the last minute before sailing, I had hoped that my old sledging companion Carl Eklund could come along. He had a great desire to sledge with me once again. Earlier I had offered him the second-in-command position with duties as chief of the scientific staff. He was with the Fish and Wildlife Service, which was reluctant to release him for two-years leave with pay. Having to support a wife and two young children, he was unable to come as a volunteer.

I knew Carl well. He was a splendid companion, had a fine sense of humor and his witty remarks were contagious to others; he always found a way to solve problems. One example of his humor was displayed when he lectured for a church group in St. Paul. After recounting our sledge-journey, he fielded questions. They came in rapid succession and every time Carl was ready for another question, a little boy about 10 years old in the front row jumped up. Carl ignored him for a while, but the young boy persisted. Finally — Carl said: "All right, little fellow, what's on your mind?." The boy shouted, "Mr. Eklund — I just wondered if there were any other members of this expedition except yourself?." With a wry grin, Carl slowly folded his arms, leaned toward the boy — and said, "Sonny boy, sometimes I wondered." The hall shook with laughter, and the red-faced lad sat down. Most explorers feel the same way.

When my ship sailed, I asked Jackie to accompany us as far as Panama in order to gain her help with last minute details since she intended to handle the domestic side while we were away. Realizing there was still much to do, I persuaded her to stay on board until we reached Valparaiso, Chile.

CHAPTER 12

M Y ANTARCTIC RESEARCH EXPEDITION 1946–48 departed from
Beaumont, Texas, on January 26, 1947. A couple of days
earlier, in the presence of many Texas officials, I had named my
ship *Port of Beaumont*. She was a renovated Navy ocean-going
tug that fulfilled all requirements. Our living quarters competed
for space with the expedition's supplies, which included three airplanes, two tractors, and 64 sledge dogs chained at every available
space on deck. But the crowded conditions could not lessen the
group's high spirits. They had one driving thought — to get down
there. With several stops along the way, the trip to Antarctica
would take more than six weeks.

The *Port of Beaumont* floating in an ice free lake off Stonington Island in
Marguerite Bay.

Any man who commands an expedition is faced with great challenge. Not only is he responsible for the success or failure of the mission, but also for the lives of his men. In the Antarctic, dangers are always present from the intense cold, blizzards, crevasses, and from one of nature's strangest tricks — the "whiteouts."

A whiteout can best be described as a paradoxical combination of being partially blind, but also being able to see illusions of things. It is like floundering in a sea of cotton; everything looks blurred and white. The phenomenon is caused by the glare of the sun on the snow. A person experiencing a whiteout *thinks* he can recognize familiar objects, but actually he can't. For instance, he may mistake a small piece of ice only a few yards away for a large hill several miles distant. The only way to overcome a whiteout is to wait patiently until it passes.

Although I was confident that my crew could take care of themselves, still they had to be warned about such dangers. Unfortunately, the warning was not always heeded.

The 19 men of the expedition had volunteered to live for a year in the Antarctic, a place most had never been. With a few exceptions they were not paid. Whether airplane mechanic, radio operator, physicist, cook, ship's captain, or dog handler, the men shared the same desire to turn their backs on the familiar and to face the unknown. Many of them had just returned from duty in a World War and could not adjust to the idea of settling down. All but five were under 30 and two-thirds were unmarried. Accordingly, they felt free to enjoy themselves and let me agonize over the worrisome details.

I was confronted with a major problem halfway to the Antarctic. A distemper epidemic hit the expedition's huskies. These tough animals can withstand incredible cold, but they cannot take hot, muggy weather. The older dogs as well as the puppies had been given shots to prevent distemper. The kennels where I purchased the dogs had certified that all the dogs were protected. A receipt from a veterinarian in New Hampshire, in the amount of $230 as payment for innoculations gave me full assurance nothing would happen to them. To make matters worse, there was no distemper vaccine on the ship. I never thought it would be needed since the dogs would be immune in the Antarctic. Still, it was sickening to watch the huskies, listless and without appetite, languish in their kennels on the ship's stern.

The *Beaumont* docked at Valparaiso, Chile, on February 21. No vaccine was to be had so I left instructions for an emergency shipment to be sent to Punta Arenas, Chile, the world's southernmost city, where *Beaumont* would put in. If help was on the way, it never caught up with us. As the ship neared the Antarctic, the gathering cold finally brought the surviving dogs back to yelping good health. But nearly half of the 64 huskies had died.

While at Valparaiso additional problems faced me. A young assistant engineer, just out of King's Point Merchant Marine Academy, was stealing supplies, sneaking them ashore, and selling them at a local bar. My commissary steward late one evening asked me to come with him. It was pitch dark. With flashlights we crawled through a small hatch into the aft cargo hold below main deck. There we saw the thief surrounded by 96 cartons of cigarettes. We had caught him red-handed. I promptly arranged for him to work his way back to New York on a Grace liner.

Finding a substitute for him in Chile was not possible; however, I persuaded my wife to go as a working member of the expedition. A reserve pilot's wife had also sailed with us from Texas, fully intending to return to New York. I allowed her to remain, with her husband. Also we took on board a Chilean mess-cook. Now we were 23.

On the five days crossing from South America to the Antarctic, we encountered unusually quiet seas. The men organized a betting pool, with a can of sardines for the one who guessed when the first iceberg would be sighted. The cook won, choosing the morning of March 12.

It is impossible to moor a ship along one of these floating ice mountains. That was one of the reasons I chose Stonington Island, in Marguerite Bay, as the base for my wintering expedition. It is one of the few spots in the Antarctic where the land slopes gradually out into the sea. Also, I knew all the landmarks, for I had wintered here six years earlier. Back in 1941, we had to fly out because the bay was frozen over. Now the big oval bay contained only loose ice, and the ship could move through.

There was now a British base on Stonington, about a quarter of a mile from our old American base. It had been set up a year before we came. In fact, England, Chile, and Argentina all laid claim to Stonington and the Antarctic Peninsula. The United States did not recognize those claims and insisted that the region remain open for exploration.

One of the many sheltered harbors of the Palmer Peninsula is Back Bay. The *Port of Beaumont* is shown at anchor next to Stonington Island. The ice cliff towers 400 feet over the vessel.

Through my binoculars I sighted the small British Base "E" of the Falkland Island Dependencies. I could make out some men feeding dogs staked out in the snow. This outpost, too small to engage in exploration, served primarily to reinforce British territorial claims. I had been forewarned about the British group. The British claimed the Antarctic Peninsula as their territory, and called it Graham Land.

Protocol demanded that I meet the Base "E" Magistrate, Major Kenneth Pierce-Butler. As soon as I stepped ashore, he immediately stressed his government's position that England claimed the land we were about to explore. He also informed me that the American base was in bad shape. Chilean and Argentine Navy ships had anchored there for a few weeks, and the sailors had amused themselves by tearing up the base. Pierce-Butler escorted me to the site, and I saw that the visitors had indeed done considerable damage. The looters had taken or broken about 80% of the property the U.S. expedition had left behind in 1941. It would take weeks to repair the damage.

The American base consisted of five buildings, all sturdily built, with four inches of rock wool insulation. The main bunkhouse measured 60 feet in length and 24 feet in width. The science building and one machinery building, set parallel to the bunkhouse, were 32 feet long and 24 feet wide. I would occupy the fourth building, a 12 by 12 foot hut that I had built on the 1939–41 expedition. The supply shack was even smaller. All the buildings were connected by tunnels.

The expedition members quickly went to work. The shore party cleaned and swept, setting fires in damp stoves, nailing canvas on the buildings, and generally trying to make the camp homelike. When we raised the Stars and Stripes over the base, Pierce-Butler protested. "I assume," he wrote, "that the United States Government has made no claims to this territory and that the flying of the flag is merely an indication of the presence of an American expedition." I replied immediately with unrestrained nationalistic fervor: "As an American expedition reoccupying this base on Stonington Island, we have reflown the American flag on the American-built flagpole at the American camp." After that I

Raising the American flag at Stonington Island in March, 1947.

heard no more from Pierce-Butler on the matter. Meanwhile the flag flew day and night, regardless of weather, in full view of the British camp.

It was incongruous that the only two expeditions on the more than 5 million sq. m. Antarctic continent had to be sitting practically on top of one another and arguing about who claimed the land.

◆　◆　◆

Already it was mid-March, almost the end of the Antarctic summer. Soon the winter night would close in, and there was still much work to be done. We brought ashore 35 tons of coal, wings for the two large airplanes, heavy radio equipment, assorted food and supplies of every description, and two snow tractors. Every day a few of the men went out to hunt seals, a ready supply of dog food.

While we unloaded the ship, I sent a pilot aloft in the small scout plane to look over the waters of George VI Sound to the south. In order to reach the southern end of the Antarctic Peninsula, a sledge party needed plenty of supplies. I decided to sail *Beaumont* down the sound about 300 miles, drop off a cache of food and other equipment, then return to the base. The scout plane returned with the news that the sound was full of icebergs. Sailing through, we saw so many of them that we were forced to turn back. However, we still had managed to sail farther south — at the entrance to King George VI Sound — than any other ship in history. As for dropping off the supplies, that would have to be done later by airplanes.

Meanwhile, my fine crew was working furiously to repair the base and construct some other buildings. They had little experience, but they kept trying.

The expedition's scientists set up their research equipment. Andrew Thompson, the geophysicist, built a tidal shack to keep records of the tides in Back Bay Cove; a non-magnetic shack held instruments to measure changes in the earth's magnetic field, and a seismograph room for an instrument designed to measure tremors in the earth's crust. Unfortunately, the young scientist was not a carpenter. The floor of the seismograph room slanted. I asked one of the ship's officers to lend a hand, and a new building soon appeared. This shack was all right, but Thompson forgot to

The wintering base on Stonington Island.

anchor it down. The first real wind knocked it apart. Stubbornly refusing to quit, he built the shack a third time, and anchored it down firmly. At the door he posted a sign: "Off Limits" so that the men's stamping on the surface in this area would not disturb the operation of the recorders. The sensitive seismograph which would record earth tremors would tie in with readings from stations around the world. Thompson's data would tell scientists new facts about the contours and thickness of the planet's surface.

While Thompson was putting up his shack, Harries-Clichy Peterson, physicist, Harvard graduate, and ex-Marine, built a weather station. He also began launching two orange-colored weather balloons each day. The direction of their ascent and their horizontal speed told Peterson the speed and direction of the air currents at various altitudes. Bob Dodson began testing some of the Army's field equipment. He slept outside in new-style tents and sleeping bags. Dodson found out — after many uncomfortable nights — that they weren't very good.

A novel threat momentarily disrupted the hectic pace. I noticed that a crevasse in the glacier near the camp had widened overnight. I feared that an iceberg, about 100 by 300 feet, would soon split and float into Back Bay, endangering *Beaumont*. The men stopped everything and conferred on what to do. If they could split the iceberg themselves, they could move the ship out of the way. Three men volunteered to try to speed up the splitting process with dynamite. But aside from shaking all the buildings, the explosion did nothing. The ice was not going to move until it was ready, which turned out to be the next morning. The iceberg neatly broke off from the ice shelf and drifted out to sea.

Toward the end of April, when the expedition had been in the Antarctic for six weeks, the sea became a mass of jagged ice chunks. The men could no longer row to shore with supplies from the ship. The freeze-in had begun. On the night of May 2, 1947, the ice turned solid. After that, *Beaumont* moved only up and down with the tide.

The last big job before winter drove us inside was putting up the radio antenna, beamed on both New York and New Orleans. The men had to raise four poles so that their tops would be a level 60 feet above the snow. Buffeted by the wind, two of the poles collapsed. Soon after, Second Mate Nelson McClary almost killed himself while stretching out one of the guy wires. He was walking backwards, unspooling wire from a roll. Because it was cold, he wore the hood of his parka over his head and did not hear the warning shouts of his friends. They watched in horror as McClary backed over the edge of a 60-foot ice cliff.

The men raced to the edge of the cliff and saw McClary had crashed through the ice and was floundering in the water. Desperately, he clawed at the two-inch sheet of ice, which crumbled in his hands. James Robertson, our airplane mechanic, quickly found a climbing rope and threw it down to McClary. There was no time for us to climb down for the rescue; McClary would have drowned before we could have reached him. With numbed fingers, he managed to place a loop of the rope around his chest and under his arms. We hitched the other end to a tractor. Larry Fiske, climatologist and an ex-Navy pilot, revved up the engine and started off. McClary, spinning on the line, was pulled straight up from the water. Robertson and I dragged him over the top — eight minutes after he had fallen off.

McClary mumbled, "Get these things off me. Hurry. . . ."

We wrapped the shivering, half-conscious man in blankets and carried him back to the bunkhouse on a small sled. Doctor McLean cut off his clothes and removed an arm cast McClary had acquired in another accident — when a turnbuckle aboard ship dropped and broke a bone in his hand. The doctor put hot water bottles on McClary's body and assigned a man to massage each limb. They were warned, however, not to touch his fingers and toes, for they would be very sensitive. During the next few days, McClary's toes and fingers turned white and peeled. Still, Mc-Clary was lucky. If the ice had been thicker, he could have been killed from the concussion.

McClary turned out to be the most accident-prone individual ever to set foot on the continent. Within six months he was out of action again, this time with a broken collarbone. It resulted from a freak accident in which he lost control of his dog team and was catapulted over the sledge as it slammed into a ridge of ice. Robertson, remembering the other injuries, remarked that Mc-Clary "must be brittle as glass."

I could have blamed the accidents on bad luck and hoped for the best. But I knew from experience that for the most part a man made his own luck — good or bad — in the Antarctic. An awareness of the severity of this place, and an abiding respect for it, was necessary at all times. In order to survive here, accidents through carelessness and miscalculation had to be avoided. Thus, I had no choice but to ground McClary, keep him off the trail, not only for his own good but for that of others his actions might have imperiled. My decision was, understandably, hard for him to accept. Thereafter he would harbor a grudge and join in an effort to discredit me.

◆　◆　◆

I had planned not to send the *Beaumont* back north for the winter, but to let the ship be frozen into the ice. The metal on the ship's engines was coated with grease or graphite, to prevent rusting. Hatches were sealed, air ducts were closed tightly, and the radios were stored away. Soon ice began to form around the ship; now we could walk the quarter of a mile back and forth from base. We had used the motor boat up to then.

At the beginning of May I thought it would be a good idea

to have a party for the whole gang. Sigmund Gutenko cooked a chicken dinner, and the sight of it was greeted with loud cheers. No, the men had not been starving. Far from it. They were simply tired of eating steaks all the time. We had no less than 6,500 pounds of it. Due to the limited refrigeration space onboard, we had to provision with boneless meat only.

The Antarctic does peculiar things to a man's appetite. Because of the hard work and constant cold, men must eat lots of food, and the fatter the better. Steak is very tasty but lean. Chickens have some fat under the skin, and the men liked that. They also craved pastry and other sweets, especially chocolate candy. Having spent four winters in the Antarctic, I knew that would happen and was ready for it. I had brought along more than 3,000 pounds of chocolate.

We settled down to face the slow passage of winter. Now the expedition entered into its calmest, and to some, its most boring and disagreeable period. I knew that the men must be kept busy, either with expedition work or hobbies. Left to himself, a man would probably start thinking about the comforts he had abandoned. The Antarctic is a perfect place for just sitting and brooding. The empty spaces and the feeling of endless time undermine a man's determination to get on with the job. Amundsen was right when he said, "Keep the men busy and you keep them happy." I made sure that the expedition's routine chores — kitchen duty, melting ice for water, hauling coal were rotated so that everybody shared the daily tasks. But the men still had a lot of free time, so I encouraged them to read or work at handicrafts. Nearly every man was engaged in some sort of a hobby, such as wood-carving. I whiled away some of the long hours in making 12-inch replicas of some of our sledges.

Halfway through May, the sun made its last appearance for two and a half months. Twilight, however, would still come once a day as the sun climbed almost to the horizon. Then the sun's rays turned the sky sunset red, the glow spreading eerily across the icy landscape. Finally the last gleam of twilight faded, and we were left in perpetual night. We lived solely by the clock, often working until 3 A.M.

During the winter, I planned our airplane and trail operations, calculating weights, distances, and consumption of food and fuel. In discussing these matters with Pierce-Butler, the leader of the British base nearby, I realized that I had strength in air power, the British in dog power. We then decided to join forces in a combined surface party down south and explore the Weddell Sea Coast. This way I would obtain the ground control points I wanted in connection with my aerial mapping program. British interests were primarily local surveying and maintaining their Base "E" to strengthen their sovereignty in this area also claimed by Chile and Argentina. Geographical exploration and aerial mapping were my independent objectives, of course, in which the British had no part.

The expedition held another party on midwinter's night, June 22. From now on the sun would be climbing back up to the horizon. With our British friends as guests, the cook again served up a feast. In the decorated bunkhouse we sang songs and drank toasts with Chilean champagne.

Most of the explorers were pretty shaggy by this time. I had told them that showers and shaves would be optional; they could be as filthy as they pleased. For the most part the men looked forward to the weekly shower. But the hair and beards of many had reached exotic lengths.

I kept a neat appearance, and befitting a civil servant — Postmaster Fourth Class, salary $225 a year, to be exact. The United States Government had designated me Antarctica's first official Postmaster. At my suggestion the post office at Stonington Island was given the postmark Oleona Base, honoring a Norwegian settlement in Pennsylvania founded by Ole Bull, the world-famed violinist. To spare the expedition the job of overloading the ship with sacks of letters for stamp collectors, the public was not told of Oleona Base until after we had reached the Antarctic. I cancelled only four letters officially, two each to the Department of State and two to the Post Office Department. I also cancelled a few for my personal interest during the year this post office was in operation, making Oleona Base, Territory of Antarctica the rarest cancellation in United States postal history.

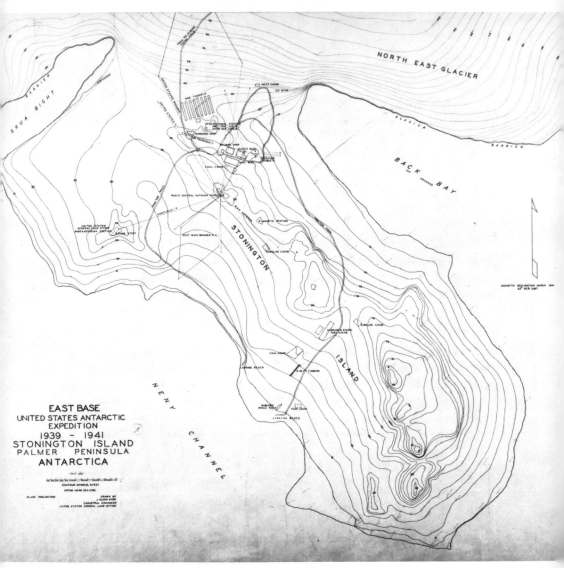

Map of Stonington Island base.

Opposite page:

Aerial view looking west onto the mountain ranges of the Palmer Peninsula.

Building layout of Stonington Island base.

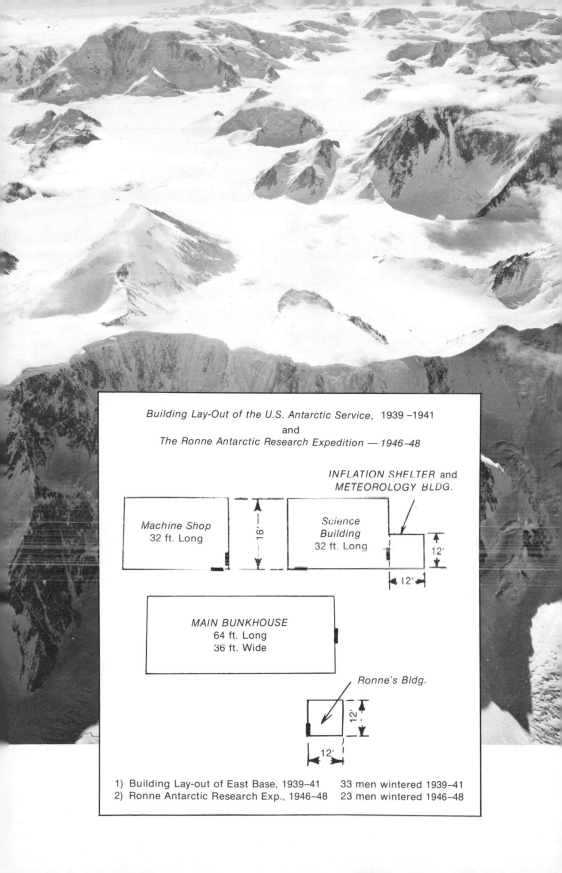

Building Lay-Out of the U.S. Antarctic Service, 1939–1941
and
The Ronne Antarctic Research Expedition — 1946–48

INFLATION SHELTER and
METEOROLOGY BLDG.

Machine Shop
32 ft. Long

16'

Science
Building
32 ft. Long

12'

12'

MAIN BUNKHOUSE
64 ft. Long
36 ft. Wide

Ronne's Bldg.

12'

12'

1) Building Lay-out of East Base, 1939–41   33 men wintered 1939–41
2) Ronne Antarctic Research Exp., 1946–48   23 men wintered 1946–48

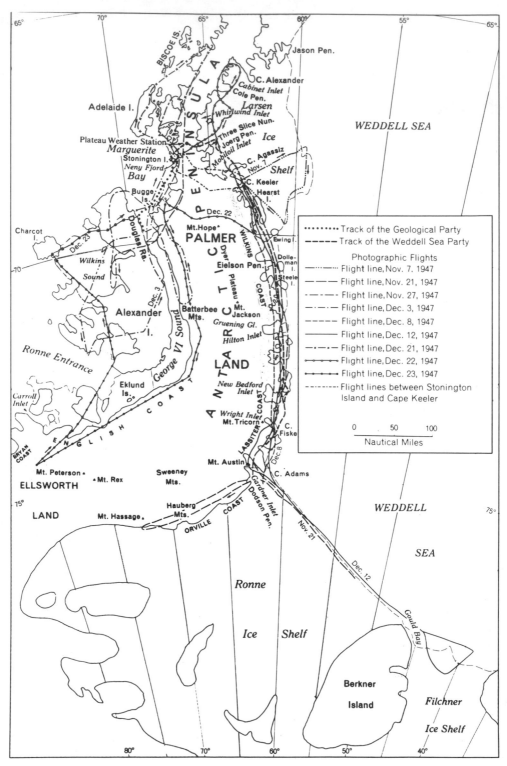

Field Operations of the Ronne Antarctic Research Expedition, 1946–48.

CHAPTER *13*

As WINTER GAVE WAY TO SPRING, the camp's pace quickened. Despite the blizzards of July and August, the men completed their preparations for the coming months of exploration. The mechanics worked over the airplane engines and the aerial cameras, while pilots calculated how many miles they could get out of the three planes with the available fuel. The men who would go on the trail parties inspected and mended their tents, clothing, sledges, and equipment. I, meanwhile, worried over the broad logistical problems: how could men, dogs, machines, and fuel best be used to cover the most ground?

In mid-July, we began our first field mission. I wanted to establish a weather station about 20 miles from camp. The best place would be on the high plateau of the Palmer Peninsula. From there, the men could radio to the base and tell us when the weather was good for flying. With five men, two dog teams, tents, sleeping bags, food, and radio gear, I set out for the plateau.

It was a difficult trip. Covering those 20 miles took two days of hard sledging. It was especially hard getting up the slopes of the plateau, for the grade was steep and the glacial ice very slippery. When the climb was too steep, we attached both dog teams to one sledge, then helped the dogs pull the sledge to the top. This was repeated with the second sledge. Everywhere there were crevasses. Several times avalanches roared down nearby slopes. Still there were some unexpected rewards. A fantastic display of aurora australis brightened the southern skies as swirling colored curtains of light danced across the heavens.

But nature also knew other tricks. After we had turned in on the evening of the second day, the freezing wind mounted to a shriek. The snow whipped against the thin tents, then covered them over. The blizzard lasted five days. We had no choice but to stay in our sleeping bags and hope the 90-mile-an-hour winds would not blow away the tents. We ate when we got hungry and passed time by talking to the base over the radio. During the storm, a husky died.

At last the winds died down and the skies were lit with a flood of stars. With the weather station set up, I prepared to return to the main base with three men, leaving Bob Dodson and Harries-Clichy Peterson to observe the weather and radio reports back to the base. Before I left, I asked the pair if they had everything they needed. Did they feel confident?

"Sure," Peterson snapped, "you're talking to a Marine."

The trip back was all downhill. It had taken two days to cover the 20 miles to the plateau, only 11 hours to return home.

The evening the four of us arrived in camp, Kelsey made radio contact with the two men on the plateau. They said that they could not work outdoors because of high winds, but they did not seem unduly concerned. The next two nights Kelsey failed to contact them. I was not particularly worried, because I knew that they had enough food for 18 days; and that could, if necessary, be stretched. Moreover, they knew the location of an emergency cache within half a mile. Bob was an experienced mountaineer, and both knew enough to use their primus stove for cooking only, not for heating (except when the tent was well ventilated) lest they be overcome by the fumes from the burning kerosene.

Finally on July 26th, the weather cleared around noontime and Adams took off in the L-5 plane. He flew from the bay ice, at that time thick enough to bear the weight of an airplane. Adams climbed to the plateau and found the tent of the meteorologists, who were supposed to signal him by laying orange panels to show the direction of the wind and the condition of the snow. He buzzed the tent, expecting to see Pete and Bob pop out to greet him. No luck. Four times he buzzed the tent without response. Adams did not dare land without information from the ground because of the stiff wind. If he cracked up he would have been stuck without help, a situation no sane man gets into in the Antarctic if he can help it.

When Adams reported back to me, I said, "Maybe the wind was making so much noise against the tent they didn't hear you. Try it again, and this time be sure to cover our sledge route in case they've left camp for some reason."

Back Adams flew, searching the surface for any sign of the men. He buzzed their tent at least six times, to no avail. The men appeared to have vanished from the face of the earth.

When Adams reported back the second time I became really alarmed. I couldn't let Adams land alone at the weather station to hunt for tracks or notes, and it was too late in the day to start removing gear from the airplane to make room for another man to go with him.

Adams said, "Pete being a Marine, maybe he went sight-seeing."

That's what I was afraid of. There had been a lot of discussion about the possibility of seeing the Weddell Sea from the plateau on clear days. Anxious to see as much of Antarctica as possible, they might have disobeyed my orders and gone off in search of new scenery. I had warned them in writing not to go out of calling distance of each other, not to lose sight of their tent, and to wear their skis at all times on the trail. Now they obviously weren't where they should have been. Had they fallen victim to kerosene fumes, got separated, become lost in a storm, disappeared down a crevasse? If both men had gone down a crevasse we'd never find them, because the wind would soon obliterate their tracks and there would not be a chance in a million of finding the right spot.

I knew it would be foolhardy to set off in the dark on a wild-goose chase unprepared. The best we could do would be to send out the airplane and a trail party the next morning.

That night we had asked some Britishers at their nearby base over to see one of our old films, "The Buccaneers." Having seen it several times, I stayed in my quarters working and wondering. At eight Kelsey tried again to raise the missing men by radio, without success. My concern mounted.

During the picture a man stumbled into the bunkhouse. "Where's Finn?" he gasped. Somebody snapped on the lights. Bob Dodson, white as the snow, pushed his way wearily through the maze of chairs toward my shack. With some of the men clustered around him, he pushed open my door and blurted: "Finn, Pete went down a crevasse! I did everything I could for him, but I had to come back to camp for help and leave him there."

For a few seconds that seemed much longer I couldn't speak. Then I pulled myself together and began to give orders: "Load the sledges, hitch up the teams. . . ." Gutenko at once set to work preparing food.

"Look here," said Pierce-Butler, in charge of the visiting group, "is there anything we can do to help?"

"Thanks, we can use help," I said. Then I asked Bob, "Where is this crevasse?"

"About eight miles up. I'll show you."

"Do you think you can make it? You look pretty exhausted."

"Sure I can make it, as soon as I've had something to eat."

Between bites he told his story: "After you left we had a tough time with the weather. The first thing that happened was that Pete's sleeping bag got wet, so he couldn't sleep on account of the cold and ice inside."

"Too bad you didn't tell us that the time you talked to us on the radio."

"I know that now but we didn't think of it at the time."

Presently, he said, the tent began to sag under the weight of snow, and a rip appeared in the canvas. Because of the deteriorating condition of the tent and the frozen sleeping bag, they decided to abandon camp and light out for the base when the weather cleared. They had trouble in taking down their tent, however, because the weight of snow that had piled up on it on the outside prevented them from lifting the tent-pole straight up to get it out of its hole. Instead they had to chop a channel in the ice under the tent to slide the butt of the pole sideways. While they were struggling with the tent, one of them accidentally stepped on the key of the radio. To make matters worse, snow clogged the microphone so that it would not work.

When the sun came out at noon, they decided to get an early start, even though they were expecting an airplane. Just before they abandoned the camp they sent out a radio message in Morse code by shorting the key-contacts with a tin can, hoping that the message would be picked up. Then, thinking they knew the way, they set out without even preparing themselves a lunch.

All went well until, after descending 3,000 feet from the plateau, they made a wrong turn and got lost in a crevassed area

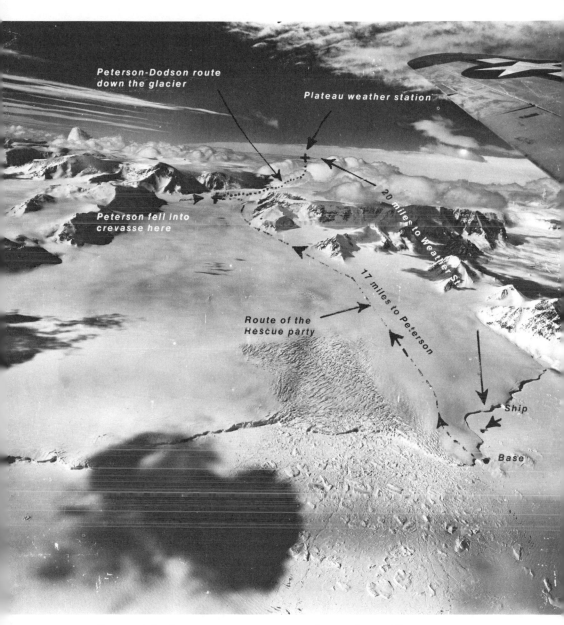

Route of the Peterson rescue party on the Northeast Glacier.

on one of the glaciers. While wandering around, they heard the noise of the L-5 on its way to their camp, but they could not get back in time to flag Adams.

They were still threading their way among the crevasses when the light began to fade. Pete slipped into a depressed snow-covered crevasse 30 feet wide. He stopped his fall by quickly grabbing and holding with his ice ax. Bob fell into a similar depression, but fortunately, the snow bridge held, and he was able to climb out.

They had now covered about nine miles and thought they were out of the crevassed area. Skiing was extremely difficult, because in the dim light they were always falling over the wavelike sastrugi, one to three feet high. Not being equipped to spend the night in the open and being in a hurry to get back to familiar territory, they decided to take off their skis and walk, dragging the skis behind them, a violation of one of the cardinal rules for safe polar travel. Pete went ahead carrying the ski poles and their one ice ax, while Bob followed pulling all four skis.

Ten minutes later Pete suddenly vanished. Bob stopped in his tracks, put on his skis, and slid over to where Pete had disappeared. There he found a hole in the snow just big enough for Peterson's slender body to slip through. Bob poked around to enlarge the hole and yelled, "Hey, Pete!"

A muffled cry came up from the depths: "Pass me a knife!"

Bob tied his knife to the end of his climbing rope and lowered it down the crevasse. The rope was 120 feet long. After Bob had dangled it for some time, Pete had not taken the knife, nor could Bob get any more replies to his shouts. It was 6:15 p.m., and there was nothing to do but ski to camp for help as quickly as possible.

Bob marked the hole with Pete's skis and his trail flags. In his excitement he committed two more mistakes: He laid the skis across the crevasse and put the flags all in a bunch instead of standing the skis upright and spreading the flags out for a distance in line with the crevasse.

He arrived at the base about three hours later.

Within an hour the men of both bases had assembled a searchlight, several climbing ropes, food, ice axes, a primus tent-heater, a sleeping bag, medical supplies, two sledges, and dog teams to pull them. Eleven of us started off into the night, slowly picking our way up the long slopes of the glaciers.

Meanwhile I kept thinking: What if Pete had been killed or mortally hurt by his fall? What if he had gone down two hundred feet or more beyond reach? What if we couldn't find the crevasse? He'd been there eight hours now with the temperature in the minus twenties. Suppose a ledge had stopped him but then had broken away to drop him? And I'd have to tell his parents, people I'd known for years. I retained very little hope that he was still alive.

When we reached the general area where Pete had disappeared, I could see even in the dark that it was intensely crevassed and dangerous even for a man on skis with a dog team. The proper procedure would have been to skirt around the area altogether.

While I held the searchlight in my hands and swept the area with it, the rest of the men, roped together, spread out, covering the region yard by yard, moving slowly and scanning every inch. In one team, the two foremost dogs broke through the snowbridge over a crevasse. One was hauled to safety, but the second twisted her body and bit through her tail trace, to disappear forever into the icy depths.

After three hours, not having found the hole, we were ready to pitch our tents until daylight when Bob shouted, "I see the place!"

He had been following his own ski tracks back, and as he neared the crevasse, the searchlight picked out the bundle of orange trail flags.

Shouts brought others clustering around the hole, coming up one by one as they threaded their way among the crevasses. Dick Butson, the British physician, spoke up: "Commander, if you think I'm the most suitable, I'd be glad to go down." Our own Dr. McLean, being a big and heavy man, was not the appropriate one to descend into the narrow crevasse.

"Thanks," I said, "I would appreciate it." Dick was well qualified for the job, being the smallest man present, experienced in mountaineering, and knowing what to do when he found Pete.

While the others got the ropes ready, Dick, Pierce-Butler, and I stood around the hole silently. Finally Dick spoke: "If I find him dead, what would you like me to do with the body?"

I thought for a moment. It was a hard decision to make. "Leave it there until I notify his family," I said. "Then, if we can, we'll try to handle the matter the way they want."

"Righto." Dick secured the climbing rope expertly to his harness. "Ready, you chaps? Lower away."

We slowly paid out the rope. The men had placed one of the sledges across the crevasse, and Ike Schlossbach lay on his stomach on the sledge holding the searchlight so that it shone down into the crevasse. Foot by foot the rope disappeared into the hole. Fifty feet. A hundred feet. Then at 110 came the shout, "Hi! Here he is!"

We held the rope fast and waited breathlessly for Dick's next word. After a few seconds it came. "He's alive! Very much so, in fact. He's talking!"

We all let out sighs of relief. It was unbelievable!

"Hi!" came Dick's voice again. "Pass down another line. Put a loop in the end, you know, for a harness."

While we tied a bowline loop in the end of a rope, I called down to Dick, "What sort of shape's he in?"

"Can't tell. Seems all right, but he is wedged head downward. It'll be a struggle."

And a struggle it was. On the surface we could only guess what Dick was doing from the way the ropes quivered, like a fisherman's lines that had hooked onto something. Actually, Pete was so tightly wedged that Dick could not get the loop around his body. Dick therefore had to untie the knot, work the end around Pete's torso, and tie another knot.

"All right," Dick shouted up. "Now pull! Carefully!"

Four men heaved on this jury rig. At about the seventh or eighth pull, like a tooth being plucked from its socket, Pete's body came loose from the jaws of the ice. Then up he came, foot by foot, back from an icy grave to the surface. As he appeared in the beam of the searchlight, we caught him with our hands and heaved him out onto the level snow, for he was still unable to move. "Kill that pain!" he yelled. His face was scratched and bruised, and his right arm hung limply.

Five minutes later we pulled Dick Butson up. Under his guidance we carefully carried Pete into a tent that had been set up and warmed with two primus stoves. Dick cut his clothing off, examined him for breakages, rubbed him, and gave him stimulants and hot chocolate, while the rest of us stood around in the cold kicking our heels together, shivering and waiting.

Bob was frantically swinging his arms and kicking his heels, his face showing relief at Pete's rescue. I said, "Bob, you must be chilled through — all the time you've spent in the open since yesterday morning."

He said, "I feel all right except my feet. Right now I have no feeling in them."

Knowing that one of the men other than the medic was in the tent, I asked him to come out and sent Bob in in his place. After a struggle, he got his boots off and began massaging his feet to restore circulation.

Though the doctor found no fractures, he put one of Pete's arms and one of his legs in splints until he could get him back to camp. By daybreak, around 9:30 a.m., both men were in a fair condition. Pete was bundled in a sleeping bag for the ride back to the base on one of the sledges.

Pete recalled that he had been walking along sleepily when the snow went out from under him so suddenly that he had no chance to save himself. The crack into which he had fallen shelved at intervals, so that on his way down he had ricocheted from side to side like a billiard ball. He finally stopped where the walls converged from both sides at once, wedged head first in a most uncomfortable position. His pack had fallen over his head, pinning his arms so that he could not move and pressing hard against his neck so that he had trouble breathing. He heard Bob call him all right and had answered, but after the first time, Bob had not heard him because he was positioned so that his voice went down into the crevasse instead of up. Moreover, when Bob's knife reached him he had been unable to grasp it because he could not move his arm. When Bob left, Pete gave up all hope of rescue. He thought he was condemned to a slow lingering death in a position that prevented him from even putting an end to his suffering. He survived his imprisonment of nearly 12 hours (which seemed to him more like a week) because his thick alpaca-lined windproof suit had kept him from freezing — except for one hand, which had lost its mitten. Furthermore, the stagnant air at the bottom of the crevasse had been considerably warmer than that at the surface. Finally he heard the footsteps of the rescue party echoing through the corridors of ice long before we actually found him. He began an intermittent shouting, and kept it up until Dick Butson was halfway down the crevasse.

When the time came to start back, Bob's feet were so swollen he could not get his ski boots on. Instead, he wore four pairs of woolen socks under a pair of felt boots and rode the other sledge.

The trek back to camp was slow and difficult, because we had to ease the sleds over innumerable ridges of sastrugi. During the morning, Lassiter flew overhead in the L-5 plane, awaiting instructions. We waved him off because the surface over which we were traveling would have made risky landing grounds. He fled away, not having fully understood us, and did not know that we had found Pete until we reached camp at 1300.

When I finally got the whole story pieced together, I was so exasperated at the many violations of safety rules that I told Pete, "You are on a twelve-foot tethering line for the rest of the expedition!"

However, I later relented and let him ski again.

The "emperors" of the Antarctic stand about 36 inches and weigh about 75 to 80 pounds.

CHAPTER *14*

I<small>N SPITE OF THEIR LACK</small> OF mature judgment in this instance Peterson and Dodson proved to be two of the very best men on the expedition. In their early twenties, they were aggressive, enthusiastic, conscientious workers. Yet, their harrowing experience makes one wonder what it is that draws a man into this sort of life. It has been said that escape, adventure, and recognition comprise all of the personal motives for man's participation in an expedition to the earth's last unexplored continent. Undeniably, these strong considerations have influenced, in one way or another, the decisions of every man who ever set foot on Antarctica.

When 20 or 30 men live in one main building, kept indoors by perpetual darkness and frequent blizzards for weeks at a time, the human personality is put to a severe test. From previous experience I knew that under such conditions monotony can become an expedition's worst enemy and that on an expedition of this kind, where wintering is necessary, the success of the project depends largely on the condition and outlook of the men when they come out of hibernation in the spring.

Every expedition has personality problems for the simple reason that the life invariably attracts not the average, steady, prosaic type of man; but aggressive, adventurous, unconventional individualists. As our Chief Pilot big Jim Lassiter aptly stated it: "I was talking when I should have been listening and ended up in the Antarctic."

When you crowd a lot of men with varied backgrounds together for a long period, with little exercise and no contacts outside the group, tempers get short; and a man must call on his inner resources to keep him interested in life or he will become a problem. Also, when a man is placed under close observation 24 hours a day, under rigorous conditions and with no chance to get away, any faults of character show up with glaring distinctness. Not only does expedition life bring out the best in strong characters and the worst in weak ones; but also it is nearly impossible to tell in advance who will stand up under such conditions. On a previous expedition some years ago I saw a man become demoralized to the extent that his desire for escape drove him to consume a quantity of denatured alcohol. Its effect on his system triggered off his mental explosion and for his own safety as well as that of others, he was placed in a straitjacket for several days.

To complicate matters further, a leader has to pick a majority of comparatively young men to stand the hardships; and, being young, they have often not learned the self control and tolerance of each other's peculiarities that an older group might possess. For all of these reasons an expedition leader tries to pick his men with the greatest of care not only for health, technical competence, and versatility; but also for the amiability and emotional maturity that makes it possible to live together in close quarters. Even so, my experience is that in general the members of expeditions do not get along very well with each other; although when they get home and write up their experiences, they feel ashamed of having acted childish and, hence, tend to gloss over their quarrels.

In one attempt to patch up a smoldering feud between two technical men whose jobs dove-tailed into one another, I invited them into my quarters. One immediately informed me he had broken diplomatic relations with his former friend. Since they both had notorious appetites, I decided a huge slice of apple pie was the key to the situation. This broke the tension, although they continued to carry on the act by neither looking nor speaking directly to each other.

Polar expeditions seem to attract aggressive individuals. For example, our Larry Fiske was not the shy type. After the expedition arrived in the Antarctic I assigned him to share a bunking cubicle with our doctor, Don McLean, a well educated man with a brilliant mind. Fiske, a Navy pilot during the war, had only two years of college. Nevertheless, he prided himself on being a walking encyclopedia — a sea-going lawyer, they call them in the Navy. When the two men first learned of how closely they would be associated, Dr. McLean asked, "Is that your bunk there?"

Fiske: "Yep. Yours up there?"

Doctor: "Yeah."

Fiske: "Well, we might as well get one thing straight right now. It's no use of your trying to trip me up on any subject, because I always know what I am talking about."

Brazen and presumptuous, yes, but the surprising thing was that Fiske could usually back up his boastfulness. I don't believe I've ever met a more versatile individual. He was our camp electrician, instructor in aerial navigation and radio code, climatologist, supply officer, tractor driver, seamstress, pinch-hitting cook, custodian of flags and signals. In fact, there were times when I wondered why any of the rest of us bothered to come along.

Occasionally an expedition member you count on, just does not work out as expected. Often it is too late to send him home, so there is not much the leader can do except relieve him of all duties. Then you have him underfoot for months, sulking and plotting absurd revenges. Not a pleasant situation. In this respect my expedition was not unlike others. While Amundsen had investigated his men for many months before picking them for one of his trips and still experienced major personnel problems, I hadn't had time to observe the temperamental suitability of my people before choosing them. As a result, I got a sharp-tongued fellow who, for reasons known only to him, tried consciously and through incompetence to sabotage the expedition. The person in question, who shall remain unnamed, whom I appointed head of my aviation division, had from the beginning misrepresented himself. Although he took flight training at the Pensacola Naval Air Station, it became increasingly clear that his knowledge of aircraft was superficial at best. Having known him as a young dog handler on the USAS expedition before the war, I did not check out his credentials as thoroughly as I otherwise might have.

In my view his irresponsibility first came to light in Beaumont when planes were being hoisted aboard the ship. By filling the tanks of our Beechcraft with about 550 gallons of gas, increasing the weight by about two tons, the added weight caused one of the lifting lugs to break, which resulted in the crash of the plane. That delayed our departure while we arranged for a replacement for us to pick up in Panama.

Before we arrived at Stonington, pilot James Lassiter informed me that my man had not taken proper care of the expedition's Noorduyn C-64 Norseman, a single-engine plane. Later, Lassiter saw him, in a fit of rage, pound his fists on the wings of our little Stinson L-5, a two-seated observation plane. His proficiency as a flyer came into question when our aviation mechanic, Robertson, had to show him how to start the twin engines of the Beechcraft. When he took the plane up on its first test hop, I asked Robertson why he didn't go along. He said he did not wish to put his life in the hands of my aviation chief.

In light of his performance, I was forced to restrict this man's activities, although I tried to be diplomatic about it, lavishly praising him for turning in routine reports. Unfortunately, even these were flawed, and I frequently had to ask for clarification. At the same time he was demanding that I keep hands off the aviation program. In a memorandum to me, he stated that "it is necessary that the Commanding Officer cooperate with me 100%. By this I mean all matters pertaining to avaition (sic) and personnal (sic) refered (sic) directly to me by you." When I advised him that I could not agree to such a preposterous demand, he barged into my quarters and, in the presence of radio operator Kelsey, informed me that he hated me and would never speak to me again. Soon after, he, who came from a wealthy Pittsburgh family, was openly declaring that he would spend $10,000 to wreck the expedition. The only person who paid him serious attention was poor Nelson McClary.

I relieved him of his duties because, as I stated in a memorandum to him, "you have finally succeeded in leaving me no other alternative . . . . I can not honestly feel that a person who admits he is disloyal, in whom I can have no confidence, and whom I consider has on many occasions not carried out my orders, is capable of managing the administration and handling of personnel as Head of the Aviation Program in which human life is at stake." That same day I named Ike Schlossbach to be in charge of flight operations.

◆   ◆   ◆

While personnel problems were being resolved, I ordered the final preparations for the intense exploration that lay ahead. Getting the planes ready was particularly difficult. It was still bitter cold — about 30 below zero — and the mechanics could not always wear heavy gloves while working on the engines. Sometimes their skin would stick to the metal, causing painful blisters. Often the engines wouldn't start because the lubricating oil had congealed. Then it had to be heated to 180 degrees on the galley stove to thin it out.

Meanwhile, another weather station had been set up. This one was at Cape Keeler, across the Palmer Peninsula, on the Weddell Sea coast. It was about 125 miles from our base camp on Stonington. Cape Keeler also served as an advance base for future exploration; 28 drums of aviation gasoline had been cached there. Instead of returning to Stonington after exploring the Weddell Sea area, the planes could fly the shorter distance to Cape Keeler, gas up, and return.

Our exploration planes were the Norseman, with its 650-horsepower engine, and the Beechcraft, with two 450-horsepower engines. While the Norseman hauled the heavy loads, the Beechcraft would serve as the photography plane, with the trimetrogon cameras mounted in the lower part of the fuselage. The Beechcraft's two additional fuel tanks enabled the plane to stay in the air for nine hours without refuelings.

One way ground-and-air worked together was by hedgehopping. The planes would go out first, scouting for good, safe trails to be used by the sledgers. The dog-drivers would follow those trails, along the way selecting good spots to be used as landing strips. Also, the men on the ground would leave small caches of emergency supplies to be used by the men in the plane in case they were forced down.

The pilots would land at these new landing strips and drop off supplies. These new supply depots would become advance bases. In that fashion the dog teams and planes could move increasingly farther from Stonington Island without having to return to our main base for more provisions.

The first attempt at hedgehopping ended in failure. Bob Nichols, the geologist, and two other men, left Stonington with three sledges and more than a ton of supplies. The sledges carried radios, tents, 100 days of food for men and dogs, sleeping bags, and other gear. But summer was coming, and the ice of Marguerite Bay was turning soft in spots. Fresh snow that fell quickly turned to slush. On such a surface one of the teams fell

Preparing to take off on aerial photographic mapping mission. *Left to right:* James Lassiter, Finn Ronne, Charles Adams.

through the ice. When Nichols tried to drag them back, he fell through the ice too. Tired, bedraggled, unable to go farther, the party regrouped and returned to Stonington. They had managed to sledge only 20 miles.

At this point, Pierce-Butler made an offer which I was quick to accept. He proposed that we combine our men and supplies for an exploration of the Weddell Sea coastline. Since I had lost so many dogs due to the distemper epidemic aboard ship, his dogs and drivers would be very useful indeed. When I learned that Pierce-Butler himself wanted to be one of the dog drivers, I knew that the party would be in good hands.

First, we had to ferry a large quantity of supplies over to Cape Keeler, on the Weddell Sea coast. Our Norseman plane could handle that job. A small British plane — the only one they had — would go on ahead, set down, and pick out a good landing strip for the larger, heavier Norseman. But the British plane did not have a very good radio, and the two planes became separated in foul weather. When the Norseman reached Cape Keeler, the British plane was nowhere to be seen. As the weather worsened, the Norseman was forced to turn back, still carrying its ton-and-a-half of supplies. The British plane did not come back.

For eight days, my pilots Lassiter and Adams flew search flights, scouring the plateaus for signs of the three missing British airmen. On the ninth day, just as everyone was about to give them up for lost, Lassiter spotted them. They were walking along the sea ice of Marguerite Bay (on the *west* side of the peninsula), still 40 miles from safety. We learned that the small plane had landed at Cape Keeler, and when the Norseman didn't show up, the airmen took off to return to their own base. But they got lost in the bad weather and, without a good radio, were unable to contact anyone. The light plane crash-landed on the ice. The three men weren't hurt, but had almost nothing to eat for nine days. They were very weak and tired when Lassiter picked them up and brought them home.

CHAPTER *15*

W E HAD COME TO THE ANTARCTIC to explore the great white continent. Now it was spring, time to begin in earnest. The sun was rising higher in the heavens each day. By the end of November, we would have light for a full 24 hours. But springtime is just as changeable in Antarctica as anywhere else on earth. Sometimes the skies are clear and bright, but storms can come up quite suddenly. In an hour, the bright sunshine can change to a windstorm, with low clouds and stinging particles of snow cutting through clothing.

Nichols and Dodson, the two geologists who had failed in their first try at a long sledge trip across George VI Sound, wanted another chance, and I gave it to them. However, this time the two of them would have to go it alone. On September 28 they started out. Theirs was a geological mission, but they would also send back weather information, which would assist us in our flying program. They would also collect rock samples.

The day after the geologists left, we began flying stores of gasoline over to Cape Keeler The flights were very difficult, for there was still plenty of bad weather. Once, the plane's crew had to remain at Keeler for five days because of strong winds and low, thick clouds. ,

The British were still eager to work with us on a sledge trip. Two of their men joined two from my expedition — Walter Smith, the mate on the ship, and Arthur Owen, the 18-year-old Eagle Scout from Beaumont. Their mission was to help map the coastline of the Weddell Sea. The Joint British-American Weddell Coast

Geologists Nichols and Dodson's isolated camp on Alexander Island.

Sledge Party left Stonington Island October 9 with three sledges and 27 husky dogs. The party covered 1,180 miles over the next 106 days in one of the longest sled trips ever made in the Antarctic. The men often traveled at "night" when the sun was low on the horizon and the surface more likely to be frozen. They reached their farthest point south 12 days before Christmas, 1947. When they returned at the end of January, 1948, the men described the wonders of the Antarctic landscape: the red sun brooding over the western ridges, silhouetting the icebergs and mountains; the low clouds that gave off a weird blue light. They described, too, the camaraderie, the struggle with the dogs, the hard days of work, the fear of frostbite, the occasional plunge through the ice or fall into a crevasse.

The geologists, Nichols and Dodson proved that they too were first-class dog drivers and explorers. Often they were short of food, but they never complained. It had been agreed that they would be given fresh supplies by airplane, but sometimes that wasn't possible because of bad flying weather. Once their food almost ran out. The two men were forced to live on a cup of lemonade and half a cup of seal meat per day.

Also, Dodson suffered from a peculiar type of "cold weather illness." The freezing air caused the metal fillings in teeth to contract. He would be chewing on a mouthful of food, and suddenly one of his fillings would plop out of the tooth in his mouth. Soon there wasn't a metal filling left in his teeth!

When I flew down to visit them one December day, they asked only one favor of me — to take back their sledgeful of rock samples. The load was getting too heavy for the huskies. When their sledge was hundreds of pounds lighter, off they went again, collecting still more rock samples, checking maps, and charging off into the mountains.

With my sledge parties working in the field, I waited impatiently for the weather to clear. Only then could aerial photography begin. Finally, on Novemebr 4, the clouds began to break. The photography plane flew to Cape Keeler and, three days later, the aerial photographic mission began.

Bill Latady had spent weeks in painstakingly mounting the aerial cameras in such a way that the photographs would be 60% overlapping from horizon to horizon.

Watching our photographer, Latady, getting ready for a flight was an amusing sight. He had a special flying suit, which had pockets everywhere, even in the sleeves. And every one of the pockets was crammed full of food. He even took the seat out of his parachute and stuffed it full of thing to eat. Latady was almost a one-man store.

"Bill," I laughed, "if you were forced down, you could live for a whole month on what is in your pockets."

Our first flight, from Cape Keeler out over the Weddell Sea, was a short one. We wanted to get used to the idea of taking pictures and spotting mountains and glaciers from the air. But even that short flight made me realize that all the maps of the area would have to be changed. In 1928, when Sir Hubert Wilkins had flown over that same area, he reported seeing some islands east of Cape Keeler. In 1941, when I too had flown over the region, I thought there were islands in that location too. On both of our flights there were many clouds in the sky. But now the weather was perfectly clear. From the little L-5 two-seater Adams and I could see for miles around. And neither of us spotted any islands, although we were aloft over the Weddell Sea about three and a half hours. This led me to believe that on certain days, when clouds formed low over the water, they *appeared* to be islands.

Other short flights showed that there were many mistakes on the Antarctic maps of this area. One dot of land, which was supposed to be an island, was really connected with the Antarctic mainland by a snow-covered ridge. One bay was 20 miles larger than the map showed. We spotted a new glacier from the air. But all these short flights, important though they were, merely made us anxious for the longer flights still to come.

On November 21, the Norseman and the Beechcraft took off from Cape Keeler for the first long flight south. The Norseman was carrying extra drums of gasoline, which would be used by the photography plane later on. In order to refuel the Beechcraft, I ordered both pilots to watch for a landmark that I had sighted previously when we flew south. I had named the prominent feature Mount Austin.

On the first leg of the flight, we saw a number of mountains and inlets and glaciers that had never been plotted on any map before. Finally, Mount Austin came close into view and the planes began to descend. Landing in the Antarctic can be very tricky. From the air, it is impossible to tell how deep the snow is. Although both planes had skis as landing gear, the weight of the aircraft might cause them to sink into the soft snow. We took the chance anyway. Sure enough, the snow was plenty deep. When I leaped out, I landed in snow almost up to my waist!

Refueling the photographic plane was hard work. Each drum of gasoline weighed 450 pounds, and it was all we could do to drag them through the snow. When that job was finished, I began to figure out where we were, how far we had come, and how long the flight had taken. And as I checked my navigaton, it seemed that something was wrong. If my calculations were correct, we weren't supposed to be as far south as Mount Tricorn at all. Still, we had passed that mountain long before we landed at Mount Austin. Determined to find out if the maps were wrong, or my calculation was faulty, I took additional sightings of the sun with my bubble sextant. Once again, I proved that the maps were wrong. Mount Tricorn was 55 miles farther north than was shown on the map. Also, parts of the Weddell Sea were 30 miles farther west than the map showed.

The Beechcraft again took off, moving through the deep snow and soaring aloft. The Norseman stayed on the ground as a stand-by. In case something happened to my plane, I wanted to have a rescue craft not too far away. As we flew on, whole groups of mountains came into view, new mountains never before plotted on any map, never seen by humans before. I named them: Sweeney Mountains, Scaife Mountains, Wilkins Mountains, Cape Smith, Lowell Thomas Mountains, Mount Horne, Mount Hassage. Yes, I was naming ranges and mountains and glaciers in honor of members of my expedition and friends who had helped me with money and equipment to get the expedition together. The last mountain I named on that first trip was Mount Hassage, for the capable chief engineer of my ship, *Beaumont*. This mountain was about 5,000 feet high. Beyond Mount Hassage I could see Mount Ulmer, which had been discovered back in 1935 by Lincoln Ellsworth and given his wife's maiden name.

Our flight had proved that the mountains running down the Antarctic Peninsula ended in the highlands I called the Joerg Plateau. This plateau was about 4,000 feet above sea level. And, because our plane was so high up, I could see about 200 miles beyond the last mountain. It was evident to me and to Lassiter that the plateau was probably connected with the Queen Maud Mountain Range, which lay just southeast of the Ross Ice Shelf. For us, as well as for the scientists who studied the Antarctic, that seemed proof enough. There was no frozen strait from the Ross Sea to the Weddell Sea.* Rather, there were highlands and plateaus of about four to five thousand feet above sea level. As far as I could determine at this time, Antarctica was one continent. Bill Latady dropped the American flag out of the opening next to the mount of the port camera. Clipped to the flag was a note describing our mission and giving our position in latitude and longitude, with the time and date. It was signed by Lassiter, Latady and myself. By this act I claimed the land in the name of the United States.

* In 1960 seismic soundings did indeed prove that a frozen strait existed.

Once both planes returned to the base, it was three weeks before we could take off again. Because of heavy clouds, there was no visibility. And the snow was slushy. That meant the Norseman could not load much extra fuel if it wanted to get off the ground. But we had to take some risks, for summer was approaching; and warmer weather in the Antarctic lasts only a few weeks. Once winter returned, flying would be almost impossible.

As soon as the clouds lifted, the Norseman and the Beechcraft were aloft again. Hours later, we spotted the British-American Weddell Coast party below. They had reached Wright Inlet, hundreds of miles down the Palmer Peninsula. When we landed to refuel, my Weddell Sea sledge party—two Britishers, Pierce-Butler and Jim Dugan, and my own men, Walter Smith and Art Owen—were breaking camp. They were to head south for additional survey work before turning back to base. I was specifically anxious to have them get an accurate location of Mt. Austin. This was a prominent landmark discovered on the first stab we made into the unknown. These four men had come a long way. They had my heartfelt thanks for a job well done.

The Beechcraft did not fly much farther that day. No sooner were we climbing high than the clouds were thick all around us. We could see nothing from the air and had to return to Wright Inlet. For two days both planes stayed on the ground. High winds, blowing at 40 miles per hour, swept over our tiny camp. It proved once again that any Antarctic weather, whether summer or winter, is not to be trusted. Even blizzards can spring up very suddenly, no matter what the season.

At last the winds died down. Because the Beechcraft had expended much needed gasoline in the abortive attempt, we would be unable to fly as far into the unknown as originally planned. But we took off, hoping to map from the air as much unknown territory as possible within our range of flying. Down along the Weddell Sea coast we went. We reached farther south in that area than any man had gone before us.

Below us stretched an unknown ice cliff, rising about 150 feet out of the water. It formed the southernmost boundary of the Weddell Sea for 450 miles, connecting Palmer Peninsula with Coats Land. I named the Palmer Peninsula stretch Lassiter Coast, in recognition of my chief pilot's extraordinary work. But the other members of my expedition also had landmarks named after them:

Latady Mountains, Dodson Island, Gutenko Mountains, Mount Thompson, Cape Schlossbach, Cape Adams.

We now headed due south into the unknown along the edge of the overcast. We could see 200 miles ahead to the horizon, but no sign of any mountains. At this time I was startled as the two engines suddenly missed and we started to lose altitude. Dire thoughts went through my mind as we flew over this white region of unknown land. Suddenly the engine started firing again. There had been no real cause for alarm; my pilot had been switching over to a full tank of gas. Here I dropped the American flag along with a claim sheet (a copy is now deposited in the State Department) whereby I claimed all of the land in this area in the name of the United States.

When our fuel ran low we returned to Cape Keeler. The Beechcraft had been in the air for 12 and a half hours. While the last drops of extra gasoline were being pumped into our tanks to bring us back to Stonington, I reviewed in my mind all we had accomplished and experienced. We had seen huge, unknown areas of the Antarctic. Our planes had enabled us to explore territory 1,000 miles or more from our main base in Stonington Island. I had a right to be proud.

Later, there were other, shorter flights, which added much valuable information to the maps of the Antarctic. One took us along the western section of the Palmer Peninsula, which Carl Eklund and I had sledged across seven years earlier. Now I wanted to go much farther south than our previous sledging limit. That flight turned out to be a little more dangerous than I thought it would be. About 300 miles south of Stonington Island, we suddenly lost radio contact with the base. If we had developed engine trouble and been forced down, we probably never would have been rescued. The Antarctic is so vast, so remote, so difficult to cross, that search parties would not have been able to find us or reach us. But we took that chance. We even landed the plane twice on purpose.

We had flown over what is now called the Robert English Coast. New mountains were sighted, one of which I named Rex Mountain; another, Mt. Peterson, was named after my physicist, who had narrowly escaped death by a fall into a crevasse. That mass of rock and snow rises to a height of about 6,000 feet. In order to plot its location more accurately, I had to take sun sights with the bubble octant while on the ground to obtain lines of position. We landed all right, and I took the sightings. But, while hurrying back to the plane, I realized what a risk had been taken. Even Jim Lassiter, who is usually very calm, seemed to be a trifle nervous.

"Hurry up, Commander," he called out sharply. "Let's get back into the air where it's safe!"

On the return trip, Latady made complete coverage in tri-metrogon photography of the west coast of Alexander Island. Off in the distance was Charcot Island, first sighted and sketched in 1909 by the French explorer, Jean Baptiste Charcot. Nobody had ever set foot on that island before. I wanted to land there; Lassiter concurred. So we did. I took a few altitude shots of the sun to

Finn Ronne, *left*, and James Lassiter taking sun sights with an octant.

determine the longitude of our landing spot. The three sharp mountain peaks on the otherwise snow-covered island were not far off. By then the clouds had formed again. We were afraid that the bad weather was mostly at Stonington, and when we came within range once more, we radioed back to the base. Our worst fears were realized. A 70-mile-an-hour gale was whipping at the base. Very likely, if we tried to land there, our plane would flip over.

At first I thought about landing along George VI Sound, and staying there until the storm died down. But that wasn't such a good idea. For we might have to stay there for many weeks. We had sufficient food to stay in the field for a month; but I knew there were pressing matters awaiting me at the base, so I was anxious to get back.

"Let's make a run for home, Commander," Lassiter said.

In order to see where he was flying, Lassiter had to keep the plane under the dark and threatening clouds. At first he reached 3,000 feet, but as the clouds kept dropping lower, he had to cut his altitude. When we were still 50 miles from base, he dropped to 400 feet, to 300 feet, 200 feet. We skimmed over icebergs floating in the open water off the coast. Once a sudden downdraft caught the airplane and snapped it down to within a few feet of the water. I saw the white tops of the waves a few feet away from me and thought surely this was the end for Lassiter, Latady, and me. The plotting board, map, dividers, pencils in my lap flew up into my face.

The radio operator told us that the winds were increasing, and a thick fog was closing in. Visibility was just about zero. Lassiter kept a firm grip on the plane's controls, veering away from icebergs, and fighting the winds, which were now buffeting our plane violently. At last he spotted some smooth bay ice down below. We were over Neny Fjord, an arm of Marguerite Bay. Slowly, he inched the plane to a landing, only two miles from camp. I sighed with relief. My confidence in Lassiter knew no bounds.

A tractor with four men was sent out to haul the plane back to base. But it wasn't an easy trip. Two men had to lie flat on each wing to break up the air-flow; otherwise the plane would have risen like a kite.

Mountain scenery at the head of Neny Fjord, close to the wintering base of the expedition.

To mask her nervousness at our predicament, my wife began washing her hair. When we landed, she rushed out to meet us, her hair dripping wet. Normally, back home this would have brought on a bad cold. Here in germ-free isolation she didn't even suffer a sniffle. That evening we celebrated the conclusion of the exploration program with a party. Chilean campagne contributed to the gaiety.

Finn Ronne and his wife, Edith, on Stonington Island, 1947.

As a full working member of the expedition Jackie edited my
articles in order to fulfill my contract with the North American
News Alliance, often sending three articles a week. She wrote her
own articles, kept a daily history of the expedition and aided the
scientific programs while several of the men were on field assign-
ments. I felt there was no reason why women could not operate
in the Antarctic along with men if it is beneficial to their career to
do so. But I do not advocate it merely for the adventure, for one
must be an extremely adaptable person to endure the mental as
well as physical stress of life on a prolonged polar expedition.

Now it was almost time to leave the Antarctic. The men at
the base began to pack our gear, take the wings off the planes, and
move the equipment back to the *Beaumont.* On January 22, my
sledge party of Smith and Owen, which had helped to explore the
southernmost area west of the Weddell Sea, returned to Stonington Island. Nichols and Dodson had come back earlier. We had
completed all our missions successfully. These men had done a
tremendous job on skis and with dog teams and had covered a
thousand miles or more. They all returned in a better physical
shape than when they departed three months earlier.

My year of scientific investigations at the base was drawing to a close. Thompson, Peterson and Fiske had taken advantage of every opportunity to record changes in man's immediate surroundings — on the surface of the earth, inside the earth's crust, as well as out in stellar space. Fiske had radioed weather data to the U.S. Weather Bureau in Washington, D.C. twice daily. Thompson had sent the results of his seismic soundings — recording earthquakes to the Geodetic Survey. He had set up the first tidal gauge ever installed along the shores of the Antarctic continent. The tidal records were turned over to the Navy Hydrographic Office for interpretation. Peterson had made extensive investigations in solar radiation, refraction and cosmic rays. The latter branch of science we did under the auspices of the Bertol Foundation, Franklin Institute, in Philadelphia. All of the scientific results garnered on my expedition were eventually released by the office of Naval Research in 14 separate publications.

This record eclipsed anything assembled by previous American expeditions and sparked interest in future undertakings.

On February 11, we received a radio message from a U.S. Navy icebreaker. The Captain, Gerald Ketchum, was an old friend and wanted to pay us a visit. They had circumsailed the continent during the two months spent in Antarctica. We had been together in the Arctic two years previously when Thule Air Force Base was built. He offered to break the ice around our ship, so that we could

Sledging 1400 pounds of medical supplies from the *Port of Beaumont* to the Stonington Island base.

follow in his wake to the open water in Marguerite Bay. We left Stonington by the end of February, 13 months after the *Beaumont* had left its Texas harbor. All about us the ice floes were beginning to break up and drift away from the coast. But, it would soon be winter, and the seas around the Antarctic Peninsula would be a mass of solid ice. We sailed steadily northward. The great ice cliffs of the Antarctic disappeared from view beyond the southern horizon.

◆ ◆ ◆

The Ronne Antarctic Research Expedition explored and mapped more than 450,000 square miles of new territory, a region two-and-one-half times larger than the state of Texas. More than half that area had never before been seen by human eyes. Much of the rest had never been mapped properly. The planes flew a total of about 45,000 miles. Thanks to the engineering genius of Bill Latady, 14,000 aerial mapping photos were obtained.

In order to understanding this marvelous accomplishment by my crew, it is necessary to use a map of the United States for reference. In his book *Into The Unknown* (Platt and Munk, 1968), Bruce Price described the expedition as follows:

"If Finn Ronne's main base had been in New York City, he would have been sending dog teams as far as Ohio. His planes would have been exploring down to the eastern coast of Florida. An area of 450,000 square miles covers the states of New York, New Jersey, Pennsylvania, Michigan, Ohio, Maryland, Virginia, West Virginia, North Carolina, South Carolina and Georgia."

At first, the Board on Geographic Names of the Department of Interior named my newly discovered region Edith Ronne Land in honor of my wife. That's how it is on many of the older maps of the Weddell Sea area and the areas beyond. But now after twenty years, the name has been changed to honor my father, my wife and me. Today, it is known as Ronne Ice Shelf.

CHAPTER *16*

As our expedition sailed out of Marguerite Bay in late February of 1948, a new group arrived to occupy the British base on Stonington Island. The leader was Dr. Vivian Fuchs. The following spring he and several companions sledged southward to Ronne Bay, following my old route. On Eklund Island they found my sealed container, learning about my claiming of the land, and brought the papers I had cached back to England where they were filed in the British Foreign Office.

In reading the report of Fuchs journey, I learned that conditions of the ice around Eklund Island had changed considerably since I was there 8 years earlier. In fact, most of the island was surrounded by open water, the sea ice having drifted out. The high barrier cliff where we had camped had broken off and drifted out to sea. Also, the lenticular depression had moved out since we were there. Had we sledged farther west toward Cape Thurmont, it would have put us later in the season, and we doubtless would have been marooned on the drifting ice. Our chance for rescue then would have been zero. The old Curtis Condor plane, almost a derelict, could never have found us; and a surface party could not have reached us even had our position been known. A ship — if one had been available — could not have broken through the pack ice to save us. But, thanks to native Norwegian instinct and Lady Luck, Carl and I got out before the ice broke. Not until eight years later, when I saw the Fuchs report, did I realize how close we had come to disaster.

In the spring of 1948 we savored triumph. Waiting to greet us were Sir Hubert Wilkins, Peter Freuchen, Bernt Balchen, Lincoln Ellsworth, Vilhjalmur Stefansson, Lowell Thomas, Larry Gould, and many others. In New York at the reception given us by the American Geographical Society, I recounted the expedition's accomplishments. But these were best summed up by Dr. Isaiah Bowman, President of Johns Hopkins University, "Exciting as adventures may be," he wrote, "they are not among the purposes of an expedition. They are warnings that lead to improved techniques and organization. We judge expeditionary leadership in terms of scientific results. With but fifty thousand dollars, plus the loan of some government equipment, the Ronne Antarctic Research Expedition 1946–48 was able to return with a harvest of scientific findings that would be a credit to a far more costly expedition."

The face of an active glacier on the Palmer Peninsula. The glacier moves about 44 feet each year and a continuous roar can be heard as the ice masses grind toward the sea.

The Explorers Club annual dinner, 1948. *Left to right:* Sir Edmund Hillary, Werner von Braun, Finn Ronne, Lowell Thomas.

My expedition marked the end of an era. No longer would it be possible for a private entrepreneur to raise sufficient funds to man and equip a modern scientific expedition for Antarctic exploration. Henceforth that role would be assumed solely by government-backed operations. Nevertheless, I wasted no time planning another expedition; and I am confident that the federal government would have supported my effort if it had not been for the Korean War. While waiting for an opportunity to return to the white continent, I lectured, wrote, and served as a consultant to the U.S. Army Quartermaster Corps.

◆ ◆ ◆

My expedition had been publicized in Norwegian newspapers through articles released by the North American Newspaper Alliance. Shortly after our New York reception by the American

Geographical Society, invitations for a visit and lecture came from the Royal Geographical Societies in Norway, Sweden, and Denmark. The Oslo lecture was attended by King Haakon VII. At the end of my presentation, the king strode to the front, climbed the step to the rostrum, and with outstretched arms greeted me in Norwegian. "I congratulate you, Commander Ronne," he said. "It was a wonderful lecture and beautiful color film." I was speechless for an instant, but finally I stammered out: "Thank you, your Majesty." He then said, "I knew your father very well. He was a 'praegtig' man." (translation: "He was a mighty fine man.")

That was an extraordinary compliment, for a "praegtig" person was one you could depend upon regardless of the challenge. My father had first met the king prior to Amundsen's departure from Oslo and his conquest of the South Pole. In honor of the Monarch's support, that remote region at the earth's end was named King Haakon VII Plateau by Amundsen.

From Oslo, my wife and I flew to Stockholm for another lecture. The next morning the American ambassador informed me that we should return to Oslo, because our embassy, in our behalf, had applied for and been granted an audience with the king. The following morning we were received in the ante-room by a military aide. At 11 A.M. the door to the king's office suddenly opened. King Haakon greeted us warmly and asked us to be seated. In the next half hour we had a wonderful time talking about polar exploration. If the king had not been destined for the throne, I am certain he would have followed in the footsteps of Nansen he admired so greatly.

My association with Dr. Bowman led to a startling disclosure about a much publicized North Pole flight in 1926. The conversation took place at Dr. Bowman's summer home on Lake Wentworth, New Hampshire in September, 1949. I later made a memorandum of our talk and had it notarized.

"Finn, I'll tell you something I don't want repeated to anyone as long as I'm around," Dr. Bowman confided. "Will you promise me that before I go on?"

I assured him I would, and he continued approximately as follows:

"Upon Byrd's return from the Arctic in 1926, I had doubt that he ever flew over the North Pole. I asked to see his compilations and what navigational aids were used to prove that he had reached 90 degrees north. Byrd always gave evasive answers and said no one should question his integrity. But he had no proof of having passed the northernmost point of Ellsworth and Amundsen the year before. I got my answer to my suspicion when Byrd returned from the Antarctic in 1930. Byrd visited the AGS and after lunch we went for a walk with one other person, whose name I will not mention, but you know him. It was raining that afternoon and with raincoats on we kept walking and talking for almost four hours around the blocks of Broadway and 156th Street. By that time I managed to break down Dicky-Byrd, and the time it took do so was worth it. Byrd confessed to the two of us then that he had not reached the North Pole, but had missed it by about 150 miles."

At that time Dr. Bowman was Director of the American Geographical Society in New York. Why, I wondered, had he not immediately let the American people know the truth about it? He replied that no one would have believed him, for Byrd was a worshipped national hero. What a dreadful thing it would be to reveal him as a liar.

My obligation to remain silent about the matter was of short duration. Within four months Dr. Bowman died of a heart attack. The third man, incidentally, on that walk in the rain was, as I suspected, W. L. C. Joerg of the National Archives in Washington, who, at the time of Byrd's confession, was Dr. Bowman's assistant.

Byrd's deception grew out of his ambition to be the first to reach the North Pole by air. He faced strong competition for the honor in the redoubtable Roald Amundsen, as determined to blaze trails in the sky as he did on the ice with sledge and dogs.

Amundsen, recognizing that the glory days of the huskies were numbered, became one of Norway's first civilian pilots. While on a lecture tour in the United States, he was visited by Lincoln Ellsworth, a surveyor and engineer in railroad building, who had been left a fortune by his father. When they met, Amundsen needed money badly. A few months earlier he had been forced to declare bankruptcy. Only because one of his wealthy friends came to his rescue was Amundsen able to keep his home by the sea, a few miles south of Oslo.

Ellsworth, who had always been interested in adventurous

Lincoln Ellsworth

exploits, proposed an idea which Amundsen eagerly accepted. He would supply the money — about $85,000, which was enough to purchase two amphibious planes — if Amundsen would take him along as part of his crew. It was an ideal arrangement. Ellsworth had the money, Amundsen the experience.

It was during that lecture tour, in 1924, that I had the opportunity to meet with the great explorer for the last time. We had lunch together at the Duquesne Club in Pittsburgh, where he gave a lecture at Carnegie Hall that same evening. He told me of his plan to fly from Spitsbergen to the North Pole and assured me that my father would again be with him, at the Kings Bay takeoff point the next year.

The two planes were purchased in Germany. In May of 1925 they took off from Spitsbergen. When Amundsen had estimated that the Pole had been reached, the two planes landed in an open lead in the pack ice. One was wrecked. The explorers were keenly disappointed when their observations proved that they were about 140 miles short of the Pole. But they considered themselves lucky to be alive. The six-man crew worked for a month on the shifting ice, carving out a runway so that the remaining aircraft could take them off.

One little-known incident pertaining to that flight concerns my father, Martin Ronne. From a bayonet he had fashioned a knife with sturdy handle and slipped it into Amundsen's flight-pack before he took off. Amundsen found it, but decided it was excess weight and in the last minute removed the knife from the pack. My father saw him do it; later, when Amundsen wasn't looking, my father put it back.

After Amundsen's planes were forced down on the ice, the men began to hack away at the rock-hard ice floes, trying to clear a runway. However, the axes and other tools splintered or dulled when struck repeatedly against the ice. Rummaging around his gear, Amundsen came across the knife my father had made. He lashed the knife to a proper length pole and began to chop away. It worked beautifully. Later, in his book, Amundsen wrote that the hand-made knife — more than any other piece of equipment — helped the group get back into the air safely.

Undaunted, Amundsen and Ellsworth began to plan for another flight, this time aboard the dirigible *Norge*. They meant to set out in mid-May of 1926. In the midst of their preparations, Richard E. Byrd, a retired Naval officer arrived at Kings Bay on his ship the *Chantier* with a tri-motor airplane lashed on deck. He announced to the world that he was going to fly across the North Pole and beat anyone else who planned such a flight, including Amundsen and Ellsworth.

Bernt Balchen, a Norwegian Navy pilot, saw Byrd and his pilot Floyd Bennett take off. Balchen jotted down in a small notebook, "9 May, 00:37 hours" — 37 minutes after midnight. But since it was spring and the sun did not set, it was still light. When Byrd returned, Balchen noted the time, "9 May, *Josephine Ford* (Byrd's plane) returned Kings Bay 1607 hours."

Shortly after the Fokker's return, the Norwegian correspondent for *Oslo Evening-Post* sent a cablegram, which was sent out by the radio operator at 17:25 hours, just a little over an hour after the plane had landed:

> "Byrd over Crossbay after fifteen and one-half hours flying; ten minutes later the two pilots landed in good shape. Pilots insisted themselves to have been at the Pole, but judg-

ing by the time away doubt having been there. Most likely no farther north than Amundsen. (Signed) Arnesen."

There was never any doubt as to how long the flight took. The reporter, who sent the cablegram, had timed it. Bernt Balchen also checked his figures with officers of the Norwegian Navy ship *Heimdal* which was in Kings Bay at the time.

The distance flown was 1,500 miles. The flight took 15½ hours. The plane was capable of a speed of 89 knots (equal to 99 miles per hour). Taking into consideration the drag of the plane's landing skis, the average speed during the flight was probably no more than 70 knots (78 miles) per hour. Therefore, in order for the *Josephine Ford* to have flown from Kings Bay to the North Pole and back, the flight should have taken 18½ to 19 hours. Winds were not a factor, for meteorological records prove there were almost none in the entire polar basin on the day of the flight. However, if Byrd's figures are to be believed, the following conditions had to exist: First, there had to be a tailwind blowing from south to north at approximately five knots per hour. Then after spending about 12 minutes flying around the pole to make certain he crossed it (and that was what Byrd said), he would have had to be blessed with a tailwind of 22 knots per hour to help push him back to Kings Bay.

Bernt Balchen, who later flew the *Josephine Ford* while barnstorming with Floyd Bennett, knew first hand its limitations and was aware of what actually happened from the beginning. But at that time, although bothered by it, he chose to remain silent. Even had he spoken up it is doubtful anyone would have listened to him. Before Floyd Bennett died, he revealed the truth to Balchen and eventually Balchen disclosed at a press conference that Byrd's claim was "based on fraud."

In the spring of 1926, I returned to Norway on my first visit since I emigrated. Shortly after my arrival, my father, who had been at Spitsbergen with Amundsen, also returned home. At the time, I had read reports in the *Oslo Evening Post* that some doubted Byrd's claim to have flown to the North Pole. I asked my father's opinion. "We all thought the two Americans returned to Kings Bay too soon. The officers on the *Heimdal* timed them and thought they had not gone farther than Amundsen and Ellsworth last year (1925)."

Amundsen recalled the enthusiastic reception when Byrd's

plane set down on the air-strip crowded with onlookers: ". . . . we were close enough to pull (Byrd and Bennett) out of the plane and give them . . . each a real and thoughtful kiss on the chin." But in the excitement, "none of us thought of asking them: 'Have you been to the Pole?' "

Although Amundsen conceded he had been beaten to the North Pole, he was determined to carry on with his plan. Two days after Byrd's return, he with Ellsworth and the Italian airman Umberto Nobile took off in the dirigible *Norge*. They flew from Spitsbergen to Teller, Alaska, crossing the pole in a 2,700-mile flight spanning three days.

In May, 1928, Nobile attempted to make another polar crossing in the dirigible, which he had renamed *Italia*. Disaster struck when the airship swooped too low and hit the ice north of Spitsbergen. Some of the crew were swept away in the wreckage, which broke away from the main part of the dirigible. Nobile and a few others managed to land safely on the ice and radioed for help.

Amundsen was in Oslo when he heard the news. Immediately he organized a rescue mission, and with five men took off in the French amphibian plane *Chatham* to hunt for survivors. No sooner did the plane rise up from Tromso — the northernmost town in Norway — than radio communication was lost. It disappeared into the Arctic seas between Norway and Spitsbergen, and neither Amundsen nor the rescue crew were ever seen again. A year or so later, part of the plane's flotation gear was found and identified.

Ironically, Nobile himself was taken off the floating ice by a Swedish pilot whose plane was equipped with skis. Later, the rest of the survivors were picked up by a Russian ship.

◆ ◆ ◆

On an April evening in 1949 some 2,500 people assembled in a Washington auditorium as the American Polar Society commemorated the 40th anniversary of Robert E. Peary's attainment of the North Pole. His daughter, Mrs. Marie Peary Stafford, was seated in the audience between me and my wife. I was privileged to introduce the principal speaker, Sir Hubert Wilkins, who had pioneered polar exploration by plane and submarines.

Choosing his words extremely carefully, the goateed Australian outlined the general plan of travel claimed by Peary, laying particular stress to the phenomenal daily distances covered. Peary was no ordinary man, Wilkins said; he was a super human, a man whose accomplishment no other would be able to duplicate. Just think of it, Wilkins said, Peary covered no less than 186 miles in two consecutive days, running on crippled feet alongside his sledge.

The subtlety of Wilkin's remarks was completely lost on some of the guests. He had written the speech in my presence. We had discussed Peary's claim to the North Pole many times over the years, and I knew that Sir Hubert put little credence in the polar claim. Wilkins had sledged in the Arctic, flown over it and cruised under the ice floes in a submarine and knew that of which he spoke. Neither did I believe Peary. Having sledged as many — if not more — miles as any explorer who ever strapped on a pair of skis, I had learned from painful experience just how much a man could push himself. While Peary's longest distance in one day's travel was something like 93 miles, the most I was ever able to cover in a day was 61.5 miles. That happened on a sledge journey I made with Albert Eilefsen in 1934, when we raced back to Little America from Byrd's Advance Base. A more meaningful comparison would be the sledge-trip made with Eklund in 1941, when our best day's work was 49 miles. Carl and I were then 33 years old — 20 years younger than Peary when he made his dash in 1909 — and we were in the pink of condition. Also, we were both expert skiers, having participated in cross-country racing over long distances. In 1941 we were skiing and sledging under ideal conditions, which meant that each step we took resulted in a forward movement of 15 to 20 feet. Peary, shuffling along on snow-shoes with most of his toes amputated because of frost bites from a previous expedition, could not have covered more than two or three feet per stride. The surface we skied on was as smooth as a waxed kitchen floor, with ridges no higher than a foot. Peary, on the other hand, well aware this was his final attempt, had to cross pressure ridges up to 40 feet high and detour around open water leads — several miles wide.

Amundsen, an excellent skier as well as a man of great endurance, averaged about 27 miles per day when crossing the Ross Ice Shelf. On one earlier occasion, when surface conditions were ideal, his lightly laden sledges returning from a cache-laying trip, tore across the ice for 71 miles before calling a halt. The effort left them totally exhausted. Needless to say, they did not cover 71 miles the following day. Not even iron-man Amundsen had that kind of stamina. And it is asking too much to expect us to believe that Peary did.

In 1910 Peary's claims caused a rumpus in the United States' Congress, and a special committee was formed to conduct an investigation. But it did not get very far, since Peary was not a cooperative witness and there was very little scientific evidence to examine. His navigational log has not been produced for an analytical scrutiny to this day in 1979.

Nevertheless he became a national hero in America, due in large part to his success in obtaining laudatory publicity. It would appear that Byrd profited later by using the same techniques. Those were the years before modern technology in navigation and communication could dispute the fanciful claims of some celebrated explorers.

◆   ◆   ◆

According to a staff member of the American Geographical Society, there is a full report on Byrd's alleged flight to the North Pole in the Society's files. However, few have ever seen it, for it is marked "Secret."

I am confident from what the staff members and others said, in addition to my own personal knowledge, that the report would discredit Byrd's claim of being first to fly over the North Pole in May, 1926.

CHAPTER *17*

S OON AFTER RETURNING FROM MY 1946–48 expedition, I had announced plans for further exploration of Antarctica. They included penetrating the Weddell Sea and wintering at Gould Bay,
which I had discovered from the air. This base on the Ronne Ice
Shelf would place me within striking distance of unexplored areas
to the south and southeast. With airplanes and surface transportation to set up advance bases, a thorough mapping of the area
could be accomplished.

My desire to mount another expedition was given a pres-
tigious boost in 1949, when a National Academy of Science committee, chaired by Dr. Isaiah Bowman, issued a special report
echoing my recommendations. "A continent-wide scientific program in Antarctica cannot be fully developed until we have at
least a reconnaissance map embracing the entire area," the report
stated. In January of 1950 my plans seemed to be winning government favor. A top official wrote me that "the Department of
State is glad to learn of your plan to take an expedition to the
Antarctic and will be interested in . . . the evolution of your
plans." Such an expedition, the letter concluded, "should be valuable from an operational standpoint as well as for the collection
of a maximum harvest of significant scientific data."

It would also be valuable in any dispute over national claims.
Although the United States Government did not recognize the
claims of any nation to Antarctic territory and made no claims
of its own, it did reserve all future rights; at the same time it
permitted American citizens to make explorations and conduct
scientific research on Antarctica.

Meanwhile, Great Britain, Argentina, and Chile were busily
engaged in establishing a series of bases to bolster their respec-

tive national claims. Their intent was to establish permanent occupancy in Antarctica. The British bases, governed by the Falkland Islands Dependencies Survey, maintained a magistrate and post offices. The Department of State presented a proposal to the interested foreign governments to internationalize the Antarctic for the future benefit of mankind. If any world area were to be under international control, what better place than the Antarctic, completely devoid of historic population and minority disputes? However, the U.S. proposal was universally turned down either in its entirety or with qualifying reservations.

The next logical step was to assert our own claims, which, on the basis of initial exploration, could be quite extensive. Although the Russians did not claim any land on the continent, their whaling activities were extensive. And they demanded to be in on any conferences dealing with the sovereignty of Antarctica.

The extension of the Western Hemisphere stretches into the Antarctic continent, separated from South America by the Drake Passage. Control of this strait would be of utmost importance to the United States should the Panama Canal be made inoperative during a war. It was vital, I believed, that we should continue our activities in Antarctica. My proposed expedition, by carrying out the recommendations of the Bowman committee's report, would serve that purpose and thereby strengthen the role of the United States in future deliberations on the fate of the white continent.

In 1951 I was busy seeking support from private sources as well as from the government. The American Geographical Society, the U.S. Weather Bureau, and all the organizations that had backed my 1946–48 expedition responded favorably. Lars Christensen, Norwegian shipping and whaling industrialist, agreed to make a suitable ship, the *Theron,* available to me for the winters of 1952–53 and 1954–55. Christensen had sponsored nine expeditions to the Antarctic from 1927 to 1938, leading several of them himself. Much of the coast from 86° E. to 17° W. was charted by his research teams. Though largely unsung in America, Christensen ranks in scientific and geographic circles as one of Antarctica's most significant explorers. I was greatly pleased to have gained not only his support but his friendship, which endured until his death in 1965.

◆ ◆ ◆

Although continuing hostilities in Korea disrupted my time-table, I stubbornly persisted in seeking ways to launch another Antarctic expedition. More than ever I was convinced that the United States must become an active participant in that forbidding part of the world. My quest for a national commitment repeatedly met with bureaucratic indifference or outright opposition. However in early 1953 I finally scored a breakthrough: Senator Francis Case of South Dakota agreed to bring my plans to the attention of President Dwight D. Eisenhower. In a letter to the senator I cautioned him that all polar matters were controlled by Pentagon people sympathetic to Admiral Byrd's interests. I had good reason to believe that they would block any expedition he did not control. "Admiral Byrd regards Antarctic exploration for this country as peculiarly his own province," I stated. "He desires no competition in this field."

During the same period, plans were being formulated for the International Geophysical Year, a worldwide program to study the earth's environment. When it was decided to include Antarctic research in the program, I was contacted by the chairman of the Antarctic subcommittee. He informed me that 21 American scientists had agreed unanimously on me as their choice to have a leading position in the program. Surprised, somewhat skeptical, but still hopeful, I consented to have my proposal serve as a nucleus for the IGY prospectus. Interest began snowballing. Congress was approached for an appropriation, and suddenly IGY took on new meaning.

Since the Geophysical Year would be a cooperative international effort, it was agreed that national claims would not be brought up or have any part in the program. However, if we were to explore and have maps before the IGY began and if the important Weddell Sea area was to be included in the program, some attention had to be called to the problem. My friends acted.

Bills were introduced into the U.S. Senate and House of Representatives to provide assistance to the non-profit, scientific American Antarctic Association, Inc., of which I was the Chairman of the Board, in consultation with an Advisory Council to carry out an expedition to the Antarctic between December 1, 1954, and May 31, 1958, for the purpose of:

1) advancing the legitimate claims of the United States in the territory and resources of the Antarctic continent;

2) determining the mineral and other resources available on such continent;
3) establishing geodetic control points for the purpose of facilitating the utilization in mapmaking of the aerial photographs taken in the course of the United States Navy Antarctic development project, 1946–47;
4) making aerial trimetrogon photographs of the unknown portions of the Antarctic continent for use in making maps of such portions;
5) exploring unknown portions of such continent; and
6) making scientific observation and surveys in the Antarctic, including, but not limited to, records of tidal movements, magnetism, gravimetric measurements and seismology.

Accompanying plans outlined the detailed program to be carried out from a base at Gould Bay in the Weddell Sea. The proposal was purely nationalistic in scope with different aims than those proposed for the IGY. It would precede the international group, could be synchronized with it, and, if desired, could assist them in establishing their bases.

At this point, the surveyor, still smarting from being left out of my 1946–48 expedition, tried to wreck my plans. He wrote senators, urging them to defeat the bill.

His efforts went for nought. On July 1, 1954, at a public hearing on the bill, I appeared before the Senate Committee on Armed Services and outlined the scope of my plans. On July 29th, a closed hearing was held on the bill and the following resolution adopted and sent to the President:

> Resolved, That the Committee on Armed Services of the Senate, recognizing the immediate need for further exploration on the Antarctic continent, urges and commends that an expedition be undertaken at the earliest possible date, under the direction of the President, for the purposes of validating the territorial claims of the United States and thereby increasing the security of this nation, exploring the mineral resources of the area, and accomplishing any possible advancements with respect to mapping surveys and scientific observations.

The White House sent my plan over to the Navy, where it fell into Byrd's hands. As I had feared, it was killed promptly. I never heard any more about it. Unofficially, I learned that Byrd had urged the Navy to send an icebreaker to the Bay of Whales. This would amount to little more than a publicity stunt.

Byrd's proprietary attitude vexed certain top government officials.

As columnist Drew Pearson reported, "they intend to tell Adm. Richard Byrd, the famous Polar explorer, that they don't want him to head the upcoming Antarctic explorations. They favor a junior officer, Comdr. Finn Ronne, instead. The Navy, however, is still backing Byrd. He also has strong political support in the Senate where his brother, Virginia's potent Harry Byrd, and his in-law, Massachusetts' long-faced Sen. Leverett Saltonstall, can block funds for the Antarctic expedition." Pearson's column pointed out that the admiral, then 67, wanted to limit American explorations to the area he discovered, Little America. He considers Little America his monument, though it has turned out to be largely an ice sheet over water . . . Comd. Ronne, on the other hand, wants to visit new areas and increase U.S. knowledge of this last great unexplored continent."

I did not know Pearson, nor was I responsible for his knowledge of current events. Pearson had shot at Byrd but hit me. After the column appeared, I phoned Byrd to tell him emphatically that I had nothing to do with the article and that I felt it would injure me far more than him. "Yes," he agreed. "I believe it will hurt you very much."

CHAPTER *18*

I N June 1956 I received a call from Byrd. He informed me that
he had withdrawn his objections to having me participate in
the upcoming ICY program. "We need you," he said, and even
asked what command I wanted in the military part of the operations. I told him that the Weddell Sea areas most appealed to me.
I was selected by the Academy of Science as scientific leader of
the station also. The other bases would have a split military-
scientific command, but at the Weddell Sea base, both phases
would be under my direction.

Within a week I reported for duty with Task Force 43,
headed by Adm. George Dufek, whom I had first met as a lieutenant on *Bear* in 1939. In 1946, I had recommended him for a command position with Arctic Operation Nanook along with Dick
Cruzen, who was named task force commander.

We had much work to do before our scientific armada sailed
to construct seven bases including Ellsworth station on the Weddell Sea. I had known Lincoln Ellsworth well and of his accomplishment with Roald Amundsen in the Arctic. Ellsworth, one
of a small group of old-time explorers didn't live to see the change
in Antarctic exploration. Nor could he have imagined that the
continent over which he made the first trans-Antarctic flight
would become as busy, comparatively, as New York's Broadway
and 42nd Street. The explorers of yesteryear would be staggered
by the changes that have taken place on the white citadel they
began probing a few short decades ago. Not many of us remained

who had spanned the change from wooden ships to steel-hulled icebreakers and M.I.T. technicians.

Amundsen's old-fashioned transport by colorful dog teams or Scott's man-hauling of sledges had been replaced by mechanization. Our largest tractor weighed 35 tons. It could pull 50 tons of cargo on sledges over level icy highways built with the aid of automatic crevasse detectors and demolition squads. The tractor burned 10 gallons of diesel fuel per mile. Amundsen considered it a luxury to illuminate his 19 by 13 one-room hut with a primus lamp; a small coal-burning kitchen range heated it.

But comparisons are meaningless. The IGY ushered in a totally new era. It was the biggest thing that ever happened to the Antarctic continent. Prior to it only small expeditions from various nations had sporadically visited Antarctic waters. Now 12 nations with great fleets of ships and planes, and thousands of men were establishing some 60 bases on the continent and its nearby islands. The IGY activities could not be considered a mere expedition but rather a scientific onslaught.

My assignment to head the Ellsworth Station was right down my alley. because it would bring me back to the general area of the Antarctic in which I had concentrated my past work. Nine years earlier I had made two long flights over the coastline at the head of the Weddell Sea and into areas south of it. At that time I discovered and named, among other things, Gould Bay, a deep indentation in the Ronne Ice Shelf. Seventy miles farther inland our radio altimeter had recorded a gradual rise in the surface beneath. Our diminishing gasoline forced us to return. I knew then from my observations of the surface that the possibility of a frozen strait connecting the Weddell Sea to the Ross Sea on the opposite side of the continent did not exist this far south and east. But what lay beyond remained a mystery. It was a challenge I could not ignore.

◆ ◆ ◆

My wife and I drove from Washington to Davisville, Rhode Island, for the sailing of the cargo ship USS *Wyandot*. Captain Francis H. Gambacorta said the ship was loaded to the waterline. Supplies had been funneled in from all over the country, everything from New Jersey-made catsup and extra tall Colorado telephone poles to bright orange Tucker snowcats assembled in Med-

An aerial view of the Ellsworth Station construction site at Gould Bay on the Ronne Ice Shelf. At left are the permanent buildings to house the research team and at right are the Jamesway Huts housing the construction forces. During the winter deep snow covered the station and tunnels were dug to connect the buildings.

ford, Oregon. After the hatches were secured, three huge crates containing our two Otter airplanes and one helicopter were hoisted aboard and stowed topside.

We had lunch on board with *Wyandot's* skipper and Captain Edwin A. McDonald, Task Group Commander of both the cargo ship and the icebreaker USS *Staten Island*. I had known Mac for eight years. We met in the Antarctic when he was skipper of the icebreaker USS *Burton Island*, which, along with another ship, visited my base at Marguerite Bay in 1948 and escorted my *Beaumont* to open water.

Minutes before *Wyandot*'s departure, a Navy chaplain gave a prayer for all hands over the ship's loudspeaker, and at 1 P.M. sharp on November 9, 1956, the mooring lines were cast off. We watched her pull away from the dock. Amid much hand waving and band music, *Wyandot*'s bow turned southward.

Staten Island had already left from Seattle; she would rendezvous with *Wyandot* at Panama. In two weeks I would fly to Valparaiso, Chile, to join the ships.

Departures from home are always hard, and I was torn in two directions. From the time we first met, my wife has always understood the drive that compelled me to go back to the polar regions. She had even spent a year in the Antarctic to aid my efforts. Now she would be left behind. At the airport she had difficulty concealing her feeling from our five-year-old daughter Karen, not, as she explained, because I was leaving them for 18 months, but because this was the culmination of our years of work and struggle.

Finn Ronne planning summer's operations during the winter of 1947 at Ellsworth Station while his wife prepares a dispatch for the North American Newspaper Alliance.

Forging ahead in the Weddell Sea off Gould Bay with icebreaker *Staten Island* in front and cargo ship *Wyandot* following.

The flight to Santiago, Chile, was pleasant and uneventful. I was met at the airport by representatives of the Chilean Navy, the U.S. Naval Mission, and the Chilean IGY. The following day I drove to Valparaiso and boarded *Wyandot*.

This was my fifth visit to Valparaiso, and I had several good friends there. Mac and other friends from the ship joined me for dinners at the homes of Dr. Olaf Olsen and Admiral Kaare Olsen, former Foreign Minister of Chile. On November 28th I gave a lecture, with the aid of an interpreter, and showed a color film of my last expedition for the Chilean Naval School in Valparaiso.

We sailed Friday, November 30, 1956, for Punta Arenas, 1,432 miles to the south.

On December 3, we approached the Roaring Forties with a rough sea on the starboard bow. Sea smoke and fog set in shortly after noon. Being a much larger ship than the *Staten Island,* we were riding rather nicely, and we could not help noticing that the round-bottomed icebreaker was having a rough time in the sea. We had several foreign observers with us. Two representatives with the Japanese International Geophysical Year found the constant rolling uncomfortable and Navy cooking without rice unsatisfying. The Chilean observer on board acted as our pilot through the Inland Passage. An interested bystander was the Argentine observer. Both nationalities claimed the sector of Antarctica for which we were headed.

Punta Arenas would be our last contact with civilization before entering the ice. For the 39 of us on board designated to spend the winter in Antarctica, it would be well over a year before we again would see the lights of a city. We arrived on the morning of December 5th. Two days later we departed from Punta Arenas and headed southeasterly for the Weddell Sea.

Our destination, some 3,000 miles away — more than half of which was choked with ice — was near an area that Dr. Wilhelm Filchner had discovered in 1913. I would some 34 years later expand the new horizons he had glimpsed to encompass what is now called the Ronne Ice Shelf. I was therefore deeply touched to receive en route a cablegram from Zurich that read: "Good luck. Filchner."

◆ ◆ ◆

In fog-shrouded seas we passed a few miles off the South Orkneys where Great Britain and Argentina maintained permanent bases. By December 15th, we were skirting the pack ice outside the Weddell Sea. Before we could set up our station, however, we had to navigate through the most treacherous ice fields on earth. A history of frustrated efforts in the ice-choked Weddell Sea had earned the area the epithet "hellhole of the Antarctic."

Ours were the first American ships ever to enter the Weddell Sea. At first we made good progress through the ice floes. Our goal was to spend Christmas at our tentatively selected base site on Bowman Peninsula. In good weather our small Bell helicopters did reconnaissance work in relays around the clock. They would radio back information on the ice conditions, guide us to open water leads, or point out heavy pressure areas to avoid. Every two hours they returned to the ship, refueled and took off again. In bad weather we relied upon our excellent radar coverage. As the pack increased in density, leaving no place to push the ice after it was broken, our forward progress slowed to a crawl.

At Cape Norvegia, the easternmost entrance of the Weddell Sea, the pack held us immobile for four days. Here we celebrated Christmas day with religious services and carol singing. Ice pressure had already caused a fuel leak in one of *Wyandot's* storage tanks, but it was fixed after 9,000 gallons of fuel oil spilled into the sea. Then, fortunately, the winds changed and created the necessary leads for us to proceed slowly along the eastern boundary of the sea.

While our ships continued to press forward, Mac and I flew by helicopter to pay brief courtesy calls on several foreign bases recently established. Dressed in rubberized cold weather survival attire, we looked for all the world like men from outer space. First we flew to the British Royal Society Base at Halley Bay, later to Britain's Shackleton Base. The ships then headed west for the Argentine General Belgrano Station. At all these bases our welcome was overwhelming. We brought gifts of fresh fruit and magazines. These couldn't have been appreciated more if they had been handfuls of diamonds.

On New Year's Day, when we were close to Gould Bay at the Weddell Sea, our westward progress was halted abruptly. The southerly cold winds that had cleared leads in the pack ice suddenly shifted. Warm winds from the north blew the heavy pack down upon us. Gould Bay, which I had discovered from the air in 1947, was jammed solid with heavy ice floes. I thought of Dr. Laurence McKinley Gould, Second in Command of the First Byrd Expedition and President of Carleton College in Northfield, Minnesota, for whom I had named the bay. At that moment he was aboard USS *Curtis* steaming to McMurdo Sound, 2,500 miles away on the opposite side of the continent, there to take charge of the National Science Foundation's International Geophysical Year Antarctic Project.

We were deep in the area where Filchner's ship *Deutschland* was locked in the ice for more than 14 months, where Shackleton's *Endurance* was crushed by the intense pressure and eventually sank. Now the devil ice had us in its tight grip.

For the next two weeks we experienced the worst ice conditions that the Antarctic has to offer. All of our efforts were frustrated by heavily rafted ice up to eight feet thick. Our 10,000-

horsepower icebreaker made numerous attempts to open a channel, but the track closed behind her, stranding the thin-skinned cargo ship. On one occasion the icebreaker made only 800 yards in a ten-hour period. Continual poundings barely dented the mighty barriers of ice. Pressure ridges rose more than 20 feet above jumbled icefields all around us. Never before had I witnessed such a treacherous mass of ice. We were isolated in a pack larger than Texas, in an area that was uncharted, unfathomed, and unnavigated.

Wyandot was virtually helpless. Ice had chipped off part of her propeller, and her steel plating was torn open below the waterline, causing flooding in a forward hold. Captain Gambacorta's crew worked desperately amid floating drums of gasoline to pump out the water and plug the leaks.

Then, just as suddenly as the ice had encased us, the wind swung to the south and the pack slackened, opening a beautiful water highway. We followed the leads for another 30 miles westward and in doing so became the first ships ever to sail in these waters. I had flown over this area nine years earlier and named it Edith Ronne Land (later renamed Ronne Ice Shelf) for my wife, a member of my 1946–48 expedition. Now on our helicopter flights the features were seen again exactly as I had mapped them in 1947. We also saw open water leads extending towards our predetermined landing site. When the ships were within 16 miles of our original destination of Bowman Peninsula, we were directed to retreat to the Gould Bay area.

Admiral Dufek's message to Captain McDonald stated: "You are not to be influenced by anyone's desire to break a record or place the base on land. The safety of your ships and men must be uppermost in your mind at all times. . . ." Mac, replying that he was "only influenced by advantages which would accrue by locating stations on land at maximum distance from other IGY stations," ordered that the two ships be turned eastward.

My feelings were expressed in my diary: "I have undying loyalty and admiration for the U.S. Government, the U.S. Navy, and specifically for Admiral George Dufek, whom I have known for many years since I first recommended him for polar service in the Navy. But I do not believe maximum efficiency in Antarctic operations is ever attained when an expedition is governed from afar by those who are unfamiliar with the on-the-spot, day-to-day conditions. If the President himself had ordered us to build a base on the shelf immediately, we could not have done so."

Indeed, *Staten Island* fired 88 rounds from her deck guns into the barrier cliff in an effort to blast out a ramp. It was a futile exercise — like the beak of a bird trying to chip a diamond. In my dairy I wrote: "The spirit of the officers and men at the moment is pretty low. The only time we laughed all day was when we received a wireless from Task Force 43.3: *Pass to Officer in Charge Weddell Sea Base. If perishable provisions exceed capacity of reefer and warm weather conditions endanger these items, dig holes in snow and store until cooler weather permits removal.*"

As we proceeded eastward Dufek continued to send confusing messages. We were told in a period of a week that "Time is running short. . . . You have plenty of time to build that base, so take it easy. . . . Gould Bay acceptable. . . . Build that base on the shelf between third and Greenwich meridian. Atka Bay is a suitable and acceptable site. . . ."

Dufek's last directive meant that we were to get completely out of the Weddell Sea and locate our station on Princess Martha Coast in Queen Maud Land. Those last instructions, contrary to the basic scientific purpose of our mission, left me no alternative but to bypass Dufek and appeal directly to IGY Director Larry Gould. On behalf of the scientists aboard *Wyandot,* I asked him to urge Dufek to reconsider his latest instructions. Several days later we were told to proceed to 41° West Longitude and build Ellsworth Station on the first suitable site. Dufek had backed down enough to allow us to remain in the Weddell Sea.

On January 27th, the 43rd day after entering the pack ice, we smashed through into open water. Moving slowly eastward, we came upon a low part of the continental ice shelf approximately 30 miles east of Gould Bay.

Henry Stephens, commander of our Seabee battalion, and I made a closer survey of the area from a helicopter. Then, landing from the icebreaker, we climbed to the top.

Skiing about three miles inland on the smooth barrier surface, we selected a site for Ellsworth Station. Beyond it lay the vast Antarctic continent stretching southward into the unknown. Mac heartily approved of our selection and directed unloading operations to begin.

The race against darkness and weather was on. Unloading

operations were placed on a 24-hour basis, in two 12-hour shifts.

Near the edge of the shelf we set up a supply dump. Then a trail party scouted for a safe route to our permanent base site. Following the skiers was a tracked weasel and a sledge carrying explosives and trail-making poles. The weasel was equipped with an electronic detector to check for crevasses.

Once the route was marked and proven safe, construction of our 18 prefabricated buildings moved forward at a good pace. As soon as a building was unloaded, it was hauled to the base station and assembled within a few hours by the Seabees. The station was made operative in 16 days, an estimated five week job.

Shortly before leaving, Captain McDonald formally turned over to me command of Ellsworth Station. Then, while some of the Seabees were still hammering nails into the last building, Captain Gambacorta headed *Wyandot* northward on her long homeward journey. The tired Seabees barely reached the *Staten Island* before her mooring lines were cast off.

We waved goodbyes as the two ships broke their way through the ice floes and disappeared into the hazy overcast. Their mission was completed but ours was just beginning. There were 39 of us — nine civilians, three pilots, eight Navy men from Experimental Squadron Six, eighteen men from Mobile Construction Battalion One, and myself. Like my father on the first Byrd expedition, I was the only person in the group who had ever been in the Antarctic.

CHAPTER *19*

ELLSWORTH STATION WAS ABOUT 70 percent completed when the ships departed. Racing the fading sun to finish the job before the winter night set in, we moved acres of equipment and supplies scattered around the station into tunnels and buildings. Within six weeks all scientific instruments were functional, and winter-routine duties had been established.

During this period I was stunned to learn of Byrd's death. Having been associated with him in polar activities spanning more than 20 years, I had seen this complex man in many moods — from white-faced anger to smiling Virginia-gentleman charm. In the truest sense he was not an explorer: He never drove a dog team, couldn't ski, and failed pathetically in his one attempt at roughing it. Yet, he achieved great fame and fortune from his polar exploits. In my view his success stemmed largely from his ability to persuade others — from Presidents on down — to do his bidding. He was a genius at raising money to finance expeditions and at finding dauntless individuals like my father to man them. Equally important, he had the knack for attracting public attention to his efforts. The press dubbed him admiral of the ends of the earth, and he was driven to live up to that illusory accolade despite advancing years and a tired, frail body. In my diary I wrote: "He certainly struggled to the last breath — not wanting to relax the grip he has held for so long on Antarctica." On March 17, we lowered the flag to half-mast and held a simple memorial ser-vice for Byrd.

Within three months I received word of the passing of another Antarctic hero — Wilhelm Filchner. In my cable of condolence to his daughter, I said: ". . . He was the pioneer in this part of the Antarctic. I admiringly followed in his footsteps here and continued his exploration into the unknown."

◆ ◆ ◆

Ellsworth Station was located on the Ronne Ice Shelf about 3 miles "inland" from the ice-filled waters of the Weddell Sea. The station was actually floating on the water — on ice 800 feet thick. By surveyors transit the height of the station was 138 feet above sea level. Delicate gravinometers determined undulations occuring regularly, bearing out the assumption that the station was afloat 2,500 feet above the ocean floor. Fifty miles south the ice shelf was 700 feet above sea level and resting on land. A sharper rise in elevation some hundred miles farther south was marked by heavily crevassed ice falls that formed an escarpment 4,000 and more feet in height. Inland from it rose massive mountain ranges. We first sighted them just before winter set in.

The long and dreaded winter night demanded that a man keep his mind occupied. Unrelieved darkness, below-zero temperatures, and blizzard winds brought outdoor activities to a standstill. Our scientists, busy recording phenomena inside and outside the earth's crust, would have plenty to do. The station's operating personnel, such as galley crews, radio operators, and utility men, would stand four-hour watches.

On earlier expeditions, I had always planned projects to stimulate my mind during the winter, building model ships or miniature dog sledges, for example. This time, my fourth Antarctic winter, I decided to try something more fanciful. Sitting at my portable Smith-Corona, I imagined a visitor suddenly dropping in to witness our actions. My task was to follow him around and record what he saw.

The Visitor — 1

IT IS EARLY MORNING on a day in mid-June. The dwellers of the ice-entombed city are ready to roll out of their sleeping bags and start the day. We meet our visitor down on the barrier edge, at the ship's docking site. It is at the cape of the icy peninsula, the only low place we could find to unload. Now it is deserted. The ice pack is close to the face of the barrier, forced there by the ocean current sweeping steadily toward the cape. It is midwinter in these latitudes. Killer-whales in packs of several dozen still poke their heads up through the ice floes, an alarming sight at close range.

Ah, I see our driver is coming down the hill. It is Crause, one of the Navy Seabee drivers; he wanted to come for us. I always seem to hit my head on that crosspiece in the door-opening on these weasels. The cabin is heated, so throw back your parka hood. We creep up the hill to the top of the barrier. Some of the old tracks are still here — those made by the tractors struggling up the slope with their heavy loads. Yes, those are crevasses, cracks in the bluff, right here, so the driver dodges them. The snow-filled ones are not safe for traversing. It was a pet project of Commander Isaac Schlossbach and Japanese observer Koreo Kinoshita, a Japanese university professor, to ski up here every morning to watch the crevasses change and shift or increase in width. But they never saw the ice move when they were here.

Rolling over the top of the barrier we see smooth terrain ahead of us. Several times we stop on the way. It is a striking view. My visitor asks if this can be real. He is not dreaming. It is true! In the direction we are traveling the level barrier is glimmering white and pure. It stretches hundreds of miles into the interior. Only wind-blown sastrugis break the otherwise unruffled surface. To the right my passenger peers into the deep rift of the bay ice. It is like a wedge southward into the barrier. It must be two miles wide here at the mouth. The cape of ice where we are

The constant motion of the surface ice in the Bay of Whales caused by the ocean currents often made small cracks in the ice into huge clefts.

The traverse party to the interior of Antarctica. Crevasse detector was attached and extended forward in front of the lead tractor.

may break loose and float away some day. We will be away from here then, I hope.

Off the sloping cliff in the foreground are ridges of age-old pressures forced high in the air. One huge ridge dominates all the others. Some seals are likely still in the water leads; but the light is not bright enough for us to see them. Those few remaining were too late in their migration north, when the waters were still open. They usually spend the winter here.

The ridge here is crisscrossed with hidden crevasses. A tractor towing a Sno-Cat was almost buried in one. The Sno-Cat was practically new, had only 100 or so miles on it, when it became immobile. The seismic man who drove it had gotten into the bad habit of starting off in highest gear. The clutch soon burned out, and a 15-ton Navy tractor pulled the Sno-Cat around from then on. In March, the five-man crew making seismic soundings approached too close to the edge of the bay ice, and the tractor crashed through under them. The crevasse was black and ugly. I will never forget the alarmed expression on the face of the senior glaciologist when he reported the trouble. It was as white as the snow he fell through. The escape was close, but now he too knows better. Practical experience is a good teacher. Our heaviest tractor, weighing 35 tons, eventually pulled the smaller one out.

We surely are hitting a bumpy stretch of trail now. I remember the tractors having a devil of a time crossing here. The driver stops again. That mound there is where we cache the explosives. We have tons of dynamite for the seismic program. The three dumps are 500 feet apart for safety. As the weasel creeps ahead, my visitor discerns a single lightbeam piercing the darkened sky. It's our searchlight beacon, burning all the time. A homing beacon for planes and men away from camp. Did I see a highway sign? Yes, I did. A sailor must have put it there: "Route 88 Illinois."

The cluster of poles on our left is the radio antenna system. They are 50 feet high and form a diamond-shaped pattern. There are two sets of four poles. The longer axis of the diamond is beamed toward Washington, D.C. One system only is used; the other is a standby. Strong winds easily blow an antenna leg down, and they are difficult to repair in the dark. The radio men had a tough time getting the poles up. They worked long, miserable hours on this project. I think it was minus 45 the day they finally called it quits. Only a few minutes now and we should be at the station.

The moon, aurora, and star-strewn sky give some light to see the gray outline of a rise. Here we are passing the Jamesway huts; 18 of them still there. The drifts have them practically buried now. Should you desire to enter one, I'm afraid you would have to shovel snow from now until Christmas. The Seabees slept here when building the station. The procedure of coming out to the camp every morning and back to ship at night was too time-consuming. The cooks served 800 rations a day — huge portions to keep the men working.

A tractor sledge caught in a crevasse on the barrier at the Ellsworth Station. The crevasse was approximately five feet wide and 50 feet deep.

We move past the last snow-encased Jamesways. They now contain all our emergency facilities — clothing, bedding, food, medical supplies. Extra stoves, galley range, generators, and radio facilities are there too. All safely stored inside in case of fire. The men feel happy about it.

Not far off looms the station. The drifts are to the top of the buildings. The blizzard last week was the heaviest so far. Two dark objects stand out high above the rest. What are they? The one on top of four columns is the "Aurora-airglow Observatory." The top of it is 30 feet above the surface. If you look closely, you will see four plastic domes projecting from the roof. Inside, the observer has unobstructed views in all directions. The other, a mosque-like dome, is part of our upper-air research program of meteorology. We call it the "Rawin-tower." It is full of intricate electronic instruments to measure conditions high above the earth's surface.

Delicate recording instruments mounted inside a light plastic box are carried skyward by a hydrogen-filled balloon every six hours. A sliver of a thermometer marks temperature, a treated plastic strip records humidity, and barometric pressure is registered. The plastic box also contains a small radio. It automatically transmits recordings or impulses indicated on the three puny instruments. I did not believe my eyes when I first saw the size of the plastic box — six-inch sides and a short transmitter tube two inches in diameter attached to the bottom. Reaching various altitudes in the balloon ascent, a tracking unit (let us simply call it a receiving radio) is mounted inside the mosque-shaped dome. It catches the impulses from the three instruments aloft and relays the information to another set of involved instruments where meteorologists tabulate and interpret the data. Inside the mosque also is mounted a radar unit that tracks the balloon until it bursts.

Let's pause now for a moment and stretch our legs. The seats in the weasel were pretty crampy — can't sit in them too long. Guess they were not intended for lengthy pleasure rides. Oh, look! These masts form another antenna system. We contact other stations within the Antarctic on it. The single mast farthest over, much taller than the others, is for another purpose — ionospheric recordings. It rises 80 feet into the air and is anchored securely in all directions. We had a tough time to raise it. On our first try, when it was almost up, a guy-wire gave way and it swung down. Tons of steel missed a man by a few inches. Masts of our radio-homing beacon you can see to the extreme right.

The aviation buildings and airplanes are in that direction. We will reach them before the end of the day.

◆ ◆ ◆

Where do we enter our fair city? Right here, follow me. In this type of morning light you can see your immediate surroundings. The piece of canvas facing us on the sloping snowdrift you may think was just thrown there; but that is not the case. It's one of seven entrances to our community. Be careful when you slide down. I should have cautioned you. There is a wooden stanchion projecting on the left. Only last week it was my misfortune to hit it with my hip. You missed it, but now you know.

In this tunnel the scientists keep the crates for the instruments. Of course, tunnel lights burn day and night now; just follow me. This passage leads to the Administration Building. We seem to be the only ones using this rear entrance. These large steel boxes contain liquor, enough for 50 years. The Navy didn't want us to run short. We keep it under lock and key.

Oh, before you go on your way, let me acquaint you with the general layout of the station. It will help you to become oriented. Not all the tunnel signs and building markers are up yet. They are still under construction in the carpenter shop. Picture yourself looking down a main street. Three cross streets terminate 100 feet or so in dead ends. In each block you find a house set back about 12 feet from the curb. At the west end of Main Street, where you stand, is a small house. At the eastern end is a fuel depot and garage. I almost forgot, a back alley ties together rear entrances of the flat-roofed buildings. These shortcuts come in handy.

All buildings in our colony, regardless of size and purpose, are fabricated on the same general principle. When I watched the Seabees put together the first building, I was surprised at the speed and ease with which it was done. Floor, roof, and wall panels are identical in size. Plywood sheathing covers the inside and outside surfaces with four-inch-thick fiberglass insulation packed between them. The protective insulation value is sufficient down to 80 degrees below zero.

The type of foundation we use in the buildings is unusual.

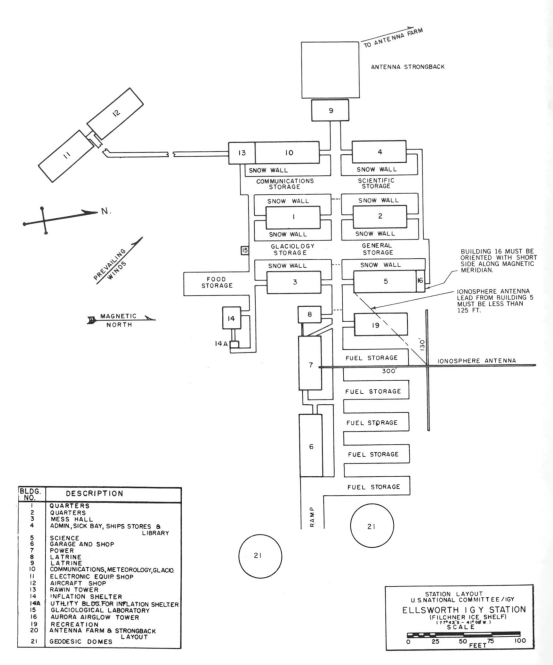

TO ANTENNA FARM

ANTENNA STRONGBACK

N.

PREVAILING WINDS

MAGNETIC NORTH

SNOW WALL
COMMUNICATIONS STORAGE

SNOW WALL
SCIENTIFIC STORAGE

SNOW WALL

SNOW WALL

SNOW WALL

SNOW WALL

GLACIOLOGY STORAGE

GENERAL STORAGE

SNOW WALL

SNOW WALL

FOOD STORAGE

BUILDING 16 MUST BE ORIENTED WITH SHORT SIDE ALONG MAGNETIC MERIDIAN.

IONOSPHERE ANTENNA LEAD FROM BUILDING 5 MUST BE LESS THAN 125 FT.

130'

IONOSPHERE ANTENNA

300'

FUEL STORAGE

FUEL STORAGE

FUEL STORAGE

FUEL STORAGE

FUEL STORAGE

RAMP

21

21

BLDG. NO.	DESCRIPTION
1	QUARTERS
2	QUARTERS
3	MESS HALL
4	ADMIN, SICK BAY, SHIPS STORES & LIBRARY
5	SCIENCE
6	GARAGE AND SHOP
7	POWER
8	LATRINE
9	LATRINE
10	COMMUNICATIONS, METEOROLOGY, GLACIO.
11	ELECTRONIC EQUIP SHOP
12	AIRCRAFT SHOP
13	RAWIN TOWER
14	INFLATION SHELTER
14A	UTILITY BLDG. FOR INFLATION SHELTER
15	GLACIOLOGICAL LABORATORY
16	AURORA AIRGLOW TOWER
19	RECREATION
20	ANTENNA FARM & STRONGBACK LAYOUT
21	GEODESIC DOMES

STATION LAYOUT
U.S. NATIONAL COMMITTEE / IGY
ELLSWORTH IGY STATION
(FILCHNER ICE SHELF)
(77°43'S - 41°08'W.)
SCALE

0   25   50   75   100
FEET

Map of the Ellsworth Station.

It's simple, and I should have thought of it long ago and been spared many weary hours of snow-shoveling. Perhaps the mind is more mechanically minded today than a decade ago. We used to dig out snow four feet into the barrier and set the floor support on a solid surface. This was not always so easy to do. A foot or so below there would be hard smooth ice. From then on it was necessary to use an ice axe. It often happened that the digging was almost completed when a strong wind would spring up. The fine drifting snow would then fill in the foundation in a matter of hours. A lull in the wind, and we would be out there digging again like mad.

Here we used a long scraper blade on a tractor. In a matter of minutes the rough snow surface was leveled. Side by side on it were laid timbers three-by-eight inches thick and three feet long. Long stringers of heavy wooden beams were then bolted at right angles on top. Two such units formed the footing for the long sides of the building. The construction men were experts; they hit it level and straight every time a new building shot up. Spanning the side footings, steel structures 25 feet long were strung across the width. Being 14 inches in depth, they were rigid and did not sag. By anchoring them on wood off the snow, heat from the building would not be lost by conduction to the foundation. Any chance of settling or tilting of the building by melting was eliminated. In this respect we are better off than our counterpart in the Arctic. He has the permafrost to fight, and that's a mean opponent. Summer's heat melts the ice of the permafrost and softens the ground. I walked over it at Thule, Greenland, and sunk in above my knees. Foundations there floated; and tilted houses were not uncommon sights.

On top of the steel structures at Ellsworth, floor panels were bolted down. Wall panels, butted against each other, were now erected along the outer edges. Thus the shell was formed. Fabricated steel structures, similar to those supporting the floor but lighter in weight, spanned the width of the building. They were fastened to the upper edge of the wall panels. On top rested the roof panels, secured firmly.

A clever device locked the butt ends of the panels. It consisted of a tapered wedge, half of it fastened to adjacent panels.

A tapered clamp, hammered on, trussed the two surfaces tightly. This assured a sealed joint, as solid as if it were molded. A few roof panels had double window-glass inlaid. It gives us no daylight now, but it will when the sun returns. I will enjoy the one in my quarters. Wall and roof panels were painted red on the outside and pale green on all inside surfaces. A heavy waterproof tarpaulin covers the roof, thus preventing snow from melting by the building's heat. I believe you understand the detailed construction of the buildings now. They are compact and solid, and 100-mile winds can't tip them over.

The Visitor — 2

I TRUST YOU ARE now sufficiently oriented to find your way through our community for awhile without further help from me. I have other things to do, you know. So please feel free to roam where you will and make your own observations.

Thank you, Skipper. I am sure that I can manage quite well without your presence. Goodbye.

It would be best, I suppose, to take up where he left off and continue on through the tunnel. Naked light bulbs glare as in a used-car lot. I see that wood framing was used extensively. Wide planks laid down on top of the snow support the structure, and upright timbers spaced four feet apart support the crosspieces of the roof. Now what is this? Chicken-wire meshing with open burlap material on the outside. How could that keep out the drifting snow? I'll tell you how. Like anthills in the woods, snow mounds had been built up all along the tunnel's south side by the prevailing winds. Snow soon covered the tunnel, and as it compacted, turned to blue ice — solid and hard as granite.

The icebox-type door is heavy to swing open. Inside, in the dimly lit vestibule, I see the reason — a strong cylindrical spring that presses against the door. In polar camps many men never learned to shut a door after them. There is no chance for perpetrators of this sin to continue it here. I let go the door and it slams shut, shaking the building. I promise not to do it again.

For years men have talked about jet heaters, but I never had seen one. Here in the vestibule, I am confronted with the monster for the first time. An ugly thing, it consists of a rectangular steel box supported by four legs. From it sprout eight tubes. The entire machine is dark green and reminds me of an octopus. The arms — or ducts — are entangled in steel crossbeam structures, snaking through them to transport heat to various parts of the building. Another jet heater takes care of the opposite end of the building. Fed through copper tubing from a 60-gallon fuel tank, the octopus-like heater comes alive at the touch of a finger on a thermostat. It spews out heat through registers fastened to the wall panels. How convenient, I thought. Amundsen would have examined such a contrivance twice to believe it. I look past the heater to a pair of skis and poles leaning in a corner. Too dark to use them now.

My eyes glance down at the floor. It is covered with tile — bright squares of light and dark green. What a luxury in the Antarctic.

Sweet, soft music falls on my ears. Which door shall I take to find the source of the music? I recognize the tune — "Galway Bay." The door immediately to my left swings open and the Skipper greets me with a smile. I never thought a Norwegian would start the day playing Irish music; I wonder if there is a reason for it. Now I knew where he went when he left me out in the tunnel. To wash up before breakfast.

The Skipper's quarters occupy a corner of the building partitioned off into a 14- by 12-foot room. A green rug covers the cold tiles. I learned that most of the men have provided themselves with floor covering. Some have used felt packing from crates; others have woven rope mats and made rag rugs.

To the left, just inside the door, I see a full-size bed with a Beautyrest mattress on it. White Navy blankets cover it. I lift the blankets a little and am disillusioned to see ironed bedsheets — without a wrinkle. I had always believed that polar explorers lived in igloos, dressed in furs, slept in caribou sleeping bags, and ate their dogs. But what do I find? Luxury and easy living. Just listen.

At the foot of the bed stands a dresser finished in rich mahogany. Next to it is a wash stand. Wall lamps cast a warm glow.

A $95-a-day bedroom suite at the Waldorf is not better arrayed. A high-fidelity record player sits on a green plastic-top table — the source of the Irish music — and a tape recorder and a stack of records are alongside. To the right of the table sits the Skipper at his desk, his typewriter in front of him. An upholstered green chair is next to the desk. The wall behind is covered with the American Geographical Society's latest map of the Antarctic. It brightens up the room, as does the American flag next to it. I see pictures of his wife and their six-year-old daughter Karen. In one corner is the red, white, and blue emblem of the Explorer's Club of New York. On top of a bookshelf are models of sledges like those the Skipper used on exploring trips when dogs were the means for surface travel in the Antarctic.

It's almost 8:30 now. The Skipper walks out, and I follow him. He goes through the other door, the one I hesitated to open when I first came in. The small office is brightly lit. Office supplies are stacked to the ceiling, and in the corner is a 500-pound safe. The doctor's narcotics are in it.

"Breakfast is on," echoes from the adjoining room. The call is for Commander Charles McCarthy, Executive Officer, who is also in charge of the aviation unit attached to the station. He has gleaming eyes and an Irish sense of humor. A bushel basket of hair covers his head, counterbalancing his enormous black, bushy beard. He declares that it won't be trimmed until his children see him. He speaks slowly and deliberately as if every word is the final result of cautious consideration. "There is nothing more beautiful to wake up to in the morning than Irish music," he says. I follow him through the dispensary, into the vestibule at the other end of the building, and onward toward the mess hall.

Men in light attire pace quickly down the main tunnel. It's 47 degrees below zero in the tunnel, but 58 below outside. The thoroughfare is wide enough for a car to drive through. The entire length is clean — not a trace of trash anywhere. Should a fire occur, the men would have room to fight it. A memorandum on the bulletin board warns: "We cannot be careful enough."

Skipper and Exec turn off to the mess hall, three buildings down. I breeze through before the door slams shut. Inside the

door is that green devil jet heater again. The vestibule opens on
the left into the mess hall and blocks the piercing draft from the
tunnel. Light green color on walls and ceiling makes the hall cozy.
Newly swabbed linoleum sparkles under a constellation of ceiling
lights. An urn on the counter near the wall produces coffee un-
ceasingly. Two electric toasters are close by. The rear part of the
building embodies the galley. The floor is covered in light green
tile, and the place is jammed with implements. A large oil-burning
range is the most irksome piece of equipment here. The cooks
have a smutty time with it. Excessive accumulation of carbon
causes burners to crystallize, crack, and chip. The griddle over
the firebox is badly warped. "Too low a grade fuel oil," mutters
one cook. The space is crowded with bake oven, meat block, sinks,
mixers, dishracks, and tables. Behind the range are mounted two
250-gallon tanks for melting snow. They are filled from the outside through a port in the roof. The loading bucket of a tractor
dumps the hard-packed snow into the opening, then it's shoved
into the chute feeding the tanks. The dishwashers alone use 350
gallons a day. Converting snow into water is a long and tedious
job. Mechanic Davis is in charge of that department. Some time
ago he started an ice pit, digging deep into the barrier for new
and clean snow, where the density is greater and yield of water
higher.

Edward Davis is boss of the galley. The Navy is his career.
He is here, he says, because he wanted to see the world's last
frontier. Davis sports an Abe Lincoln beard and an expanding
waistline; he has gained 15 pounds since setting up shop on
the ice.

Assistant cook and baker Richard Grobb grew up with Germans in Wisconsin, where he started mixing bread dough at the
age of 13. He has baked in the Navy for 16 years. At present he
is president of a coffee klatsch advisory council on how to run the
Navy and the world. No one recognized him this morning because his bushy beard had disappeared during the night. Alvin
Mathis, assistant cook and helper in the galley, is a Navy hospital
corpsman. Dutifully pursuing dishwashing for two weeks in the
galley, he became attached to it — and again found life enjoy-

able. He had been down on it until then, because he and our young, inexperienced doctor saw eye to eye only in different directions. The doctor didn't want to share his domain in the dispensary, so Mathis asked to be transferred to the galley. He is a charter member of the coffee tribunal.

Tables have bolted-on stools without backrests. They are inelegantly designed and uncomfortable. It is the prevailing thought that they were mistakenly sent to the Antarctic instead of to a concentration camp in the Soviet Union.

A variety of juices are on the counter — orange, lemonade, pineapple, grape. My hosts gulp them down. Fresh fruits and vegetables are not obtainable. The nearest fertile soil is 2,000 miles away. The doctor has placed small bottles of "decavitamin" tablets on the counter, and most men take two every morning.

At the counter the men give the cooks their breakfast orders. Rations are not scanty at Ellsworth Station. The Exec has scrambled eggs, French toast, sweet rolls, milk and a large cup of black coffee. A complaint is heard from one customer: "Cheese omelet again from Wisconsin?" A voice from the end of the table reassures him: "Heck no, the cook just told me it's imported from Brooklyn." By now the table is filled with 14 hungry men. They put away food like a football team in training.

"You know, Mac, it's a rare sight to see so many ugly faces right here at one time, Thiel and Brown excepted — they shave for breakfast." Behrendt's wisecrack draws a quick retort from the Exec: "The three of you can't grow a beard; if you could, you would raise seeds in the face and transplant to the top of the head this winter."

On Sundays and holidays only two meals are served. From 8:30 until 12:30, the men can then order anything they want. A hard-working enlisted man and a leisurely civilian each consumed four large steaks twice in one four-hour period. "Steak twice a week is not enough for these fellows," the cook snorted. The men are all gaining weight fast. Leonard Crause, the youngest at 19, gained 40 pounds and grew three inches in five months.

I amble toward the door to continue my tour, checking the bulletin board on the way out. The film listed under "Movies Tonight" draws a comment from one of the men. "Saw that one 20 years ago." Of 290 full-length films, about 75% of them are classified as bad motion pictures. The men watch them just the same; it gives them relief from routine life. Commencing every evening at seven o'clock, the mess hall is converted into a picture theatre by rearranging the tables and adding a few extra folding chairs. A collapsible screen is set up in front of the bulletin board, the projector on the counter.

During the movies, beer is allowed. Some men drink two dozen or more cans in an evening. It is cheap, only 11¢ each. Although some of the men drink too much and get drunk once in awhile, an order from higher authority condones it: "Let the men have all the beer they want, provided they pay for it."

The Visitor — 3

By 9 A.M. the men have left the mess hall to begin their working day. There must be a reason for the punctuality, I guessed, even here. Perhaps it is best for morale that the men keep busy. Amundsen believed that. His men always had strict working schedules. The cooks by now are busy washing and stacking dishes and swabbing the floor. It is said there is no dirt in the Antarctic, but . . .

From what I know of the station layout, I think it best to retrace my steps to the Administration Building and walk beyond it to the photographic laboratory. The icy steps into the building are slippery. I regain my balance and hang onto the tightening bar of the door. It must be pulled upward to unlock. I lean my weight against it, and the massive door swings open. The vestibule is poorly lighted, but I make out "Photolab" on a door. I push the door partly open.

Walter Cox sits at his desk, a spotlight illuminating his tiny working area. He is making negatives, putting them in envelopes, and filing them. Stacks of film are in front of him. The laboratory was completed only a short while ago. It now has hot and cold running water, and the electrical connections and outlets are in place. Cox did much of the work at night, in his spare time. He has served six years in the Navy, first seeing the Antarctic on a summer trip when attached to the photographic staff on *Deepfreeze I* ° the previous year. He is of the opinion that he is the best photographer in the Navy. His goal is to be promoted to Navy Chief, and he has ambitions to be a Hollywood photographer. Of medium height, rather chubby, Cox has a round face and a small stubby nose that points as high in the air as his aspirations. He claims to hold the beer-drinking record at the station — 35 13-ounce cans consumed in one evening. Mathis, the hospital corpsman turned assistant cook, is runner-up with 31 cans.

I follow Cox into the darkroom, softly lit by a safety light mounted on the wall. There seems to be good order here. Everything is clean — new, too, of course. A long stainless-steel sink covers the left wall. It holds the washing tanks for developing and fixing prints. Spigots for hot and cold water are at the end. Drainpipes lead through the floor panels down into the snow. No problem here with waste water. It melts the snow and sinks into the barrier. It is said that there are large caverns underneath the buildings from the constant pouring of water.

A large picture is stapled to the wall. It is a vertical shot taken of the buildings before the drifts started to cover them. The long shadows indicate that the sun must have been on the rim of the horizon. A comparable picture taken at the end of winter would show the great changes drifting snow can make. But I will not be here to see it.

Across from the photolab, on the opposite side of the vestibule, is the washroom for officers and civilians. A long wash bench fills the space to the left, and individual wash basins are on it. Over the sink, next to it, are spigots for hot and cold water, and a shower stall is in the corner. A sign reads: "Check the water-level in the tank." Should the tank run dry, serious damage would result. Posted on the wall is the modern-day explorer's schedule for using the laundry equipment. The machines are in constant use. Heavy woolen pants, shirts, socks, and long woolen underwear are loaded into the washer after breakfast, transferred to the

---

° *"Deepfreeze"* was the original code-word for all the U.S. Navy's Antarctic operations with the years added — *Deepfreeze 59."*

dryer at lunch, and picked up at supper. This must be the age of softness. The old-timers woud rather freeze to death than wash heavy underwear.

There is Walter Davis now, the machinist, putting a new gasket on a valve flange that was leaking water. He is a huge blond man, heavily set, and powerful as a giant. A quiet and hard-working soul, he is one of the most dependable men in camp. Up at six o'clock every morning, including Sundays, he can always be found repairing tractors, heaters, washing machines, pumps or motors. Davis now lives in the garage, where he built a sleeping space. "Too boisterious in the bunkhouse — could not sleep," he said.

A door in the vestibule leads into the ice-crystal palace. I go in to take a look. It is as cold as the outside and more drafty than a windtunnel. Shivering at the thought of it, I quickly sprint back to the door leading out, firmly pull it open, and jump down the three steps to the level of the main tunnel. I'm afraid the door slams shut. Again.

The radio room, glaciological office, and weather central are located across from the Administration Building. From the weakly lighted vestibule, I enter a narrow passageway. The first opening I come to is on the right. An "Exclusion Area" sign is suspended from the ceiling structure. I have to duck down to miss it. What can be the reason to keep the other men out of here? Something secret? More likely, the radio operators do not want to be disturbed while sending and receiving Morse code.

A high workbench to the right of the door opening has a mass of electronic gear on it, and small tools are spread around in a jumble. At the far end, Chief K. K. Kent is bent over an instrument, soldering tiny terminals onto small studs protruding through a mass of multicolored wires underneath the panel. He hangs the soldering iron on a hook, straightens up, and grunts "That should do it." Kent, slender, blondish, has a mustache he twirls to sharp points. Doing it is his pastime. Kent has spent 11 years in the Navy, and he wants to finish 30 before retiring. Bagpipes and plaids hang on the wall in the radio shack. He plays on them, too — mostly at night when on watch. Men sleeping behind a partition wish those squeaky pipes never had been invented.

Three radio receivers, each about the size of a breadbox, sit on shelves over a desk next to the transmitter. Robert Haskill, an operator, adjusts dials on the one in the center and puts a new sheet of paper in the typewriter. He now dons headphones and begins typing. I hear signals coming through his phones. He is copying traffic from Balboa, Canal Zone. An amateur wrestler, Haskill shows off his manly tricks in the recreation hall. Bruises, puffed eyes, and some discolored noses are often seen — usually on Sunday mornings.

The radio shack is a busy place. Charles Forlidas, another radio operator, sits back-to-back with Haskill. Forlidas is a pipe smoker and is working hard to grow a beard. A member in good standing of the beer-drinking fraternity, he enjoys making wisecracks during motion-picture showings in the evening.

Being invisible, I cannot walk up to Chief Kent and ask, "What's behind that curtain?" I have to be more subtle and appeal to his subconscious self to open the drape. My silent command is obeyed immediately. Aha! There sits the Exec with headphones on, working the amateur radio.

The ham set is the greatest morale builder at the station, enabling the men to speak to families and friends back home. The Radio Amateur League helps them send and receive ham-grams.

I watch the Exec turn the dials. Suddenly, a voice crackles through the set: "This is ice island T-3 in the Arctic Ocean calling." The Exec gives his own call signal — KC4USW — and they chat all about their radio equipment. Now another voice comes in. It is Ike from Glenview, Illinois, ready to put a phone patch through for one of the men. Soon a young IGY civilian is in intimate conversation with his sweetheart at a midwestern university. They should have a little privacy, I think, at least here, although ham operators all over the world listen in. I'll move on.

I tiptoe down the corridor. Sparsely lit, it ends in a section spanning the width of the building. One must go through it to reach Weather Central in the rear. A partition splits the glaciological space into two rooms. The first one is full of instruments, gauges, racks of thermometers, ice axes, rope, and other outdoor accessories. Large cabinets are filled to the top with paraphernalia. On a table I glimpse a drawing showing tabulations in ice and snow at various depths. Next to it I see a calculating machine and a typewriter.

Through a slit in the green curtain that shields the opening into the second room I discern two men. They are crouched over a table, their backs towards me. Table lamps brighten their working space. One's nose is so close to the table it's almost touching. Nearsightedness probably. A look over his head divulges a notebook with the tiniest handwriting in it. Hugo Neuburg is senior glaciologist and one of nine civilians here. A six-footer with massive shoulders, he is as powerful as a bull. He sports a goatee not envied by anybody. His nose is not begrudged either. When exposed outside, it easily gets frostbitten. When the mercury drops below zero, he rushes inside to restore circulation. Losing a nose must be terrible. As far as I know, it has never happened in the Antarctic.

Next to Neuburg sits Paul Walker, another glaciologist. Walker, also a six-footer, has a dense beard and a mop of hair sorely in need of trimming. In another month it will be difficult to tell whether he is coming or going.

Neuburg struggles to get into his heavy polar clothing. A nose protector is held in place with an elastic band around his neck. Walker now pulls on his parka. Their destination is the deep pit, 200 yards south of the station. There the character of the snow and ice is studied. Sample cores will be taken at intervals, until the 100-foot level is reached.

When the glaciologists complete their studies in the pit, the seismologists will take over. Borings will be made with augers to reach another 50 feet into the barrier. That would then be below the waterline. Deep in the small hole of three inches diameter, explosives will be set off to determine the velocity of sound and vibration through snow. The third man in Neuburg's party arrives. Nolan Augenbaugh, geologist and helper, is quartered with the aviation group in Barrack II. Short, chubby, exceedingly serious in looks, he has a red face with fiery eyes and a wild-growing beard. It is rumored he has a bad temper — probably brought about by two hitches in the Marine Corps. Clouds rim his horizon, but the sunshine is there if one looks for it.

Neuburg is visibly jittery and anxious to get started. The

Digging in a 100 meter "deep pit" to study snow and ice characteristics.

Paul Walker, *left,* weighs snow sample from coring auger while Hugo Neuburg takes data to determine snow density.

three men have enough work carved out to keep them busy until
the ships come in January. Ice axes are used to break the hard-
packed snow. At the present level it's more like ice. The men re-
move the snow from the pit by means of a wooden box on runners.
The slope of the pit is about 15 degrees from the vertical. A weasel
is used to raise the loaded snow on a jury rig employing block and
tackle. A tent covers the pit so blowing snow won't fill it.

Density measurements are made by driving a two-inch-
diameter tube of calibrated length into the hard, crusty snow. The
content thus collected amounts to 500 cubic centimeters. Melted
down it gives about 300 cubic centimeters of water.

Until a few weeks ago, shallow-pit studies were made once a
week. Small thermometers were inserted a few inches apart along
the sides of the six-foot-deep trench. It was found that temperatures decreased by degrees with depth. In March, stakes were set
out in the snow over an area of several square miles southeast of
the station. Surveyor's transit tied them together accurately to
within inches. In the spring, they will be rechecked to determine

variations caused by the shifting of the ice shelf. The most impossible weather doesn't stop them from going to inspect their network of stakes. They hate to miss a single reading.

Now, as the three men duck out the door, I ponder what benefits derive from these ice and snow studies. Is is worth all the effort? I am reminded that glaciers once covered 32 percent of the earth's surface (now only 10 percent). Changes in glaciers provide information on climatic trends, and the Antarctic continent has an immediate influence on the weather. Continuous melting of glaciers and ice caps may have an effect on economic and political situations years ahead. Ports now ice-locked may open up to trade, or low-lying lands may be flooded.

I thought it best to leave the serious looking icemen; they have so much important work to do. The thought of digging a 100-foot-deep pit haunts me. I fear I will be shoveling snow in my sleep.

A flimsy partition divides the icemen's abode from the meteorology office. Poking my head through the wide entrance, I notice that, excepting the mess hall, this is the roomiest working expanse I've seen here. I remember when coming up the road from the barrier edge this morning that the Skipper pointed out the mosque-shaped structure at the right end of the station. Now I am directly under it. Senior Aerologist Walter May is in charge here. Fortyish, a little heavier than average, he has a jovial face with a beard — and stogie — like General Grant's. A good sense of humor, his free time is occupied in the study of philosophy and splashing paint on canvas. He is quite capable at both. With 17 years in the Navy, he admits to chasing hurricanes in the North Atlantic, typhoons in the Mariannas, and slant-eyed brunettes in Japan. "A good Navy Aerographer," he says, "has the ability to look into a girl's eyes and tell weather." Whether?

Three young enlisted men assist in the met program. Gary Camp is only 20 years old and is as strong as a prize fighter. The others are Thomas Ackerman and William Butler. Both are quiet in their daily behavior but rebels on weekends, when they want room for their feelings. Gerard Fierle, the only civilian IGY employee in the section, is here to install the automatic recording instruments for the U.S. Weather Bureau. His former abode was the wilderness of Alaska, where he adopted some of the traits familiar to the sourdough. Some of his adjectives would put a bo's'n's mate to shame.

The two enlisted men go outside to inflate a balloon. I follow them. At the rear entrance of the met building, a tunnel leads between the galley and the food cache. The walk is well lighted. Set back in a wall of snow is the jet-heater room that provides heat for the inflation shelter via long tubes buried in the snowdrift. Indirect heating is necessary because sparks or an open flame could cause an explosion where hydrogen is generated. The building, 20 by 16 feet, has large doors on top for vertical release of the balloons. A gas producing generator about seven feet in height stands in the corner. The opposite wall is cluttered with cans of chemicals stacked halfway to the ceiling.

Closing the side door carefully, Camp prepares to produce gas for the upper-air balloon run. He puts on safety goggles, rubber apron, and protective gloves. He goes about it in a familiar way, having performed the routine twice a day for almost six months. Utmost safety precautions are followed, because making hydrogen gas is a tricky and dangerous process. Camp brings over a five-gallon mixing can for mixing the chemicals and pours 6.5 pounds of aluminum chips and 10 pounds of caustic soda into it. He clamps on the lid and turns the can many times to mix the dry chemicals thoroughly. I notice he is very careful that none of the mixture touches his hands, because it can cause burns. Camp next pours the chemicals through a fill-pipe into the reaction chamber. Thus charged, the hydrogen generator is ready for operation. Never having seen such a machine in operation before, my curiosity mounts as Camp proceeds. He pours 10 gallons of water into the reservoir and mutters, "That should do it." Slowly he opens the reaction valve. Water trickles through a plastic tube into the generator reaction chamber. Within 20 seconds there is a faint rumbling, and the needle on the pressure gauge begins to rise. Now he opens the valve more, so that gas producing is accelerated, pouring into the balloon until proper lift is reached. He ties off the neck of the balloon, and it's now ready for use.

Butler, who entered the inflation shelter a few minutes earlier, attaches a small plastic instrument box to a line around the neck of

Aerographers releasing balloon that carries transmitter to record barometric pressure, humidity, temperature and other weather data.

the balloon, then pushes the large hinged walk-out doors open. Balloon and instrument in hand, he releases it into the cold Antarctic air. The balloon moves horizontally for a short distance before rising. Many of the instruments have been smashed to bits by striking buildings and antennas. The problem could have been eliminated had the camp layout been turned 180 degrees, as originally planned. Unfortunately, the officer in charge of the arrangement had his own ideas; and they were followed. Protest was to no avail. If the release point had been located on the lee side of the station, the balloons could have been launched in prevailing southerly winds. But it is too late to change now.

Retracing my steps, I pass the icemen's space and enter the passageway. My next stop is one of the two bunkhouses.

The Visitor — 4

As I TREAD THE planking, a rolled fiber-glass curtain across the main tunnel catches my eye. I had failed to see it before. Now I notice many fire curtains spaced along the passageway. In case of a fire, one has only to pull a drawstring, and the heavy, fire-proof curtain drops, cutting off draft. CO_2 chemicals under high pressure in red painted tanks are spaced in alcoves for easy access. Fire hoses, 250 feet long, are attached to each unit and can reach any spot at the station. A triangular steel frame, two feet to a side, brushes my shoulder at the corner of the narrow passage to the bunkhouse. Next to it hangs the clapper. Whirling the clapper inside the triangle produces enough alarm to wake the dead. This supplements the automatic fire-alarm system.

The cross streets are brightly lit from naked lights hanging from frost-encrusted overhead beams. Packing cases line the tunnel walls. Empty crates saved by the IGY civilians are in the left alley along with photographic stores and a confused assembly of reflector lights. The alleyway to the right is filled with all types of radio spares, reels of cable, pallets burdened with cases of motion-picture film, office supplies, and general stores. The second cross street, next to the mess hall, is similarly arranged, cluttered to the top with general household supplies, ropes, tackle, ladders, and recreational items. The rear alley leads to the food cache directly behind the galley. Narrow passageways wend between stacked food crates. At the far end is the meat cache. It is crammed with steaks, turkey, chicken, ham, pork, veal, and other products. Enough food is stored here to feed the men for six years. Davis, the cook, has no problems with food spoilage, because in Antarctica nature provides the best deep-freeze in the world.

I step into the quarters occupied by the eight enlisted men and two civilians of the aviation group. When spaces were first assigned, they expressed the wish to bunk together, and the Exec granted their request. They get along nicely.

The first room to the left holds the ship's service store. The lower half of the Dutch doors has a counter on the inner side. On it is fastened a "no admittance" sign. Probably to prevent men from helping themselves. A strict credit system is in force. The men can draw what they wish, but deductions will be made from their pay when the ships get here. Some of their monthly bills are quite high — mostly for beer. Earl Herring, Navy storekeeper, is in charge here and keeps an accurate account of items drawn.

The lounging area next to the ship's service store extends one-third the length of the building. It has tables, chairs, and benches; and the men spend much of their free time here. Fred Dyrdal, aviation tinsmith just off night watch, works at his favorite hobby — dabbling in oils. With 16 years in the service, mostly in aviation, he has covered the greater part of the globe. His strongly hewn face radiates a powerplant of energy. Word has it that he is one of the three hardest working men at the station.

Young airmen Ronald Brown and Larry Larson are sitting here with him. Brown, 19 years old, has already been in the Navy for two years. He has a pleasant way about him and is popular with the others. Larson, 20 years old, is the blond, Nordic type, rather slow in his movements. He plasters the bulletin board in the mess hall with his cartoons.

David Greany, aviation electrician, is his principal target. He is short and on the heavy side, with a boisterous manner. He passed out cigars a few days ago upon learning that he had become a father. When operating the movie projector, he provides a running commentary that some believe is more interesting than the soundtrack. With others in the aviation group, he works on spare parts during the day — between coffee breaks.

The room on the left beyond the lounging area is shared by the civilians Gerald Fierle and Nolan Augenbaugh. Neither is a housekeeper; clothing and gear are scattered as though struck by a tornado. The other side of the bunkhouse is divided into three rooms, sleeping the eight airmen. Each room is about 14 feet long and eight feet wide, sufficiently roomy for bunks and Navy lockers. Walls are covered with pictures of pin-up girls. Larson, Brown, and Herring share the first room; Atles Lewis, John Beiszer, and Allen Jackson the second. The far corner one is shared by Dyrdal and Greany and is the most orderly.

I slowly withdraw toward the front. The vestibule light is dim; perhaps a brighter one would disturb sleepers behind the partitions. In the dimness I lose my footing before reaching the tunnel. No cause for alarm. A spectator is not easily bruised.

Directly across the tunnel in the other bunkhouse are quartered the enlisted men of the Navy's Construction Battalion. The first room inside the door is shared by Bob Haskill, Charles

Forlidas, and Clyde McCauley. Next comes the lounging area, then innermost on the right are the three Navy Chiefs — Spear, May, and Kent. Their room is the largest one. On the other side sleep Cox, Mathis, and James Ray the utilityman. Next to them are Camp, Ackerman, and Butler. Finally, in the third room are Hannah and Crause. Their lounging area is crowded with models, beer cans, magazines, and books. I note that a light bulb is burned out in the vestibule. The lights are of necessity kept burning continuously. As a result, the base is running short of them. Hannah the electrician does not think they have enough to last out the winter. When the temperatures drops down into the minus 60's, the bulbs burn out quickly.

◆ ◆ ◆

Walking farther down the main tunnel, I approach the entry to the science building. In the vestibule is a wall of cabinets filled with office supplies and instrument spare parts. After John Brown snaps a padlock on one, I shadow him into the first room. Brown, senior physicist, is tall and slender with a sharply carved face. The scholarly type, he possesses an air of dignity. In his brightly lit laboratory stands our Ionospheric Sounder, six feet in height, four feet wide, and three feet deep. Mounted on casters, it can be moved around.

Walking to the rear of the intricate electronic machine, Brown removes a panel and exposes an array of small instruments. A multitude of colored wires connect them. This transmitter sends out radio-frequency impulses through transmission lines which lead to an antenna atop the 80-foot-high mast outside. I saw the tall pole this morning, before entering the underground labyrinth. An old grandfather's clock hangs on the wall behind the Sounder. One may wonder what part it plays in the instrument's function. Actually it's an important one. The clock is electronically tied to the Sounder's timing device and is set nightly for accuracy by time signals sent out by the National Bureau of Standards. Slamming doors made it difficult at first to keep such a precision instrument accurately controlled. A slight jar would throw the thing out of kilter. A sign on the door cautions: "Don't slam it — Damn it."

Donald Skidmore, Brown's assistant, tears an electronic unit apart at the workbench. I wonder if he can get it together again. Small and stocky, he has the stride of a Kentucky-Derby winner. Of the civilians, Skidmore is the only one married; his fifth child was born after he got here. A dynamo in perpetual motion, he has more projects underway and fingers in more activities than there are stars visible in the southern hemisphere. Sharing a room with Brown adjacent to the laboratory, he displays energy even when asleep. Men sleeping in the building are often awakened by Skidmore's sudden outbursts: "Oh, no you don't — Oh, no you don't." A graduate in business administration, Skidmore is also an ace in electronics. His varied experience has taken him many places and qualified him for many jobs, from male nurse in a mental hospital to supervisor in a manufacturing plant. He is ready to discuss any subject at the drop of a snow crystal. The men call him a walking dictionary.

A black eye and bruises on the right side of Skidmore's chin show up as he stands in one of the bright overhead lights. His association with Saturday night's celebrants resulted in him getting the worst of a tangle with Haskill. In a recent message to his wife, Skidmore alibied that "the same corner on the same door struck again."

Brown's and Skidmore's room is adjacent to the Sounder. Double bunks are tucked along the end wall; Navy lockers, writing desk, and boxes fill most of the floor space. Wooden slats across the roof structure support bundles, bags, and traveling cases. When Skidmore first came ashore, he was appointed "Chief of the Dunnage Patrol." Had stray animals been around, he would doubtless have started a dog pound as a sideline. His duties were to collect scraps of lumber, packing cases, and dunnage from unwrapped material used by the builders. His dump of rubbish soon was the greatest heap on the continent. At times, on scavenging walks through construction areas where Seabees were working, he came upon tools carelessly thrown aside. A hoarder by nature, Skidmore quietly picked them up and cached away in a safe place; he thought they might be put to good use in the wintry days ahead. His accumulation of tools soon took on the proportions of a hardware store. The tools would have been lost forever, covered by drifting snow, had not Skidmore collected them. Although he willingly shared the loot with others if done on his terms, he is first to be blamed when tools disappear — no matter where, how, and when. By the way, a supply of electric light bulbs, accidentally placed in Skidmore's belongings, have been found. Now the men will have plently of light during winter's darkness. Once again all in serene. And so is Skidmore.

The Visitor — 5

A NARROW PASSAGE down the center of the building leads to the science library. Edward Thiel's quarters are on the left. Sharp facial features and thinning hair give him the look of a scholar, which he is — the only one here with a Ph.D. Bunking alone, he enjoys more space than the other IGY civilians. Thiel's field is seismology. On graph paper in front of him are zigzag lines, and mathematical equations are scratched on sheets of paper. At the barrier's edge this morning, I had wondered how thick the ice actually was. Thiel's graph indicates it to be about 800 feet.

The science library is next to Thiel's room. It is well stocked with polar books and technical publications. A dark cylinder about a foot and a half high and about the same dimensions in diameter stands on the floor. A red light on top indicates that it is active; cables lead to a battery next to it. The machine is a gravity meter. It weighs about 40 pounds, is portable, and will be taken into the field next summer. It is so sensitive that the gravity change over a vertical distance of a foot can be detected on the instrument scale.

John Behrendt is Thiel's assistant in seismic work. The tallest man in camp at six feet, four inches, he is broad-shouldered and rawboned. Except for eyes, nose, and forehead, everything above his collarbone is covered with long, shaggy hair, blooming out like weeds in an uncultivated field. His strides are those of a giant. Some men here think that the two-man mountain tent he will use during traverse in the spring will be torn to shreds as he tries to get in and out of it. Although Behrendt appears to be even tempered, he enjoys an argument. He always has his verbal sword unsheathed.

The customary green curtain covers the opening into Behrendt's and Kim Malville's room across from the library. Sparingly lit, it's difficult to make out what's in it. Through a clutter of clothing hanging from the ceiling, I see double bunks at the left wall off the rear vestibule. Perhaps their wardrobe is there to dry. Behrendt works on Neuburg's deep pit, and despite sub-zero temperatures, a man will perspire freely. Windproofs and inner garments get wringing wet.

By the dulled vestibule light it's barely possible to make out shelves laden with camera equipment, chemicals, boxes, and odds and ends. Four dark-green hoses snake through newly cut holes in the outer wall and disappear into the rear tunnel. Malville's small office fills the corner on the other side of the vestibule. A star chart covers the wall above his work table. On this are film, graph paper, notebooks, and technical instruction manuals. A table lamp furnishes a soft glow in the chilly room. In fact, Malville uses it as a darkroom at times.

Malville, an aurora physicist, had a hard time last night when observing in the tower. Sleep suffers during aurora displays because he hates losing a single chance to record what he sees in the sky. Ellsworth's youngest IGY civilian, Malville finished school short months before the expedition sailed. Charged with the aurora and air-glow recordings, he is busiest on clear nights when the southern lights puts on their dazzling display. His youthful look and large dreamy eyes have won him the nickname of "Sleeping Beauty."

I saw the aurora tower with its four plastic domes at a distance this morning. Now I'll get to see it from the inside. Following Malville out the rear door of the building, I am led to four steel columns supporting a wooden platform. This is reached by a metal ladder in the center. Malville ascends first and, in the dark, quickly fades out of sight. Soon the beam of a flashlight shows through a rectangular opening, illuminating the shaft; the trap door is open. I should have taken gloves; bare hands on frigid metal rungs burn like fire. The 30-foot climb to the top through air seemingly filled with ice crystals leaves me gasping.

Malville snaps on bleary lights and slides the trap door shut. In the 20- by 8-foot observatory stands the aurora spectograph, mounted inside a steel housing about four feet high. Its upper portion extends into the plastic dome. Malville's head and mine are inside it now, looking out through plexiglass. Stars never visible in the northern latitudes flicker off and on. A brilliant moon high in the northeast shines over the frigid landscape.

The most distinctive and characteristic color of aurora is yellow-green; occasionally during spectacular displays patches of blood-red color flash into view. Very rarely, during twilight, is a blue-gray aurora observed. All these colors are produced by specific excited atoms and molecules in the upper atmosphere, and the exact elements responsible for such colors can be determined by the spectrograph. Using an instrument similar to a prism, the faint auroral light is split into a spectrum extending from deep purple and blue into the deep reds. This spectrum is photographed by an extremely fast fisheye lens — that has an angle of 180 degrees — using high emulsion film.

Moving to a crudely built wooden stand, Malville positions himself before the "All-Sky" camera, which takes pictures of the entire sky visible from the dome. On clear night he sets it to snap a picture every minute. How is this done? Uppermost on the camera, clear of obstructions in all directions, is mounted a convex mirror. It throws the light from the sky onto a flat mirror above it. This in turn reflects the visible sky into an automatically operating motion-picture camera mounted directly underneath the mirror. Auroras occurring within a radius of 250 miles are photographed with a 16-millimeter motion-picture camera, a frame of film advancing automatically after each 10-second exposure.

Under the third dome is the photometer, which measures the intensity of aurora displays. On a slow moving strip of graph paper is recorded the brightness. Turning my gaze toward the opposite end of the tower, I see a bunk with a mattress on it — but only 18 inches from the ceiling. Hardly room enough for a man to sleep; and of course, he doesn't. Malville takes visual observations from there. Fieldglasses mounted on a vertical frame give clear views directly above when the sky is clear of aurora and moonlight. He can then count faint meteors and record their direction and brightness.

That metal ladder was still cold; I was glad to be back in the science building again. Surely Malville cannot have more projects going on than those I have just seen, but he does — in the magnetic hut, some distance away from the other buildings. A magnetograph mounted inside constantly records changes in the earth's magnetic field. It consists of a small magnet suspended by a fine quartz fiber. Attached to the magnet is a mirror that reflects light from a projector onto a moving strip of film. As the earth's magnetic field changes, the motion of the magnet causes the reflected light to move back and forth, leaving a fine wavy line on the film. The magnetic fluctuations Malville records in the hut are best observed during periods of high sunspot activity.

Malville's magnetic hut is now buried in the drifting snow. To reach his instruments, he braves blinding blizzards and perpetual darkness. But these obstacles mean nothing to him. Obviously he is greatly attracted to his work.

As I pass through the building and out the vestibule, I notice that Brown and Skidmore have the front panels of their Sounder on the workbench; they are tracing wires to find a short circuit. Careful not to disturb them, I close the heavy door quietly.

The Visitor — 6

I AM ON MY WAY to the recreation hall, which is located next to the science building. No chance of anyone stumbling here. The place is well lighted. The common meeting place, it is open 24 hours. Except for a locker at the rear, it is one room — the largest single open space at the station. The ping-pong table at my left is in use, and to the right stands a shuffleboard where bearded men slide a polished weight back and forth with precision. A hi-fi record player in a mahogany cabinet stands on a table next to the locker. Popular songs are most favored, but a few of the men

enjoy listening to opera and the classics. They formed the southernmost opera group in the world with Chief May presiding.

Wrought-iron couches and chairs with bright red and green
cushions are spaced along each wall. Here the men can relax and
enjoy the music. Through the door opening into the hobby-shop
locker I see shelves lining the walls. Stacked here are boxes containing handicraft materials the Navy sent down. Probably the
best morale-builders in a polar camp, these keep the men occupied through the long winter. Building ship and airplane models
is a popular pastime. Some of the men tool leather, fashioning
handbags and billfolds. Oil-painting kits are also much in demand.
A great many finished products are already in the lockers, waiting
to be taken to the folks back home. With little more than pocket
knives to keep hands and minds busy, previous expeditions had
nothing comparable to these creative diversions.

In the rear corner to the left stands the only jet heater in
the building. Eight heating tubes fan out to registers spaced
around the room. A birthday party is held there every second
Saturday of the month for those born in that month. Grobb the
baker makes a huge birthday cake and decorates it with the
names of the celebrants. It is served with coffee after the movie.
Later in the evening a punchbowl is produced. It is emptied in a
matter of minutes.

When the recreation hall was first finished, Protestant church
services were held here. They lasted a few Sundays only. With
only four or five men in attendance, the religious effort was abandoned. Catholics did not fare any better. Seven of them held
Mass in the dispensary a couple of Sundays, when the medic of-
ficiated by playing services on the tape recorder. But it soon became evident that sleep was preferred to prayers.

More popular is the gymnasium, a few steps outside. A short
tunnel covered with heavy duck canvas leads to a Jamesway hut.
A small light bulb illuminates it. The wooden floor is covered with
a thick wrestling mat. Boxing gloves hang from the ceiling, and
weights are stacked in a corner. A space heater keeps the temperature right for a workout, perhaps; but it feels chilly here
now. I retreat through the darkened passage back to the rec hall.

Leaning on the pool table is William Sumrall. Born and raised in Mississippi, he is our expert on life in the deep South. The Exec thinks he is so far south now that when he returns to the small town named after his family, he will consider them all a bunch of damn Yankees. Like Conrad Jaburg, he is there to pilot a small airplane. They bunk together in the BOQ, a building 16 by 12 feet in size that was thrown together as the sun dipped below the barrier edge.

My next objective, via a short diagonal tunnel leading off the main tunnel, is the generator building. The passage is poorly lighted, and cold winds whistle through openings in the burlap-covered framework. The temperature has fallen to 53 degrees below zero in the tunnel. The red end-wall of the generator building is barely visible in the dim light from the main tunnel. Just then, the massive door swings open. James Hannah, first class Navy electrician, holds it wide, allowing me to walk through — unseen, of course. Hannah has 11 years of service and has hinted that he intends to stay in until his 20-year hitch is completed. He and Davis the mechanic are the hardest working men here. Both are tops in their fields and tackle any job in good spirit. They have been seen doing outside work with the temperature 60 below zero. Not smiling, but doing it. Hannah's walk is as smooth as a panther's. Proud to be a Texan, he thinks Heaven is the next best place to it. Part Cherokee, he has a profile like the one on the old nickels.

The generator building is 56 feet in length. Dull lights cast a pale glow over the cavelike room. Buried deep in snow, it is sheltered from the cutting winds and kept warm by heat from the generators. Evenly spaced in the center of the building, the five generators occupy the full length of the room. Rated at 30,000 watts each, they produce enough electricity to satisfy the needs of a small town.

Inside the door at the left are two huge galvanized tanks, one directly on top of the other. These, the emergency water storage, hold 2,000 gallons each. Exhaust pipes from the generators melt the snow, and the water then flows to the tanks below by gravity. Should snow melters in the galley or washrooms break down, water is available here. On the other side of the room, battery-charging units hum in harmony. Automobile batteries are kept fully charged so that tractors and other vehicles, now deeply buried in snowdrifts, can be started in January. Cabinets for storage of electrical spares and testing instruments are at the rear end of the building. Nearby is Hannah's workbench. High above his desk is mounted the heart of the automatic fire-alarm system. From the red box, wires lead to all the buildings. Should fire break out anywhere near small sensitive detectors fastened to the ceilings, solenoids located in this box will be immediately energized. A relay will set off the siren. It's a penetrating sound, one that can be heard, I suspect, as far away as the South Pole.

The rear door of the building leads to the garage. I enter a snow-laden tunnel and find "anthills" of snow on the south side, where fine snow particles sift through. It is pitch black at the door, and I fumble for the handle. Finally inside, I discover that the garage has the same roominess as the generator room. Referred to as the public works department, it's a busy place. Superintendent, general manager, owner, and laborer is Navy Chief Albert Spear. His responsibilities are vast, and he makes the garage function as he would a large industrial plant. During Chief Spear's 16 years in the Navy, he assisted in construction in many parts of the globe. One of the original Seabees first sent overseas to construct runways on Guadalcanal, he later took part in the battle of the Coral Sea. In his late 30's, he is a short, broad shouldered man with flashing eyes and a massive head of black hair. Cleanly shaven, he is always among the first to reach the galley in the morning. As a general rule the Chief abstains from alcohol, but he's addicted to cigars — and they are always the best obtainable. He is meticulous about his personal habits. Looking into his lockers, I see nothing out of order as much as an inch. The items appear to have been laid out by transit.

A typical Navy Chief, he can blow off steam and calm as quickly as wind after a storm. He came here for adventure, expressing a desire to stay over the second year. When darkness crept in on him in April, he changed his mind. Now he can't reach civilized shores too soon. Such is now the case with a few others, too. The Exec says, "I believe the demons got hold of my brain and made me volunteer to come to the Antarctic. Only been married 10 years — just a good start on my honeymoon — and I cracked."

Inside the door at right is the mechanic's "penthouse," built on a platform five feet off the floor. A slanting set of stairs provides entry to Walter Davis's 9- by 7-foot home. Bunk, Navy locker, table lamps, all shine above the tiled floor. An assortment of footwear and beer cases are stowed underneath the bunk. Davis has much to take care of from six in the morning to after evening chow. Twice daily he braves the outdoors. In temperature and wind that would force many a seasoned polar man inside to shelter, he drives the 15-ton tractor over the station area. First, he plunges over high wind-blown ridges on the south side to reach the mess hall snow melter. With the two-and-a-half-yard scoops on it, he piles snow on top of the galley roof, where the cooks shovel the snow into a chute. Davis then moves the tractor to the men's washroom roof, and a similar chute is filled with snow. To reach the other washroom is more of a problem. The one at the end of the main tunnel used by officers, civilians, and Cox's photo lab, it requires that Davis circle the station area. The heavy tractor's rumbling can be heard in every building. Davis then returns to the garage vestibule, where the tractor motor is kept running constantly. Because it's hard to start when cold, it has been allowed to run for months; it will continue to do so until January.

The end wall of the garage consists of doors reaching from ceiling to floor. Hinged on top, they swing inward and are hoisted with block and tackle. Vehicles can then be driven in and out. A vestibule outside the hinged doors is as wide as the garage and extends the same length. Tunnel construction is used here also — chicken wire covered with burlap. Except for the ramp outside, the place is covered by snow. Davis uses the shelter to stow tractor parts and oil.

A narrow passage leads from the vestibule directly to the eastern end of the main tunnel. I found it almost impossible to get through here because of the many cases of beer stacked to the roof. Across from them, on the opposite side of the tunnel, are fuel depots that form three side streets. Each holds about 500 drums of fuel, enough to heat the station for years.

The aviation group has the fuel detail for the winter months. Drums stacked four high are brought down by wedging out the bottom one in front of each layer. Usually six or eight drums then slide down to tunnel level. Lewis, aviation mechanic, loads them on a lightweight sled and drags them to front entrances. With hand pump and long extension hose, he fills fuel tanks in the vestibules. It's a seven-day-a-week job.

Lewis, another six-footer, is a powerful man. His strong arms and sledgehammer hands are the largest on any man here. He swings a 400-pound fuel drum around as if it were cotton. Pulling the sled, he moves into the main tunnel with a drum of fuel supported by aviation mechanic John Beiszer. Married, he thinks the Antarctic should be incorporated into a resort area for single men. He says, "I shall always appreciate seeing ice only in a glass from now on."

Beer cases on the tunnel floor provide a seat for a short rest. It is my first chance to relax and reflect on what I have seen. Skipper appears suddenly and walks to the garage vestibule. I follow him. He throws the canvas flap aside, and a cold breeze hits my face as we step outside. "I will take you as far as the Jamesway huts," he says. "The rest of the way down to the barrier edge you can manage yourself. Now you know what a polar base is like. Hope you've had an informative visit." There he turns and waves, then heads back to the station, its towers silhouetted against a cold moon in the southern heavens.

CHAPTER *20*

S HACKLETON BASE, ESTABLISHED BY THE British under Dr. Vivian
Fuchs, was constructed about a month before we started to
build the Ellsworth Station, although the Britishers landed on
the Ice Shelf the previous January, leaving only a skeleton crew
to over-winter. Ice conditions then had been the worst possible
and when their ship drifted northward in a violent storm, the
seven marooned men dug in on the ice-edge, setting up a pre-
carious shelter. With limited supplies, their winter-night had been
spent under the most austere conditions.

When the U.S. Navy's icebreaker *Staten Island* first reached
the barrier fronting this small British base, I flew in a 'copter to
pay them the first visit since they became marooned.

At the time we cruised westerly along the 150 ft. high barrier edge in ice-free water. The seven men who manned this
scanty temporary base were certainly glad to see us! We were
the first outsiders they had seen for about a year. They had gone
through a very rough winter in their small shack without a generator for light and living on a very limited supply of food. Fresh
fruit and other "goodies" from the huge deep-freeze and cooling
rooms of the *Wyandot* boosted their spirit. They were awaiting
the arrival of their own supply ship — once again stuck in the
Weddell Sea ice-pack with their leader, Dr. Fuchs on board.

Eventually their ship did arrive to complete the base before
the winters' darkness encased their tiny camp.

The British trans-Antarctic party was to winter during the
same time we were at the Ellsworth Station. Once settled into a

working routine, we communicated by radio with Fuchs and his men at Shackleton Base, about 65 miles to the east. Later we exchanged visits by plane. The British party's main objective was to make a crossing from the Weddell Sea, via the American South Pole base to McMurdo Sound on the Ross Sea.

At the first sign of spring, the entire group of 11 men, using tractors and two teams of sledge-dogs would commence the cross-continent trek. It was the aim of Dr. Fuchs to follow the exact route outlined by Shackleton in 1914–15 when he attempted to penetrate the Weddell Sea in his sailing ship *Endurance*. Unfortunately, at that time Shackleton's ship became beset in the treacherous pack-ice, causing it to drift helplessly for many months before being crushed and sunk by the tremendous ice-pressure caused by the violent ocean-currents that flow across the most treacherous of all the oceans in the world — the Weddell Sea.

As you may recall Shackleton's original plan turned out to be a life-struggle for survival. Miraculously, after drifting northward more than 450 days in the hostile Weddell Sea on a huge ice-floe, the men with Shackleton eventually reached open water in the vicinity of Elephant Island and landed on that lonely island. Shackleton departed with four companions in a twenty-two foot lifeboat with the hope of reaching South Georgia to obtain outside help. Meanwhile, the rest of the men in Shackleton's party made the best of it by settling down under the overturned life-boat and living on seals while awaiting a possible rescue. After a hazardous trip, Shackleton's party did reach South Georgia, but were forced to climb a huge mountain and make a dangerous slide down the other side before reaching safety at Grytviken whaling station. It is said Shackleton's hair turned snow-white from the rigors of the experience. It was a well-planned operation, however, because the following year a rescue ship picked up the men who had wintered on Elephant Island. Miraculously, not a man was lost on this — the greatest of all adventures ever enacted inside the Antarctic Circle. Now 42 years later Dr. Fuchs was ready to try the transcontinental journey.

Upon the sun's return, mechanized tractors of the British party fought their way about 250 miles south from Shackleton Base. One tractor fell into a crevasse but was pulled to the surface after much effort and the expending of hundreds of gallons of fuel oil. Upon reaching South Ice Station, calculations indicated a shortage of fuel due to the crevasse mishap.

In a radio conversation with me, Dr. Fuchs expressed doubt that the crossing would be continued unless fuel supplies for his snowmobiles were replenished. He asked if I could help by flying twelve drums to South Ice Station. In a cable to Dufek, I requested permission to assist the British. In the same cable, at the request of Fuchs, I asked that special permission be granted for the entire British party at Shackleton to be evacuated on our ships, together with my Ellsworth Station personnel, in case the transcontinental trip had to be abandoned that year.

I made arrangements to land at Shackleton, load the fuel drums, and fly them — plus a load of scientific gear left behind — to the British. Upon landing at South Ice, we were greeted by Fuchs and his men, eager to get underway again.

With my movie camera, I filmed the British fellows rolling the fuel drums out of my plane. Then Bunny Fuchs and I shook hands, and I wished him and his crew a safe crossing.

Returning to my Ellsworth Station, we flew over the rugged terrain that had plagued the British party. Gaping black holes were all over the area. Looking down over one crevassed ice field, I wondered how the British managed to get through without losing a tractor or a man. At the South Pole, Fuchs's party was welcomed by more than 100 men, including one of his own supporting parties led by Edmund Hillary, who had come by tractor from the American facilities at McMurdo.

Originally, Hillary's support party was told to await Fuchs's arrival, off the Beardmore Glacier; but being ahead of schedule and knowing that "Uncle Sam" would back him if need be, he decided to move on to the pole. The temptation to be the first to reach the South Pole in a tractor was too great for Hillary to resist. While they were en-route, the two "knights of the ice" had a strong discussion over our open radio frequency. "Stick to the plan!" Fuchs barked. But Hillary, not accustomed to take orders from the boss, did what he wanted anyway.

After about a week at the South Pole to rest and let the U.S. Navy mechanics get their vehicles in top shape, the Britishers continued to McMurdo.

Theirs was the first surface group ever to cross Antarctica

from one end of the continent to the other. It was an historic event. For it Fuchs was knighted by the Queen. I am glad we were helpful to our friends.

◆ ◆ ◆

Meanwhile, at Ellsworth Station our field program had begun in earnest. With hundreds of square miles of new land within reach of our airplanes, I was anxious to continue where I had left off on my 1947 flights when I had to turn back due to diminishing fuel. On most of these flights I sat in the co-pilot's seat and took notes on the geographical features unfolding below. From the 600 to 700 foot height of the ice shelf, the elevation rose sharply to an escarpment of more than 5,000 feet. As we came out of a cloud cover, a huge mountain range, brilliantly bathed in the sun, rose right in front of us. We obtained several lines of position by shooting the sun and thus established the general location of the mountains. Later we were to learn that what we thought was a new mountain range (which included *Dufek* Massif) had been sighted and named by a U.S. Navy flight-crew of a long-range Neptune plane from McMurdo Sound in January 1956. I had not thought it possible that the Navy crew had seen these mountains because their declared positioning of the range was about 140 miles in error. I also learned later that what is now referred to as Dufek Massif and the surrounding mountains were actually mountains first seen by the leader of the Belgrano Base, General Hernán Pujato, as early as October, 1955.

◆ ◆ ◆

Some 80 or 90 miles south-southwest, I discovered another impressive cluster of mountains. The highest summit I estimated to be about 10,000 feet, with other peaks almost the same elevation. Again I would experience the unique thrill of sighting unknown land. After several weeks of painstaking air-exploration, I delineated the outline of a huge new island south of Gould Bay. This was the high land I had glimpsed briefly nine years earlier. From the west cape of Gould Bay the island extends almost 200 miles to 80 degrees latitude South. It extends westerly about 120 miles with its highest elevation about 3,200 feet above sea-level. When the five-man traverse team from my station crossed the island, its seismic soundings proved land underneath to be 1,700

◆ 247 ◆

"Snow cats" used by small traverse parties to penetrate into the unknown during the International Geophysical Year Program, 1956–1958.

feet above sea-level at the highest point. It also discovered a deep ditch on the ocean-floor that extends part way around the island. Subsequent seismic soundings the following year eliminated the possibility that this ditch divided the continent between the Weddell Sea and the Ross Sea. The escarpment of the island, which generally forms the contour along the entire outline, was about 1,000 feet in height. This new discovery, geographically the largest and most significant of the IGY, was named after Lloyd Berkner, chief scientist of the U.S. contingent, and a friend of many years. I did not quarrel with the choice, although I had recommended that my greatest discovery be designated Case Island, honoring the senator who helped me fight for United States' leadership in Antarctic exploration.

CHAPTER *21*

B EFORE TURNING ELLSWORTII STATION OVER to our replacements,
I made certain that the base was shipshape. Floors were
scrubbed and polished, and the accumulation of ice and snow on
the buildings and tunnels was removed. Visiting Navy and Coast
Guard officers said the station was the best-maintained that they
had seen in the Antarctic. During departure ceremonies on January 17, 1958 — our two ships had arrived a week earlier — com-
mendations were presented to a number of the outgoing officers
and enlisted men for extraordinary performance of duties during
the year just past. The station was then transferred to the new
command.

With the icebreaker *Westwind* leading the way through practically ice-free waters, the ships made their way northward to the
vicinity of the South Sandwich Islands. There *Westwind* headed
for the Bellingshausen Sea, and *Wyandot*, the ship I was aboard,
set a course for Buenos Aires. Waiting for me there was my wife
Jackie and friend Kay Sweeney. Our brief stay was highlighted
by an invitation from Argentine Navy officers: Would I be their
guest the following winter on a cruise to their bases in the Antarctic? Frankly, I had not anticipated returning so soon to the
frozen continent; however, if the U.S. Government didn't object,
there was no reason why I couldn't make the trip. It turned out
that the State Department not only gave its approval and financial backing, but even arranged for me to take a cram course in
Spanish at the Foreign Service Institute. I would return to the
Antarctic not as an explorer but as a good-will ambassador.

Meanwhile, *Wyandot* proceeded to Santos, Brazil, where the IGY civilians and the military personnel of the wintering party were flown to Anacostia Air Station in Washington, D.C. Having accumulated much military leave, I remained in Brazil for a week with my wife and Kay. Then we flew on to Lima, Peru, where we spent 14 days in beautiful tropical surroundings. This was a great contrast to the rigors of the frozen continent, but it did not take me long to get accustomed to the luxury.

Upon my return home I was honored by the Washington Board of Trade with a luncheon at the Mayflower Hotel, where I addressed guests from government, the military and the scientific community. Lecturing subsequently took me from Hawaii to cities in western Europe. At the request of the Department of State, I told the world of U.S. activities under the IGY program. This lasted until it was time to visit the Argentine bases in Antarctica. I flew to Buenos Aires, went on board their icebreaker *General San Martin,* and headed south to the Weddell Sea.

After about 14 days in the pack ice, we landed at Belgrano Base. A tour of the facilities ended with us climbing into a puffing diesel vehicle for a 60-mile ride down the barrier edge to my old Ellsworth Station. I was disappointed and embarrassed to see it had deteriorated badly. With mixed feelings I participated in ceremonies transferring control of the American base to the Argentines.

Back aboard ship, we steamed northward, rounding the Antarctic Peninsula northward through Bransfield Strait to Deception Island, the huge volcanic crater that has provided a safe anchorage to mariners for more than 140 years. It was from the southern rim of this crater that Nathaniel Brown Palmer first sighted the Antarctic mainland on January 22, 1922. From the Argentine base here I climbed the steep mountainside to the spot where Palmer stood. From there, I too could clearly see the mountainous mainland over the southern horizon, one of the thrills of my life.

◆　◆　◆

In 1961 I returned to the lecture circuit. In Hamburg, Germany, the USIA office informed me upon arrival that a family living there would like to meet me. Accordingly, an appointment was made for me to have dinner at the home of Captain Alfred Ritscher. I recognized the name immediately.

In 1938–39 he led a German expedition to the coastal areas off Queen Maud Land in the Norwegian sector of Antarctica. In his ship *Schwabenland,* he was sent by Hitler to discover and claim land in the Antarctic. The expedition did an excellent job, as I learned after World War II ended. A friend of mine with the Department of the Interior phoned me one day and asked me to come to his office. He then presented me with two volumes of the Schwabenland Expedition. They were beautiful books with color photography mapping and a full report on the expedition.

Captain Ritscher spoke some English, and with my poor German, we had a most interesting conversation during dinner. He told me about the method used to launch his plane and how it was hoisted on board after flights. A most congenial person, he seemed fit enough for another voyage to Antarctica. But it was I, not Captain Ritscher, who was destined to return.

While lecturing in Europe during the fall of 1961, I received a cable from the Navy Department that I was to fly to the South Pole in a party of distinguished visitors to commemorate the 50th anniversary of Amundsen and Scott's expeditions in 1910–12. After an 11-hour flight from Christchurch, New Zealand, we reached McMurdo Sound, the Navy's Antarctic logistic operational base. Here we were assigned quarters in Jamesway huts — mine was named the Ross Hilton Hotel — and given a briefing on Antarctic operations. We were advised of the methods used in construction of the new Byrd station and of preparatory work to install an atomic reactor at McMurdo. The unit was then aboard the USS *Arneb,* scheduled to reach McMurdo within a week.

An amusing incident took place at our first briefing conference, attended by representatives of several countries. One, a member of New Zealand's Parliament, stood up and, in a loud voice, said: "We New Zealanders have been very much interested in hearing all the speeches about what you Americans are doing here in the Antarctic, and specifically what you are doing here in the Ross Dependency. But, I would like you to know that whatever your intentions are, you are all now on New Zealand territory." This completely serious man was greeted by an outburst of uproarious laughter.

During the next ten days we had the opportunity to inspect the McMurdo base, the old and new Byrd stations, and the South Pole station via flights in the ski-equipped C-130 airplane. We also had helicopter flights to Cape Royds, the wintering base of Sir Ernest Shackleton in 1908, and to Cape Evans, the wintering base of Scott in 1911, when he departed on his sledge journey to the South Pole. While at the Pole we celebrated the 50th anniversary of Amundsen's attainment of it by presenting a plaque to the station. Along with it was an autographed photograph from Olav Bjaaland, the last to die of the five Norwegians who first stood here on December 14, 1911.

◆ ◆ ◆

On June 8, 1962, I voluntarily retired from the Navy — prematurely, it turned out, for I learned later that I was up for promotion to rear admiral. But that summer I had my mind on things other than the privileges of rank. I was headed north to beyond the Arctic Circle.

Ever since I first started reading books on polar expeditions, I had been fascinated by Spitsbergen, an isolated group of islands halfway to the North Pole from northern Norway. My dreams of visiting this part of the Arctic had long been shared by my close friends, Kay and Ed Sweeney, President of the Explorers Club. I had met him in 1942, when Ed was Byrd's aide serving in the Chief of Naval Operation's office in Washington. We became fast friends. Our families vacationed together skiing at Aspen, Colorado, and spent summers sailing in Chesapeake Bay. But a cruise to Spitsbergen was something else.

Joining the Sweeney's, my wife Jackie, and daughter Karen, just before sailing were Ann and Ralph Becker of Washington, D.C. Fritz Oien, an experienced hunter and trapper, came onboard as our guide. The clan, strengthened by my nephew Jahn, gathered in the city of Tromsø, northernmost in Norway, where we boarded the ship *Heimen*. *"Heimen"* means "home" in Norwegian. Numerous expeditions had sailed from this city in quest of the North Pole. Amundsen sailed from here, and a monument commemorating him stands in the center of town.

As we sailed out the fjord and left the Norwegian coast behind us, the 97-foot sealing ship bobbed like a yo-yo on the turbulent Arctic Sea. Wind shrieked in the rigging and waves constantly washed over the decks. We were caught in the heavy seas of the fishing banks, roughest part of the Arctic Ocean between Norway and Spitsbergen. Our 11-year-old daughter Karen, seasick for the first time, began screaming, "Stop the ship! I want to get off!" Finally — late in the evening — she cried herself to sleep. But next morning, she was first in the mess hall for breakfast.

In the early morning hours of the third day out, the mountainous silhouettes of the southernmost islands came into view. Soon we were abreast of South Cape, the beginning of cold, hostile peaks, glaciers, and fjords that extend poleward for hundreds of miles. Short but 10 degrees of the North Pole, the lonely northern coasts of the island chain are unmercifully battered by the polar ice pack.

Nevertheless, it was a welcome sight. For two days, swells and strong winds had made the ship roll continuously, leaving the galley with more food but considerable less crockery than anticipated. In the lee of the land, the swell calmed and we would again venture on deck. *Heimen*'s bow cut through the mirror-like surface with barely a ripple. She nosed gently into the pack ice, picking her way through the open leads. At times the ship was unable to push aside the heavy floes, and had to back off and try again. For 30 miles we butted our way through like a stubborn goat.

Eight hundred miles within the Arctic Circle and nestled deep among the mountains and glaciers lies New Aalesund, a small Norwegian mining community. It was once called Kings Bay, a significant name in Arctic exploration. During the 1920's the history-making flights of Amundsen, Ellsworth, and Byrd took off from Kings Bay. On a rocky promontory overlooking the fjord stands a granite obelisk in memory of the Amundsen and Ellsworth flights. Below the monument, the names of those who have made pilgrimages to this spot are set with small white stones in the soft tundra. Most prominent was the emblem of King Olav V of Norway, who visited the site a few weeks before us. We watched while two cousins, my 11-year-old Karen and 15-year-old Jahn Ronne, placed their initials on either side as a tribute to their grandfather Martin Ronne. Having served on Amundsen's expeditions for 20 years, he was at King Bay during the flights from here in 1925 and 1926.

Reluctantly we took leave of the little city and cruised along a rugged shoreline to the inner passage of Kings Fjord. Breathtaking grandeur surrounded us — glaciers flowing towards the sea between majestic mountains, the splendor of Arctic flowers that bloom as soon as the earth is freed of its snowy mantle, the spectacular midnight sun. Along the northern shores of the fjord Sweeney and Becker found salmon plentiful.

Underway all through the night, we anchored next morning at Isfjorden, in front of Longyearbyen, capital of the territory. Here, most of the Norwegian and Russian claims are located. The governor of Spitsbergen has his residence and office here. At Sassenfjord, a scenic inlet of Isfjorden, I met Hilmar Nois, an old trapper. As we walked down the beach, he stopped at a small shed and pulled out parts of an old sledge, the wood bleached white by the sun. "I would like to give you this as a memento of your visit," Nöis said. "It belonged originally to Amundsen. He used it on his sledge-trip to the South Pole in 1911." Nois had acquired the sledge in 1913 from Norwegian scientist Adolph Hoel. Nois had used the sledge on his hunting trips over Spitsbergen and on the sea ice to the north. I was touched by his sentiment and delighted with his gift. It was restored by my brother John in Oslo and placed in the Roald Amundsen's Polar Museum of Consul Lars Christensen in Sandefjord, Norway. Amundsen's only other known sledge remaining from his conquest of the South Pole is at Poleheim Museum at Holmenkollen in Oslo.

Returning to Longyearbyen, I sent the following message to the Russian consul Gregory Barulin at Barentsburg:

> A group of Americans visiting Svalbard with Antarctic explorer Finn Ronne, three families, a total of 10 persons would like to make a short visit to Barentsburg Sunday 12 August. If this is convenient to you we would arrive on M/K *Heimen* to Barentsburg at 1100 or 1600.

We had been speculating as to whether or not the permission would be granted, and were pleased to receive the message:

> We expect you at 1100 *Moscow time* on 12 August.

Promptly at the appointed time the *Heimen* maneuvered into the dock at Barentsburg. As Sunday was not a working day, some 100 people, mostly men with cameras, waited on the dock. As I stepped ashore, an interpreter came forward and introduced me to Vice-Consul Yvdowok, who asked what our plans were. I replied that we were three families touring Spitsbergen. We had nothing specific in mind, but would be pleased to see whatever they wanted to show us.

Hilmar Nöis, *third from left*, presents Finn Ronne, *second from left*, with Amundsen's sled at Sassenfjord, Spitsbergen, 800 miles due north of Norway in the Arctic. Other members of the party: Captain Jack Jacobsen, *left;* Captain Fritz Oien, *right.*

The Vice-Consul suggested we start walking up the long stairs leading to the settlement. Barentsburg is located on a steep slope with leveled terraces where stand many substantial buildings. High on the hillside was the residence of the consul, Mr. Barulin, a man in his late fifties. He came down the wide stairway and greeted us in a most friendly manner. He was a top diplomat. After a friendly word to each of us, in his perfect German, he escorted us up broad carpeted stair to a large reception room, ornately furnished with Persian rugs, upholstered settees, red velvet draperies, and wonderful oil paintings. Members of the Consul's staff joined us, including the wife of Vice-Consul Yvdowok, arrayed in printed chiffon dress, stole and fan. Our ladies nervously brushed their stretch ski pants and straightened their Norwegian sweaters.

In a short welcome speech, the consul asked us to join him in refreshments in a larger dining room. When we were all comfortably seated, Mr. Barulin proposed a toast to our presence and to the friendship of our two countries. We toasted the U.S.A., Russia, science, and the cosmonauts then orbiting the earth. Finally I expressed briefly the fine cooperation we had with the Russian scientists during the International Geophysical Year when we had worked together in the Antarctic.

We all enjoyed a most delicious dinner, and our glasses were constantly filled by the white-jacketed waiters. I was seated to the left of the consul, my wife at the right. A most congenial and friendly person, with a pleasing smile he suggested that our conversations should not dwell on politics. I noticed that he filled his glass from a decanter of what looked like either vodka or water. I did likewise. Yes, it was indeed water that consul Barulin was drinking. From then on, I had the same.

Our host surprised us when suddenly he rose, glass in hand and proposed a toast to Tirpitz. At first this baffled us; then he ex-

Barentsburg, the largest Russian mining community on Spitsbergen.

plained that he meant "bottoms up" — referring to the German battle-cruiser *Tirpitz* sunk in 1944 by British bombers in a surprise attack. Camouflaged, the ship was hiding in a Norwegian fjord. We had sailed past her on our way up here, noticing the keel sticking high above the water close to a rocky shoreline.

Finally, after two and a half hours, we withdrew to the reception rooms. We felt we should leave, but the consul insisted that we stay. Dance music forestalled further immediate attempts to leave. But how do American ladies dance in ski boots with a Russian consul?

Our hosts had treated us royally. Now the consul and others walked with us down the flights of steps to the dock. At least 300 people were on the dock to give us a friendly farewell. As unofficial Polar Ambassador of good will, I was, it seemed, improving U.S. relations at both ends of the earth.

◆ ◆ ◆

At the conclusion of the annual banquet of the Explorers Club in 1965, at the Waldorf in New York, I was introduced to a skyscraper of a fellow who spoke with a Swedish accent. His name was Lars-Eric Lindblad. "Travel agency is my business!"

He was exactly the kind of man with whom I could share an idea. I told him that ever since my father's return from Byrd's expedition in 1930, I had harbored the dream of starting regular tourist cruises to Antarctic. I recalled that in 1932 my father had persuaded a Norwegian shipping firm to conduct such a cruise. . . . The *Stella Polaris*, the most deluxe passenger ship afloat, was set to sail from France in the fall of that year, My father was scheduled to sail with them. But at the last minute, the cruise to Antarctica was cancelled, another victim of the worldwide depression.

Off and on since then I had brought the idea to the attention of shipping and travel agents, but all expressed doubt that tourists would pay to visit a frozen continent, just to see a few penguins.

Lindblad, however, was interested. After hearing me out, he accepted my idea. "Let's try getting off next January," he said. But, he specified one condition: that I be the leader. . . .

During the summer and fall months preparations were made for the first American tourist cruise to the Antarctic. A ship with accommodations for about 100 passengers was charted from the Argentine Navy. Brochures were made and advertisements placed in newspapers and magazines. The cruise was presented as a semi-scientific expedition with ship-board lectures in oceanography, biology and ornithology. There would also be illustrated film lectures on famous polar expeditions, using films from my lecture library. Requests began to pour into the office. By the end of the year 52 paying passengers had signed up for the January 1966 flight by Avianca to Argentina.

The ship, *Lapataia* was comfortable, and the crossing of Drake Passage was smooth from Beagle Channel to Deception Island. Inside the boundary of the northern fringes of the Antarctic Peninsula, we made courtesy calls at several bases. We met with scientists there and were given lectures in the scientific fields pursued. Our ship sailed close to rugged mountains and steep glaciers sliding into the sea. The tourists were awed by the spectacular scenery, the grandeur of the high and rugged mountains and the variety in the shapes of the ice bergs.

The success of that voyage inspired similar cruises by Lindblad to other remote corners of the earth. Lars' "gamble" with my idea had proved to be a very good investment. As for me, I once again visited the continent of my destiny, and took deep satisfaction in carrying out my father's ambition to open up Antarctica to tourists.

◆ ◆ ◆

It was natural, therefore, that in 1966 the Japanese Alpine Club contacted me. They had decided to launch an expedition with the principal aim of being the first to scale Antarctica's highest peak Mount Vinson (16,860 feet), located in the Ellsworth Mountain range. The Japanese requested my views on the best method of reaching their goal by ship, planes, climbers to be involved, the needed logistic support, etc. This correspondence ended with their request that I come to Japan and convey my knowledge of the area in person. To this, of course, I had no objection. I was well aware of their active participation in the International Geophysical Year program.

My wife and I flew comfortably on the Japanese Air Line from San Francisco to Tokyo with a brief stopover in Hawaii. I gave lectures in Tokyo and other Japanese cities, two television programs with my color film, and interviews for *Yomiuri Shinbun* — a newspaper. I instituted regular working sessions with the mountain climbers and assisted in the planning of their Antarctic expedition. We flew to North Island and visited with the Shirase family. Lieut. Shirase had led the first Japanese expedition 50 years earlier. We met governors, mayors, Shinto and Buddhist priests; went on the world's fastest train to Kyoto; visited the pearl divers and were taken to the Ginza district of Tokyo for various shows. Before we left the Far East, we took a two-week sidetrip to Hongkong and Thailand.

The week after we returned to Washington, an announcement was made that an American team of mountain climbers had just scaled Mount Vinson. The Navy and the National Geographic Society had cooperated in the planning of this somewhat secret operation. It was most embarrassing, since both organizations undoubtedly had heard of the upcoming Japanese expedition, which had been planned for a year!

The only fair way out of this international dilemma would have been for the American team to invite a couple of Japanese climbers to join them perhaps even to have made it an international climbing team, as other nations had expressed an interest in the project. This was a bad time for American sportsmanship. I wrote my Japanese hosts and apologized for my country's bad manners. I had no prior knowledge that such a plan was in the works.

♦ ♦ ♦

I made additional trips to the Arctic in 1963 and 1969, again landing at Longyearbyen and New Aalesund on Spitsbergen. Both times the ships penetrated the pack ice beyond the 82nd parallel, my farthest north. These trips were of special interest to me because they afforded me the opportunity to study at close quarters the condition of pack ice found in these high latitudes.

Swept by ocean currents flowing across the Arctic Ocean, broken ice floes piled to a height of 40 feet or more above the waterline. I could see that teams of dogs pulling loaded sledges over such obstacles would have tough going; even with men pushing the sledges to the top of the rafted ice, the pace would be slow — perhaps no more than 10 to 12 miles a day. I also noticed many open waters leads too wide for sledges to cross. They would have to be detoured around the leads, adding miles and hours to the journey. My observations were borne out by young Norwegian skier and dog driver Bjorn Staib, who started from Cape Alert on Ellsmere Island. His party struggled to repeat the journey supposedly made by Robert Peary. But, after covering less than half the distance to the North Pole, Staib's men managed to reach an ice island manned by American crews, where airplanes evacuated them to Thule.

Another party, a British one led by Wally Herbert, started from Point Barrow; aided by air drops, men and dogs succeeded in crossing to Spitsbergen. But the effort required two winterings on the polar ice cap and it took the party two years to get across. On the final stretch of the journey, a British ship with helicopters picked up the party and brought it to Longyearbyen. I saw some of the dogs at the coal-shipping docks in 1969. They looked like a bunch of crummy animals then — simply worn out.

In 1969 most of our time was spent in the Isfjord area where the Norwegian Polar Institute conducts scientific studies. Four helicopters were available here that summer. Unfortunately, due to constant overcast weather, we were marooned at Longyearbyen for 10 days without seeing clear sky overhead. A collier eventually brought us south to north Norway.

CHAPTER 22

I N DECEMBER 1971, ANTARCTICA AGAIN BECKONED. The Department of Defense invited me to participate in the celebration
of the 60th Anniversary of Amundsen's triumph at the South Pole.
Jackie and I packed our bags and boarded a C-41 Skymaster at
Andrews Air Force Base in Washington. We made brief landings
in Honolulu, the Fiji Islands, and Christchurch, New Zealand,
where we were outfitted with cold weather clothing and briefed
by experts on what we could expect to experience at McMurdo
Sound, our destination.

After six hours we saw on the right the snow-covered mountains of Queen Victoria Land. On the left stretched the Ross Sea.
We landed at Williams air strip, where helicopters brought us the
ten miles to McMurdo Naval Station. The next day, December 7,
we flew to the South Pole.

The terrifying beauty we saw when flying up the Beardmore
Glacier defied description. Bordered by forbidding mountains,
this wide river of ice flowed down from the high polar plateau to
the Ross Ice Shelf. Numerous crevasses scarred its surface. I mar-
veled at Scott's fortitude in picking a way through this multitudi-
nous maze. In a brilliant sky, with only scattered clouds on the
horizon, we could see the sharp ridges of 14,000-foot Mount
Markham. As we streaked above the vast polar plateau, I scanned
the endless white vista for the Amundsen-Scott station. Finally I
saw movement on the shimmering snowy surface, indicating the
base personnel were preparing for our arrival. It had taken us three
and a half hours to fly from McMurdo to the 9,200 foot high

South Pole Station. Scott's party in 1911–12, manhauling their sledges, took 76 tortuous days to attain the Pole — only to perish on their tragic return journey. Soon we were on the ground at 90 degrees south, the first couple ever to set foot there.

About 30 of us were in the plane to commemorate Amundsen's party first reaching this isolated spot in 1911. In "Club Ninety," the recreation Hall, the Admiral gave a resume on the station and its personnel. It was followed by a short ceremony with my presenting a small gift to the South Pole Station from the Norwegian Geographical Society. It consisted of two color enlargements framed in gold and with an inscription engraved on the white surface. The first picture showed Amundsen's party of four men facing the tent my father made. On top of the extended flag pole, swayed by the wind was a simple pennant with POLE-HEIM (the polar home) embroidered on it. Underneath was the Norwegian flag. The other picture showed Scott and his men standing by the same tent. It was taken 31 days after the Norwegians had departed on their return journey to their wintering base at the Bay of Whales.

All the South Pole guests next went to the mess hall for a farewell dinner before we headed back to McMurdo. The two planes coming to pick us up were already in the air, crossing the Ross Ice Shelf on the way to the Beardmore Glacier. We had two hours or more before they would land. The dinner was a hearty one, topped off with a huge cake and, in true South Pole style, home-made ice cream. Before leaving we hurried to use the mail equipment with the coveted South Pole cancellation.

My final minutes at the South Pole were spent in the radio shack, where my friend, Lowell Thomas was on the short wave frequency. My chat with him was recorded to be broadcast later on his 7 P.M. program.

"Finn," Lowell said, "I have a dinner date tomorrow at the White House. Is there a special message you may wish to convey to the President?"

"Yes, Lowell, there is. Tell him that the American boys down here in the Antarctic are doing a splendid job. This they do in spite of the cold and stormy isolation. The boys tell me the mean annual temperature here is fifty-five degrees below zero. I have a particular praise for the Navy, which is providing the logistic support. Admiral McCuddin, the commander of all U.S. activities here sends you his best. See you in New York soon, Lowell."

"Right, Finn, in far off Antarctica — and so long until to-morrow."

◆ ◆ ◆

Our mission completed, we returned to McMurdo that evening.

Early next morning at the appointed hour our party of 18 took our seats in the helicopters, and we were soon on our way to Cape Royds. We had intended spending only an hour at this historic site, the hut built more than 60 years ago by Sir Ernest Shackleton. Our party had come merely for a brief view of the austere conditions endured by the early explorers and to photo-graph nesting penguins in a nearby rookery. Then the helicopters, standing ready, would whisk us off to Scott's hut at Cape Evans.

Suddenly, in one of those chameleon changes of temper char-acteristic of the continent, a fierce blizzard swept in. Winds howled at 40 miles an hour, driving before them a wall of snow. From the hut I could not even see the rookery 75 feet away where moments before I had been photographing the penguins.

We milled nervously about inside the rickety old wooden structure. We stomped our feet on the squeaky floor, clapped our hands to keep warm. Jokes and a cheery bravado hid the general chill of spirit, but everyone had the same dreadful thought: How long would we be marooned in this old room covered with vol-canic ash and filled with decaying mementos of another era? Ironically, in this scientifically advanced day when men walked on the moon and dwelled comfortably all year in a weather-proofed Antarctica, we seemed destined to relive the bitter ex-perience of pioneer explorers — but without the simple neces-sities Shackleton had six decades ago. Flight crews of the two copters had already begun to count the available sleeping bags and assess our emergency food situation. There were six bags and food for two and a half days, if we were careful.

The pilots quickly hustled us back to the copters when the blizzard slacked. But by the time we were strapped in our seats, visibility was gone. Conditions deteriorated so rapidly that after five miles we had flown into a white-out. There was no visible horizon — no depth perception. Ice, glaciers and sky all appeared as one. We seemed to be maneuvering in a sea of milk. I was sit-ting next to the exit door, looking into the white void when I sud-denly saw a jagged outcrop shoot by. My breath stopped. The pilots radioed McMurdo that we were returning to Cape Royds.

Back in the hut, we huddled together in the cold. The crew brought our survival gear and lit a small gasoline stove. Several men went in search of some pure, clean ice from the pressure ridges near the coast. It took a long time to melt the hard blue ice formed by glaciers millions of years ago. Into the water went chicken, beef, spaghetti, and other canned items to make the most delicious 18 cups of "hoosh" any of us ever tasted.

Warmed and cheered, we all gave a loud whoop when the pilots announced they were going to make another try. There had been a slight clearing.

This time they followed along the coast of Ross Island, hoping we could stay close enough to the glacier fronts of rocky outcrops abutting the sea to find our way back to McMurdo.

Suddenly, the curtain of white dropped in front of us again. Another white-out! Our pilot banked sharply toward the last visible crevasse at the edge of the barrier we'd been following.

As the copter swung around, it looked as though we were going to crash into the glacier front. The white wall loomed before us, and impact seemed imminent. But, at the last second, the pilot skillfully righted the craft and set it down at Cape Royds. He left the engine running until the second copter had landed. Disheartened, we trooped back to the cold hut. The pilot told me later that this was the closest call he had ever had!

♦ ♦ ♦

By now it was 4 P.M. — six hours since we had left McMurdo. Everyone needed to "take a little trip over the hill," as toilet facilities at Cape Royds did not exist. It was snowing hard, and the wind was howling. My wife described the ordeal: "I had on five layers of clothing from waffle-weave underwear to outer windproof survival gear — a boon until this moment. My escape to privacy from 17 men in the cabin was a painful struggle that left me shaken and frozen. I stumbled back to the hut convinced that I really didn't want to become a hero, after all."

By now all of us had seen more than enough of Shackleton's hut, but it was out of the question for us to walk the 40 miles back to McMurdo. The terrain was dotted with crevasse-filled glaciers that poured down from Mount Erebus to the sea. Nor could we reach the base over the sea ice, furrowed with open leads impossible to cross. Our return depended solely upon the two copters.

We had to make it on the next try, because there was not sufficient gas to fly us back to McMurdo if this attempt failed. However, if that happened I felt certain that the men of the top command would figure out a way to get us out of here. Later I learned that Admiral McCuddin had considered sending tracked vehicles over the sea ice or a dog team from a nearby base.

As time wore on, the dingy hut took on new dimensions. In spite of a New Zealand Government notice on the wall cautioning all visitors from removing any items from this historic shrine, we began to eye the corroded cans of bird's-egg powder, cabbage, ox-tongue, and weathered boxes of hardtack. Only a musty bottle labeled as a remedy for dysentery provided the necessary restraint.

Dirty socks, worn mukluks, ragged blankets, scraps of canvas, and old seal skins covered with volcanic dust had borne mute testimony to the hardships of the seemingly long past when we first arrived. Subconsciously, each of us was picking out a spot on the floor where we might spend the night. It was impossible to remain in the hut for any length of time; the damp cold was too penetrating. Every 30 minutes or so we had to move around; even the snow and wind outside offered some respite. There was a stove but no fuel. Even if there had been kerosene, a note warned that the old relic did not function properly. An overnight experience under these conditions was something none of us wished to contemplate.

Fortunately, we were not put to the test. On one of our forays out for exercise, we noticed a break in the cloud cover. Slowly the patch began to grow. When the sun finally broke through, we bounded across the volcanic slag to the waiting copters without a backward glance. Less than an hour later we were thawing out at McMurdo.

◆ ◆ ◆

Next morning we were up early. We were to fly back to Christchurch, New Zealand, late that evening. A review of present activities began after breakfast, with the scientific programs dominating the agenda. Eklund Biological Laboratory, our first stop, was named after ornithologist Carl Eklund, who had died shortly after returning home from Wilkes Station during the International Geophysical Year. Carl had been my chosen companion on one of the longest Antarctic sledge trips on record, in which we covered 1,300 miles in 84 days.

In the Ross Sea sector "Eklund's Lab" teams are kept busy researching the nutritional aspect of the vast protein accumulation in the waters surrounding this isolated continent. Here perhaps are untapped resources to feed an over-populated world.

Geophysical branches of science were explained as we made our rounds to the various installations. Moving from building to building, my eyes focused on Observation Hill, overlooking the base. A huge wooden cross on top was a reminder of Scott and his four companions entombed in the Ross Ice Shelf, south over the horizon. Time had not allowed me to scale it when I was here ten years earlier.

After lunch I started up the steep grade. The day was crystal clear with not a cloud visible. It afforded a brilliant view in all directions. A third of the way up, a young Naval lieutenant caught up with me. Westerly I saw the Victoria Mountains, cold and isolated with rivers of ice flowing between the tall and massive ridges. Twenty-five miles north was Mount Erebus, guarding the rest of the Ross Island where British expeditions first came to winter at the turn of the century. Looking southerly, I located Minna Bluff and White Island imbedded in an ice sheet. In the distance lay the Ross Ice Shelf, shimmering like a mirror on the horizon. Scott and Shackleton had sledged across it on their way to the pole, and their heroic deeds are forever associated with their discoveries, the Beardmore Glacier, Mount Markham, McMurdo Sound, Cape Evans and Cape Royds. Mount Erebus was still spewing hot lava and smoke, as it did on the 28th of January, 1841 when James Clark Ross first sighted the snow-covered summit. It is the only active volcano found in the Antarctic.

For the next few minutes I relived not only the saga of Antartic exploration but also my own part in nine expeditions spanning almost 40 years. Up to this time probably no other man had sledged as many miles on Antarctic ice as I, nor had anyone spent as many days and nights there. Indeed, of all the explorers who had visited these frozen shares, undoubtedly none could claim to have seen as much of the unknown as I had beheld.

By this time the sun was nearing the western horizon. Busses drove us out to the airstrip where our Skymaster awaited. Before entering the plane for the return flight to New Zealand, I had a final visit with Leo McCuddin, expressing our appreciation for all we had seen. He asked if I would like to return some day to observe the changes at McMurdo and the South Pole Station.

"Yes," I answered enthusiastically, "if I'm invited."

"Finn, you are invited right now for the 75th Amundsen-Scott anniversary in 1986," Admiral McCuddin assured me.

"Thanks, Admiral," I replied. "I hope to be here."

Index

Index